D1276199

REAL ESTATE
101

OTHER BOOKS IN THE TRUMP
UNIVERSITY SERIES

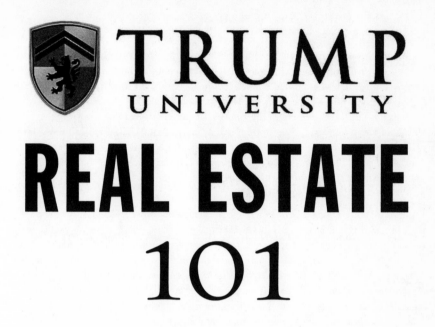

TRUMP
UNIVERSITY
REAL ESTATE
101

Building Wealth with
Real Estate Investments

SECOND EDITION

FOREWORD BY DONALD TRUMP

GARY W. ELDRED, PhD

WILEY

JOHN WILEY & SONS, INC.

Published by John Wiley & Sons, Inc., Hoboken, New Jersey.
Published simultaneously in Canada.

For general information on our other products and services or for technical support, please contact our Customer Care Department within the United States at (800) 762-2974, outside the United States at (317) 572-3993 or fax (317) 572-4002.

Wiley also publishes its books in a variety of electronic formats. Some content that appears in print may not be available in electronic books. For more information about Wiley products, visit our web site at www.wiley.com.

Library of Congress Cataloging-in-Publication Data:

Eldred, Gary W.
   Trump University real estate 101 : building wealth with real estate investments / by Gary W. Eldred.—2nd ed.
      p. cm.
   Includes index.
   ISBN 978-0-470-45582-1 (cloth)
      1. Trump, Donald, 1946–   2. Real estate investment—United States.
3. Real property—Valuation—United States.   4. Entrepreneurship—United States.
I. Trump University.   II. Title.   III. Title: Trump University real estate
one hundred one.   IV. Title: Trump University real estate one hundred and one.
   HD255.E37528 2009
   332.63'240973—dc22

                                                                              2009007451

Printed in the United States of America.

10   9   8   7   6   5   4   3   2   1

Contents

CONTENTS

Acknowledgments

First, I wish to thank Donald Trump and Michael Sexton, CEO, Trump University, for inviting me to become the content expert for their real estate mastery program. Mr. Trump has said on many occasions, "I only hire the best." That's certainly true for the team at Trump University, and I am honored by their request to join them.

Specifically, in working on this second edition of *Trump University Real Estate 101*, I want to thank my colleague in the UAE, Zouheir Jarkas, whose far-ranging knowledge of finance and investment markets has again proven invaluable. I would also like to recognize my assistants at the American University of Sharjah: Omer Shabbir Ahmed, who not only went beyond the call of duty to help meet deadlines but also produced work of the highest quality; Mohsen Mofid has also helped, and I thank him for his years of extraordinary service in assisting me in whatever way I needed. Also, new to this edition is Mohammed Ghassan Hannoun who has shown himself to be quite capable in all assigned tasks. And finally, I want to thank my long-time assistant, Barbara Smerage of Santa Fe, New Mexico, who has now worked with me to complete more than 20 book manuscripts. Barbara's work is always flawless.

Foreword to the Trump University 101 Series

by Donald J. Trump

PEOPLE OFTEN ASK me the secret to my success, and the answer is simple: focus, hard work, and tenacity. I've had some lucky breaks, but luck will only get you so far. You also need business savvy—not necessarily a degree from Wharton, but you do need the desire and discipline to educate yourself. I created Trump University to give motivated business people the skills required to achieve lasting success.

The Trump University 101 Series explains the most powerful and important ideas in business—the same concepts taught in the most respected MBA curriculums and used by the most successful companies in the world, including The Trump Organization. Each book is written by a top professor, author, or entrepreneur whose goal is to help you put these ideas to use in your business right away. If you're not satisfied with the status quo in your career, read this book, pick one key idea, and implement it. I guarantee it will make you money.

Donald Trump congratulates Gary Eldred for his outstanding work on Trump University's mastery program in real estate. (Photo by Karen Slavick, Trump University)

Preface to the Second Edition

Why Building Wealth with Real Estate Just Got Easier

W E HAVE PREPARED this second edition of *Trump University Real Estate 101* especially for today's marketplace—a market where you can make money with property investments much easier than you could have when the first edition of this book was written in late 2005. In the first edition, I emphasized that the "motivated" seller approach to finding good buys had lost much of its viability. Back then, the great majority of sellers wanted top dollar, and foreclosures, preforeclosures, and REOs (bank owned properties) still represented quite a small part of the market. In addition, during those boom days, amateurs (meaning people who thought that anyone who buys property is sure to make a quick and easy fortune) and speculators who followed the "greater fool theory" drove property prices much higher (in many cities) than sensible investors (such as myself) were willing to pay. That's why in the first edition I emphasized the entrepreneurial approach—which involves seeking out undervalued areas and/or creating value through improved marketing and management strategies.

Because both Donald Trump and I strongly favor entrepreneurial investing (which works in all times and all places), this second edition still shows you how to profit big through that approach. But now, not only can you profit entrepreneurially, you also (once again) can gain through buying properties from those motivated folks who overextended themselves (either financially, managerially, or both) and the banks that carelessly underwrote those loans and now hold hundreds of thousands of foreclosed properties. Entrepreneurial ability + bargain price = extraordinary potential to build wealth.

"But wait," you might say, "you expect me to invest in real estate when financial news is so bad?" Well to answer that question, I quote Warren Buffett who advises, "Buy when others are fearful, sell when the buyers are greedy." Plus, much of the news is actually good for property investors—if you know how to interpret it correctly. For example, many articles in the press recently carried headline titles such as "Grim news as housing starts fall to their lowest level since before 1959." If you work as a painter or carpenter in construction, that is bad news. But if you invest in property today, plummeting new construction represents investment opportunity. The lower the number of new homes, condos, and apartments that get built, the more certain I am that prices of existing properties will again begin their long-term upward climb.

Likewise, all of the depressing news about record levels of mortgage delinquencies and foreclosures—bad news for distressed sellers and their banks, but such news signals an abundance of opportunities for investors. Yet, do not wait too long to act because both the banks and the federal government (especially the president's "homeowner rescue" plan) will be working the next several years to keep people in their homes through various types of debt forgiveness and loan restructuring.

What about the U.S. government debt levels? The stimulus package and multiple bailout programs will add a trillion dollars or more to the U.S. national debt. How can such news display a positive angle? The answer for property investors is inflation. To make it easier for debtor nations to pay their debts—throughout the world and throughout history—governments have always inflated their currencies. Today, property investors with good credit can borrow at quite attractive interest rates. Lock in low rates for the long term; pay back in much cheaper dollars in future years while also reaping the benefits of increasing rents and property prices.

One last point here: Although the press has made much of the cyclical downturn in property, stock prices both in the United States and in many countries abroad have plummeted far more quickly and steeply than the prices of properties in even our most irrationally exuberant cities. Anyone over age 50 who was counting on "stocks for retirement" has definitely had his or her faith shaken in that asset class. Moreover, in planning for retirement, the income that an asset yields becomes much more important than any cyclical swings in price. And again, the facts show that the net rents retirees can collect from a million dollars of property total more than twice the amount of income that the same amount of stocks would provide in dividends.

As to which asset class performs best during years of inflation, we can look at the longest and most severe inflationary period in United States' history: 1966 to 1982. During those 18 years, the Dow Jones Industrial Average actually fell in real, inflation-adjusted dollars. Stock market investors saw their wealth shrivel. In contrast, the median home price during those inflationary years nearly tripled from $25,000 to $75,000.

In other words, when evaluated in terms of downside volatility, attractive yields from income, and gains from inflation, property outperforms stocks. With 60 million people now age 50 or older in the United States (and many other Western and Asian countries face similar demographics), property will become the investment asset of choice. We will see more upward pressure on prices (which of course will drive yields down for future investors—even though the cash yields will still exceed those available from stocks).

So, you now see why building wealth with properties today is easier than it has been in years. Unsold inventories are high, distressed sellers are many, interest rates are low, competition for properties has diminished, and prices are low relative to where they will stand 5 to 10 years from now. Donald Trump went from beginning investor to real estate billionaire in less than 15 years. *When* did he begin? It began in the depths of the mid-1970s recession when New York City was essentially bankrupt and pleading with the U.S. Congress for a bailout (which was never granted). *How* did he do it? By creating and executing an entrepreneurial action plan.

Get started now in today's opportunity-laden market. Create your own entrepreneurial plan. You can rely on this new edition of *Trump University Real Estate 101* to guide you to achieve the financial security and financial freedom that you know lies within your reach.

1

ENTREPRENEURING IN REAL ESTATE WITH DONALD TRUMP

To BUILD WEALTH with property investments, "Buy at the right price, at the right time, and in the right place." That's why today, you enjoy perfect positioning. Because of the recent property slump from London to Hong Kong, from Shanghai to Dubai, from LA to Santa Fe, from Miami to Moscow, from Barcelona to Boston—you can find extraordinary bargains nearly everywhere throughout the world. As newspaper articles and the television talking heads fret about the downturn in property, those of us who have seen and heard it all before are out shopping for the deals of the decade.

PERFECT STORM CREATES PERFECT OPPORTUNITY

Mr. Trump and I have each experienced and keenly studied property markets and mortgage markets for more than 30 years—all the way back to the 1970s. And we both agree: This perfect storm of tight money and excess property supply (especially foreclosures) has created perfect opportunity for you. Historical experience has proven many times: Investors who move forward to acquire properties in times of distress and perceived uncertainty become the property multimillionaires of tomorrow.

During the past several years, I have logged 200,000 miles of national and international travel—looking at properties, attending property shows, speaking at investor conferences, and evaluating conditions of emerging property demand and supply. From such travels, I have discovered a cornucopia of profitable possibilities. Several centuries ago, Baron de Rothschild famously advised, "Buy when the blood is running in the streets." The Baron paints a more vivid picture of market conditions than "right price, right time, right place." But his message counsels the same experience-derived wisdom—that same wisdom recently espoused by Warren Buffett: "Buy when others remain fearful, sell when others become greedy."

ENTREPRENEURS ACT ON FACTS

We all know that emotion dominates markets. During boom times, irrational exuberance infects peoples' thoughts. They speculate wildly—yet persuade themselves that they are placing their money into a sure thing. When the party ends, they feel sick with a financial hangover and vow never to get into real estate (or stocks, or gold, or commodities) again.

Entrepreneurs behave differently. When markets boom, they pull back as the price growth of an asset class greatly exceeds the growth of its supporting income. For example, at the peak of the boom, Las Vegas houses costing $350,000 would bring in no more than $1,200 a month in rents. By that time, the smart money had exited. Speculators were merely selling to each other. The greater fool theory once again triumphed. ("I may be a fool to pay this much, but I will find a greater fool who will pay me even more.")

As price corrections occur in response to speculative excess (and ignorance), entrepreneurs know that recovery always follows a downturn. Rather than freeze in fear, entrepreneurs act on facts. They wait for speculators to vanish from the buy side—as they certainly have—and then real investors step in to relieve those financially strapped owners who now must sell at whatever price they can.

Of course, not all distressed sellers today were yesterday's speculators. And not all of today's sellers are distressed. But the extra supply created by the distressed sellers, when matched against the vanquished demand, opens the door to a bank vault of profits for entrepreneurs who focus on facts rather than fear.

What facts? Here are just a few:

- *Population:* During the next 20 years, the population of the United States will grow by 40 million persons. The population of the world will grow by more than one billion. These additional people will not only fuel demand but will likely push up the costs of resources (lumber, energy, steel, skilled labor) needed for new construction.

- *Yield:* When we measure income relative to asset price, property outperforms all other asset classes. With property you can earn an unleveraged (cash purchase-no financing) annual yield of 6 to 9 percent (i.e., not counting future appreciation). Bonds pay 4 to 6 percent, CDs pay 2 to 5 percent, and stocks pay current yields of 1 to 3 percent. With 60 to 70 million baby boomers seeking income during their retirement years, they will bid up the price of property as they attempt to invest to earn retirement income.
- *Inflation:* We do not merely need income during retirement, we need *inflation-protected* income. On that score, bonds fail. For long-term bonds, your coupon payments remain unchanged for the entire period to the maturity date of the bond—which typically ranges from 10 to 30 years. Even worse, yields on safe, investment-quality bonds fall below 6 percent—and yields on (perceived) safe U.S. Treasuries now fall below 4 percent.

  Although stock dividends, over time, tend to outpace inflation, stock prices themselves can lag the Consumer Price Index (CPI) for decades (e.g., 1929–1958, 1966–1988, 2000–?). Property? Since the 1930s, the prices of properties and rent levels have outpaced the CPI in every decade. (Though some individual markets have lagged, that's why Chapter 6, "Where's the Area Headed," tells you how to forecast economic growth, population increases, and potential appreciation.)
- *Volatility:* How would you like to approach your retirement age and painfully watch your nest egg shrink by 40 to 60 percent? Retirees who hold their wealth in stocks frequently experience such shocks (1973–1974, 1987, 2000–2003, 2008). Even in the worst national economic downturn in property since the 1930s, the median house price has fallen just 15 percent—though some areas (those dominated by speculative borrowers and buyers) have suffered more extensive drops. Prices in well-selected areas (as per the lessons of

Chapter 6) have fallen little—and in some cases are still appreciating. When you avoid speculative markets and follow the tried and true principles of location, you will not suffer the volatility shocks that Wall Street brings investors.

- *Leverage:* The credit crunch and piles of foreclosures have once again proven the age-old wisdom if you borrow unwisely, if you borrow speculatively, you can lose big in stocks, bonds, or property. But when you borrow sensibly, over time leverage will multiply your original cash investment many times over.

  What is *"sensible leverage"*? Financing that provides you positive cash flow after you make your mortgage payments—and mortgage payments that cannot spike upward within a period of just a few years.

- *Create Value:* Unlike any other asset class (stocks, bonds, gold, annuities, commodities, foreign exchange collectibles), property permits you to earn large entrepreneurial rewards in two major ways: (1) The first principle of making money in real estate tells you to buy at the right time, at the right price, and in the right place. With know-how, you can buy properties for less than they are worth. In the chapters that follow, you will learn how to master this entrepreneurial skill.

  Property principle number (2) tells you to create value. Here's where opportunity with property really builds your wealth. When you buy stocks, you merely hold for a hoped-for gain. With property, you not only can earn immediate gains through savvy buying at a bargain price—you earn even more when you improve a property's market strategy and management practices.

Buy Right—But Go Further, Create Value

In this book, you discover how to *buy* right, but even more importantly, you learn the *practice of entrepreneurship* as lived and practiced by the ultimate entrepreneur, Mr. Donald Trump. More than ever, Mr. Trump's experience is needed because throughout the United States and around the world we can see the carnage created by the mindless speculators who merely try to surf a wave of momentum to easy riches. We are returning to an arena where to win the game of property you must go beyond luck and a fortuitous (short-term) boom. You will profit most with the least risk when you create value, not just rely on windfall gains.

As Mr. Trump told me when we planned this book, "For all too long, the infomercial guys of late night television who promote 'nothing down,' 'pennies on the dollar foreclosures,' 'quick flipping,' and other supposed techniques to get rich quick have dominated the field of real estate seminars, boot camps, books, and CDs." Then he added, "Life rarely works out that way. If you go for get rich quick, you are really going for broke." Quite prophetic.

We don't want you to go broke—or go for broke. We will not promise that the entrepreneurial principles of Donald Trump and Gary Eldred will turn you into an overnight millionaire. (Although it does happen occasionally.)

We do promise that our advice and counsel shows you how to buy right *and* create value that will help you build wealth, achieve your potential, and provide excellent service for your customers (tenants and buyers). Even better, like us, you just might have a lot of fun along the way.

"Think Big, Live Large"

Entrepreneuring means more than just property investing and building wealth. You can apply it to live a richer, fuller life in every respect. "Think big, live large." With that now famous axiom, Mr. Trump encourages you to "see each day as an important day for your future and a special day just because you have it. Energize your existence. 'What a great day!' Say it right now and feel the positive thinking it generates. Give yourself a chance to do your best, and everyone will benefit. Know that you can fill today with possibilities and opportunities."

Open Your Mind to Possibilities

To achieve your potential, educate yourself to think and expand your possibilities. It turns out that both Mr. Trump and I began reading books on real estate while we were undergraduates in college. Both of us began investing in property when nearly all of our fellow students were hoping to buy a sharp car or find a cool apartment to rent.

Why did we act differently? Why did we begin to build wealth at an age when most of our peers settled for lame excuses? Because we refused to accept the conventional wisdom that we were too young, too inexperienced, or too anything else.

We achieve more because we open our minds to new ideas. We search out information and knowledge. Both of us read to learn the facts of real estate markets and the wider national and world economies—and we read in the field of (for lack of a better term) *self-improvement.*

We encourage you to think positively, create possibilities, and see beyond your current horizons. When we see headlines like, "Builders' Inventories of New Unsold Homes Reach New Highs," or "Tight Credit Stalls Property Sales," or "Foreclosures Jump 42 Percent," we do not run in fear to stuff our cash into government-insured bank CDs. We know that such headlines spell B-A-R-G-A-I-N-S G-A-L-O-R-E.

Know the Details

When you open your mind to possibilities, you open your mind to profits. But positive (I like to say exploratory) thinking will work only when you prime your mind with an ever-growing flow of knowledge. As Mr. Trump likes to say, "I'm not young enough to know everything."

Indeed, he keeps Kipling's six honest men ever present to build his knowledge. Their names are What, Why, When, How, Where, and Who.

"To get a building built in New York City," says Mr. Trump, "requires knowledge of zoning, contractors, architects, air rights, tax laws, union rules, and a thousand other things—which most importantly includes intimate knowledge of the intended customers. When I started, I had to learn it all. No one else could learn for me. But every day, I would learn something, apply it, and make progress. Believe me, becoming a world-renowned developer didn't happen overnight.

"I always warn people not just to jump in. First prepare. It's that fine line between bravery and stupidity. Before you dive in, know the flow of the tides and the depth of the water. Danger lurks everywhere. By danger I mean the unknown. Even in shallow waters, you can drown. Sometimes you don't see the risks until you swim past the point of easy return. Keep risks in mind no matter how sensational or foolproof you think your deal might look.

"In those early years, I worked endlessly to research every detail that might affect the deal I wanted to pursue. I do the same today. People often comment on how quickly I operate, but I can move quickly when opportunities open because I've done the background work first—which no one else sees. I prepare thoroughly. Then, when the green flag is dropped, I can stay ahead of competitors."

THINK FOR YOURSELF—ACCEPT RESPONSIBILITY

Of course, you will incorporate the facts and opinions of others into your investment decisions. But never abdicate your decisions to your advisers. Do not be swayed by others without verifying or applying the lessons of the past. Watch closely for errors of facts and judgment. The bank failures, foreclosures, and personal bankruptcies that have recently made the news occurred (for the most part) because too many people merely followed the crowd and ignored their individual responsibility to think, research, and exercise well-reasoned, reality-grounded judgments.

"Adopt a mind-set of personal responsibility. When I say, 'adopt the right mind-set', I emphasize responsibility. People who accept responsibility do not blame or find fault with others. The shirkers, the excuse mongers, and the naysayers rarely contribute much and rarely amount to much either. The dues paid to belong to that club cost far too much.

"I knew a guy that I used to call up just to see who and what he *blamed* that day. I don't think that guy ever thought he had made a single mistake in his life. Nothing was ever his fault. He was his own worst blind spot. He eventually became a perpetual loser because he never learned the reason for his biggest failure: himself. Learn from his example. When things go wrong, look first to yourself.

"I've been in business long enough now and have had my share of ups and downs, so I can go from seeing the problem to seeing the solution. Instead of dwelling on a problem so much, visualize solutions. Especially in today's market, losers see problems and hide from risk. The property millionaires of tomorrow realize that problems generate profits for those smart enough to act.

"Such a mind-set works: Highlight and enumerate the positive things you can do. Use the negatives to steer a productive route around, over, or through obstacles. It's your responsibility, but also your rewards."

Goals and Habits

"Give your goals substance," advises Mr. Trump. "Give them value that supersedes money. Make your goals count on as many levels as you can. Write a subtext that will provide benefits not only for you but for other people as well. That's an important aspect of thinking big—and a big step toward greater success.

"Too many people in recent years wanted to make money, get rich, spend lavishly—yet they did not understand nor acknowledge the reciprocity of wealth-building. In fact, I dislike the term '*make money*.' It's too crude. I prefer the word '*earn*.' The word 'earn' reminds you that before you reap, first sow something of value for others.

"Only then will people respect you for your habits, your character, and your performance. As Aristotle points out, such habits reflect your qualities. Ensure that your character sets a high standard. Review your habits, behavior, and performance. Discipline them to lead you in the right direction. Advance toward the life you want to live and know that to achieve it will distinctly define your own boundaries of behavior, your own goals—without being influenced negatively by anyone else."

THE ART OF THE DEAL

Place yourself into your deals. Commit! Mr. Trump likes to quote Thoreau's passage: "I know of no more encouraging fact than the unquestioned ability of a man to elevate his life by conscious desire [commitment]." Desire encourages; it empowers. You succeed when you apply your brainpower, then move forward. Without action, thought is stillborn. Action without thought endangers your wealth. The art of the deal, the path to success, remains simple: Discover, learn, think, act, achieve, revise, achieve more.

2

YOU CAN STILL ACHIEVE WEALTH IN REAL ESTATE

> **I love Rudyard Kipling's "Six honest men." Their names are "What and Why and When—and How, Where, and Who." Ask questions.**

I ENJOY PROPERTY. And I hope that by the time you complete this book, you will, too.

Property offers more people more opportunities than any other type of investment. Great economy, poor economy, high interest rates, low interest rates, boom market, bust market—it makes no difference. I have made money through all types of markets and economic conditions. And so will you—if you learn to think and act as a real estate entrepreneur. To achieve your dreams:

1. Guide your daily life with an entrepreneurial mind-set, character, and action plan.
2. Apply a systematic possibility-driven method to discover, create, and harvest real estate value.

THINK AND ACT AS AN ENTREPRENEUR

Popular culture frequently mischaracterizes (and often criticizes) the entrepreneur. For many people, the entrepreneur represents the brash, bold risk taker who charges ahead come hell or high water. He or she is often falsely portrayed as a promoter who slick-sells hype over substance. In this warped scene, greed motivates base behavior. This type of person will do or say almost anything to make a quick buck.

Sure, the real estate business attracts more than its share of practitioners and gurus who more or less match this dark perception. Nevertheless, at Trump University, we see the world more positively (and more clearly). Our view of entrepreneurs aligns with a passage from a speech that the late President Ronald Reagan delivered at St. John's University:

We have lived through the age of big industry and the age of the giant corporation, but I believe this is the age of the entrepreneur.... That's where American prosperity is coming from now, and that's where it's going to come from in the future.

The ultimate resource—as economics Professor Julian Simon emphasizes in his book by the same title—is people. Professor Simon reasons that we need not worry about running out of oil, gas, water, platinum, or, for that matter, money. As long as people demonstrate the "can do" spirit and as long as people grow their creative abilities to solve problems, we can look to a brighter future. "The main fuel to speed progress," Professor Simon emphasizes, "is our stock of knowledge, and the brake is lack of imagination. The ultimate resource is people—skilled, spirited, and hopeful people who will exert their wills and imagination for their own benefits, and for the benefit of us all."

To experience success, pursue life with a purpose.

Here's our Trump University pledge to you: When you choose to go into real estate and when you choose to motivate your life with an entrepreneurial spirit, you will enjoy unlimited opportunity to work for your own benefit, for the benefit of those you serve, and, through responsible, ethical behavior, for the benefit of us all. By combining knowledge, effort, and imagination, you will create real estate value.

Today's property and mortgage markets spell o-p-p-o-r-t-u-n-i-t-y for you—when you adopt an action plan that brings this entrepreneurial spirit to life.

Life is like an act; perform to the best of your ability; captivate your audience.

Entrepreneurial Thinking versus Motivated Sellers

In today's world of troubled owners and lenders, motivated sellers present a time-tested way to negotiate bargains. Yet, even so, you profit most when you view *motivated sellers* as one great possibility, but not by any means your only possibility.

Most get-rich-in-real-estate books preach only the gospel of motivated sellers. They tell you that to seek your fortune in property, focus on those many desperate souls plagued by divorce, layoffs, credit card debt, medical bills, the threat of foreclosure, and bankruptcy. In the United States and throughout the world, such misfortune has struck millions people.

When you successfully close deals with such troubled folks, you can sometimes buy a property at 20, 25, maybe even 30 percent below its current market value *potential*. Skilled negotiating can earn you instant equity.

But does the motivated seller approach to buying really work? Yes, it can. However, only jump in with your eyes open. Some get-rich-quick gurus overstate this technique's promise and understate its ability to deliver solid gains: They mislead in three ways: (1) violations of ethics and law, (2) practical difficulties, and (3) stunted entrepreneurial vision.

Violations of Ethics and Law

Some investors who negotiate with troubled sellers violate ethical and moral boundaries. They pressure, deceive, and extend promises that they do not intend to keep. To combat such unethical practices, various governments have enacted laws that specifically regulate sales by motivated (distressed) sellers in preforeclosure and/or bankruptcy. Although ethical entrepreneurs can profitably negotiate with troubled, motivated sellers, when doing so, they tread lightly with full, honest disclosure.

Practical Difficulties

The motivated seller approach adds practical difficulty to the issue of ethics. You cannot easily find motivated sellers who own substantial amounts of equity in their properties and at the same time will sell to you at a price substantially below market value. It happens. But it takes knowledge and effort. Through short sales, too, you can sometimes overcome the "no equity" problem. That technique also requires substantial planning and patience.

Stunted Entrepreneurial Vision

Although motivated sellers present some ethical, legal, and practical difficulties, the biggest mistake lies elsewhere. When they emphasize motivated sellers, too many authors stunt the entrepreneurial vision of investors. I have heard or read the following advice dozens of times: "Never buy any property unless you can get it for at least 20 percent under market." Not really. To make a sound decision, you figure out the *total* profit potential of a property.

By all means—as in many of today's property markets—search for and negotiate a bargain price. Ferret out those motivated sellers whom you can help resolve their most pressing concerns. But do not let this one technique push aside all other potential sources of profit. These other sources include (but are not limited to) cash flow, appreciation potential, below-market terms and costs of financing, mortgage payoff, and, most significantly, opportunities to add value to the property.

As you become a knowledgeable and experienced property entrepreneur, you will find profits lurking in dozens of hiding places—when you put on your rose-colored glasses to see them.

Don't let anyone tell you that you can't price yourself higher than the competition. We break the comps on all of our projects.

Entrepreneurial Thinking versus Property Market Appreciation

Property gurus often say that motivated sellers offer you the best chance to achieve wealth through real estate. In contrast, the popular press seems obsessed with short-term price changes—up and, more recently, down. According to hundreds of recent articles, investors should look for ways other than property to make money.

So let's address two issues:

1. Do you need market appreciation to build wealth in real estate?
2. What does experience teach?

Do You Need Market Appreciation to Build Wealth in Real Estate?

In the fast-moving property markets of the early to mid-2000s, investors, homeowners, and speculators made bundles of money from market increases in price. That's great. But this boom period generated a false presumption; that is, without appreciation, profit opportunities disappear. You might as well put your money into a savings account: less risk, greater expected return.

This simple conclusion misses three other major sources of real estate profits: cash flow, amortization (mortgage payoff), and value creation. Let's focus on cash flow and mortgage payoff. I will show you how to create value in later chapters.

I first invested in a no-growth town in Indiana. One of my first properties cost $100,000. I paid $10,000 down, and the seller financed the balance over 10 years. This older (I should say aged) apartment building did not appreciate. After 12 years, I sold it for $100,000, the same price I had paid.[1]

---

[1] For ease of illustration, this example uses rounded numbers.

To anyone who only judges returns by increases in price, it would seem that my apartment building proved to be a lousy investment. Instead, a closer look at the numbers actually reveals a bonanza.

After operating expenses and debt service, that property netted $2,500 a year in after-tax cash flow. Just in terms of cash flow, I earned an annual return on my $10,000 cash invested of 25 percent. In addition, that $10,000 down payment grew to a total equity of $100,000 (recall, I paid the note off at year 10).

Without appreciation, without value-creating improvements, I earned a total annual rate of return in excess of 30 percent. Can you still buy such properties? Yes, even today you can find similarly attractive deals in some parts of the South and Midwest and other areas that lie outside those more widely publicized, high-priced cities and neighborhoods.

Never focus only on market price increases. Just as the "dogs of the Dow" sometimes outperform the Microsofts and Amazons, so too can various low-to-moderate income, out-of-favor, no-, or slow-growth property markets offer attractive yields. The entrepreneur knows that he or she can achieve strong returns even in those times or areas where price increases take a long vacation. (However, as you will see in Chapter 6, due to the powerful force of leverage that multiplies gains from appreciation, I would encourage you to invest in areas that show more promise than the neighborhoods and towns like those I first chose, albeit without thinking through alternative buying strategies.)

What Does Experience Teach?

Are you discouraged by the negative news that fills the newspapers, magazines, and TV news shows? Don't be. Such media babble really signals opportunity, not despair. Every time property prices stall—or take a downward cyclical move—the press (and its media molls) announce "the end of real estate as an investment." Indeed, for the past 60 years, economists, Wall Street analysts, and other supposed financial experts have wrongly predicted a halt to future price gains. Take a quick trip through their far-off-the-mark forecasts from years gone by:

- "The prices of houses seem to have reached a plateau, and there is reasonable expectancy that prices will decline" (*Time*, December 1, 1947).
- "Houses cost too much for the mass market. Today's average price is around $8,000—out of reach for two-thirds of all buyers" (*Science Digest*, April 1948).
- "If you have bought your house since the War ... you have made your deal at the top of the market. .... The days when you couldn't lose on a house purchase are no longer with us" (*House Beautiful*, November 1948).
- "The goal of owning a home seems to be getting beyond the reach of more and more Americans. The typical new house today costs $28,000" (*Business Week*, September 4, 1969).
- "Be suspicious of the 'common wisdom' that tells you to 'Buy now ... because continuing inflation will force home prices and rents higher and higher" (*NEA Journal*, December 1970).
- "In California ... for example, it is not unusual to find families of average means buying $100,000 houses. ... I'm confident prices have passed their peak" (John Wesley English and Gray Emerson Cardiff, *The Coming Real Estate Crash*, 1980).
- "The golden-age of risk-free run-ups in home prices is gone" (*Money*, March 1985).
- "If you're looking to buy, be careful. Rising home values are not a sure thing anymore" (*Miami Herald*, October 25, 1985).
- "Most economists agree ... [a home] will become little more than a roof and a tax deduction, certainly not the lucrative investment it was through much of the 1980s" (*Money*, April 1986).
- "The baby boomers are all housed now [1989]. They are being followed by the baby bust. By 2005, real housing prices

will sit 40 percent below where they are today" (Harvard economist Gregory Mankiw, "The Baby Boom, the Baby Bust, and the Coming Collapse of Housing Prices," *Journal of Regional Economics*, Fall 1989).

- "We're starting to go back to the time when you bought a home not for its potential money-making abilities, but rather as a nesting spot" (*Los Angeles Times*, January 31, 1993).
- "Financial planners agree that houses will continue to be a poor investment" (*Kiplinger's Personal Financial Magazine*, November 1993).
- "A home is where the bad investment is" (*San Francisco Examiner*, November 17, 1996).
- "Your house is a roof over your head. It is not an investment" (*Everything You Know about Money Is Wrong*, 2000).
- "But the real question is, how will [housing prices] look longer term? As I've said, I do not think that housing values will be higher ten years from now" (Yale economist Robert Shiller, quoted in *Newsweek*, January 27, 2005).

Now think ahead. Who enjoys the highest net worth today? Those fear-induced folks who believed the press pundits and economic pontificators of yesteryear? Or those property entrepreneurs who ignored the Chicken Little naysayers and proceeded to acquire properties (especially in periods of down markets blessed by relatively low interest rates—opportunities such as those presented to you now)?

Most importantly, 10, 15, or 20 years from now, who will enjoy the highest net worths and greatest degree of financial freedom? Those who follow today's end-of-real-estate forecasts? Or those who follow the entrepreneurial principles and philosophy of Donald Trump?

Caution: We do not advise you to buy any thing, at any price, at any time—although history proves that even that unthinking strategy would generally have yielded good returns—over the long run. And yes, some (but certainly not all) property markets show wide cyclical downs and ups (with each new up surpassing former peaks). Yes, great deals typically require work and creativity. Yes, sometimes your properties might experience downward pressure on prices or rent levels. But these concerns miss the point.

All property markets and economic conditions present entrepreneurial opportunities for profit. Donald Trump began his career in the dark years of the mid-1970s, when virtually no one wanted to buy or develop property in the nearly bankrupt New York City. More impressive, Mr. Trump sowed the seeds for his present prosperity during his bleak loan workout days of the early 1990s—surely a strong example of turning lemons into lemonade.

So consciously choose your future: Will you accept those gloomy forecasts again flooding the media—forecasts that in the past have erred 180 degrees? Will you imbibe cliché and half-baked conventional wisdom? Or will you ignore the whirlwind of babble to become a real estate entrepreneur? Will you look beyond the journalistic pundits and so-called economic experts to trust the voice of reason, hope, and experience? In other words, will you let fear and a lack of knowledge keep you benched on the sidelines of wealth? Or will you choose to control your own life and actively navigate toward the financial and personal destiny that you would like to achieve?

If you answer, "Yes! Sign me up. I'm coming on board," good for you. In the pages that follow, you will discover the road to wealth and financial freedom. Let us show you how to think and act as a real estate entrepreneur—someone who can see a partially boarded-up hotel located in a deteriorating neighborhood—yet envision a Grand Hyatt Hotel surrounded by upscale shops, restaurants, and cafés; someone who can read site zoning rules that restrict the height of a building to 40 stories—yet obtain legal approval to build New York City's tallest mixed-use structure of luxury condominiums of 80 stories (twice the height seemingly written into law); *someone* such as yourself who can read fear-mongering headlines—foreclosures growing, and unemployment rising—yet still recognize that big problems create huge possibilities for profit.

As a knowledgeable, motivated entrepreneur, you can put together deals that provide win-win solutions. They may not match Trump deals in size or amount. But in like manner, they will engage your power to imagine, create, and build a richer life for others—and yourself.

3

How You Can Become a Real Estate Entrepreneur

TRUMP ADVICE
FOR ENTREPRENEURS

When I began working with Donald Trump, I was pleased to learn that he loves to read as much as I do. But even more surprising (although on reflection, it shouldn't have been), Mr. Trump shares my belief in the value of emotional discipline, and, for lack of a better term, self-improvement books.

Mr. Trump always emphasizes that "your attitude determines your altitude." Even though most so-called experts in the field of *academic* finance and investments dismiss such advice as mere "pop psychology." To the professors who teach investing, success requires only skill with numbers, quantitative methods, and portfolio diversification. In fact, until recently, most university business schools did not teach even one course in behavioral finance—a field in which a noted researcher has been awarded a Nobel prize.

As Mr. Trump has said, "Although in business school, I would not have believed that psychology could pave the way to financial success, I now realize that success starts from the castles your mind builds." Without the right habits of mind and corresponding habits of action, no would-be entrepreneur is likely to accomplish much. To Mr. Trump, the characteristics that lead to success include the following:

1. *Think positively:* It's your choice. You can find excuses or you can accept responsibility. You can find those who will complain with you. Or you can surround yourself with people who believe in what you (and they) can do, not what you can't do. Your attitude powers you toward (or away from) your wants and goals.

2. *Don't do it (just for) the money:* "Choose your goals so that you can pursue them with passion and enthusiasm," says Mr. Trump. "You will hit tough times. Your passion and enthusiasm will juice your momentum. Your passion and enthusiasm, your sense of accomplishment will get you over, around, under, or through those brick walls that will undoubtedly appear to block your progress. With enthusiasm, problems provide nothing more than a challenge, not a reason to quit."

3. *Set the standard:* "Ask yourself," says Mr. Trump. "What standards do you want to display to the world? What standards will exceed the expectations of your customers? My father set high standards for his bread and butter—houses and apartments. When I built Trump Tower, it opened to wonderful reviews and established itself as a landmark building. Like my father, I set and then surpassed my own standards, and in a big way."

Today, Mr. Trump continues to set new, high standards, not just with luxury buildings, but also with his golf courses. One leading golfing magazine has written that Mr. Trump "settles for nothing less than the best. If he puts his name on it, it's got to be great." Trump's first two golf course "masterpieces"—Trump International at Mar-a-Lago in South Florida and Trump National in Westchester County, NY—are undeniably great. They've won awards and converted naysayers. And he's already gone on record with hopes of someday bringing the U.S. Open to his course in Bedminster, NJ, which is built on the former estate of the one-time auto company executive, John DeLorean.

Simply stated, these three Trump principles will guide your entrepreneurial success: (1) develop and nurture positive habits of mind, (2) enjoy the money but motivate yourself with passion and enthusiasm, and (3) set the standard that pleases yourself and your customers—and a standard that others follow.

I'm not young enough to know everything. I'm always asking questions.

HISTORY PROVES THAT even average mom-and-pop property investors have achieved returns that would make the investment manager of a superstar mutual fund drool with envy. The more than 30 percent return that I earned on my first apartment building did not represent anything out of the ordinary. Recall that my gain with that property occurred without price increases or value creation. In fact, during my early years as an investor, I mostly milked my properties for cash flow to support myself during college and graduate school.

My Entrepreneurial Awakening

Luckily, after completing a PhD, my entrepreneurial vision broadened. Through a referral from the dean of the business school where I was then teaching finance and real estate, I got involved in property development. In addition, I landed a plum consulting assignment on a property deal for Roger Miliken (a Forbes 400 billionaire).

These experiences opened my eyes. Although my early property investments paid off handsomely, I soon recognized that an entrepreneurial approach to real estate would pay much larger dividends than anything I had previously imagined.

As Charlie Frazier (the original developer of Sea Pines Plantation on Hilton Head) once told me, "You can make money with real estate, but you can make far more with your ideas. My balance sheet shows property is my largest asset. But that's wrong for me and it's wrong for you. Your mind holds far more promise and potential than this entire island [Hilton Head] we're standing on."

Since those days in South Carolina, I've met and become friends with many more top-level entrepreneurs—some you've probably heard of, such as Mary Kay Ash, Ebby Halliday, Mark Victor Hansen, Frank McKinney, Trammel Crow, and, of course, Donald Trump. Others lead less visible lives, much like those profiled in *The Millionaire Next Door* (by Thomas Stanley). But no matter—famous or not-so-famous—all exercise emotional discipline and believe in the power of ideas.

Mind over Matter

Although each of these entrepreneurs differs in style and personality, every single one has affirmed to me the critical importance of mind over matter—or perhaps I might say "mind matters most."

Cosmetics did not make Mary Kay Ash wealthy. Mary Kay happened to earn her wealth through cosmetics (actually by creating a world-class sales organization). Textiles did not make Roger Milliken wealthy. Roger Milliken built his wealth through textiles. Property did not make Donald Trump wealthy. Donald Trump achieved his wealth through property development, renovation, and revitalization. Do you see what I'm saying? Entrepreneurs succeed because they guide their lives with the right principles and philosophy—not as a result of a particular product or industry per se.

Compete with yourself to be the best you can. Entrepreneurs know that to merely compete with others lowers their standards.

Donald Trump and I favor property. But we do not want you to merely rely on property to make you wealthy (although it might). We urge you to think, "I can create wealth through property." Entrepreneurs stress active personal control and responsibility.

Magnify Your Favorable Odds

Does an entrepreneurial approach guarantee success in every endeavor? Of course not. That's precisely why entrepreneurs differ from the majority. Few of us get through life without taking at least a few hard knocks. But the entrepreneurial approach offers the principles and philosophy necessary to bounce back.

Running into an obstacle doesn't necessarily mean going through it; you can go around, under, or over it. I never give up until I've exhausted all of my possibilities.

Even though an entrepreneurial outlook does not guarantee success, it sure magnifies the odds in your favor. With 25 years of experience in real estate and other ventures, I can look back for a postmortem diagnosis of my own screw-ups. Each and every time I let "misfortune" get the better of me, I violated a key entrepreneurial principle. I now see that within the center of such storms always lay an eye of opportunity that I missed because of confused thinking. This malady in turn blocked my ability to imagine and execute one (or some combination) of multiple promising outcomes.

Guide Your Life with Entrepreneurial Principles

Lest I sound maudlin, I would like to report that, like Donald Trump, overall my life has been blessed with good fortune. Both Mr. Trump and I have experienced far more successes than setbacks. And we are convinced that when you adopt our entrepreneurial principles and philosophy as your own, you too can take your personal and financial life to a much higher level of satisfaction and wealth (while avoiding some of the mistakes that each of us has made).

So here are the thoughts of Mr. Trump and myself on how you can become a top-gun entrepreneur who earns your wealth through real estate:

1. Elevate your attitudes.
2. Program your positive self-talk.
3. Dig your well before you're thirsty.
4. Cease your destructive spending and borrowing.
5. Plan your time, shape your life.
6. Honor your appointments, promises, and agreements.
7. Learn continuously, improve continuously.
8. Make great decisions.

For proof that these principles work, observe the failures and achievers you see each day. Who are the people who live the most emotionally satisfying, prosperous, and financially independent lives? I will bet that they are the people who find ways to move forward rather than wallow in complaint. Achievers do what they plan and plan what they do. Achievers envision possibilities when others see obstacles. Achievers elevate their attitudes.

Elevate Your Attitudes

"Your attitude determines your altitude." To achieve large goals, think positive, think big. It's the mind-set that powerful motivators such as Donald Trump, Zig Ziglar, Tony Robbins, and Les Brown prescribe for their audiences. Do not dismiss the power of positive attitude as mere pop psychology. Today, no one can seriously question the power of positive attitude to bring welcome and lasting change to your life.

> **So many books and examples preach the power of positive thinking that it seems unnecessarily repetitive to even mention it. Yet, every day I see examples of how negative thinking defeats spirits and destroys lives. So, either people haven't gotten the message or they're not paying attention. I hope that failure doesn't include you because I cannot abide by self-defeating attitudes.**

In the field of medicine, for example, Dr. David Burns has scientifically pioneered the practice of cognitive therapy to help patients develop positive attitudes and beliefs. Clinical tests confirm that such attitudes help people conquer debilitating depression. (See Dr. Burns' best-selling book, *Feeling Good*, Collins Living, 1999.) "As a man thinketh, so shall he live" even formed the theme of self-improvement books published in the 1800s. Both science and practical experience prove that can-do attitudes sharpen performance. Yes, we do live as creatures of habit. But we form those habits through our prevalent and persistent attitudes and beliefs.

You've heard people say, "I'll believe it when I see it." Psychologist Wayne Dyer turns that phrase around to say, "You'll see it when you believe it." As Dr. Dyer points out, believing that you can achieve the goals you want encourages you to find ways to realize them. If you fail to believe that you can realize your life-affirming goals, you'll never try.

At one time in my career, I conducted a national seminar program called "Stop Renting Now!" In talking with the people who attended, I learned that negative attitudes and beliefs had vanquished more dreams of home ownership than the lack of credit, income, or cash. Most of these people could have bought a home years before I met them. (Surprisingly, these folks were not in their 20s, as I expected they would be. Rather, most were over age 35.) Because they falsely believed that they could not own, they never searched out the knowledge that would have opened their eyes. Blinded by their distorted beliefs, they could not see their real possibilities. To remove this disabling affliction, in my book *Yes! You Can Own the Home You Want*, I titled the first chapter "Attitude + Education = Homeowner."

Your attitudes and beliefs do influence the height of your achievements. Drs. David Burns and Wayne Dyer are right. You will see it when you believe it. Set your goals high. Then, through knowledge and continuous education, figure out a way to conquer your obstacles and challenges. Entrepreneurs think positive and big. Whatever the mind's eye can envision, the spirit can achieve.

Program Your Positive Self-Talk

What do you say when you talk to yourself? Do you frequently critique yourself, yet, perhaps at the same time back away from responsibility for your own behavior? Do you find yourself saying anything similar to the following:

- I can't remember names.
- It's going to be another one of those days!
- That's just my luck.
- I'm just not creative.
- I can't seem to get organized.
- I can never afford the things I want.
- I never have enough time.
- I never know what to say.
- Things just aren't working out for me.
- I don't have the energy I used to.
- I'm really out of shape.
- I never have any money left over at the end of the month.
- Nobody wants to pay me what I'm worth.
- I'm just no good at math.
- I lose weight, but then I gain it right back again.
- I always freeze up in front of a group.
- I get a cold this time every year.
- I'm always running late.
- If only I had more money.

If some of these self-put-downs sound familiar, you're programming yourself to fail. In his action-directing book, *What to Say When You Talk to Yourself*, Dr. Shad Helmstetter writes:

> You will become what you think about most. Your success or failure in anything, large or small, will depend on your programming—what you accept from others and what you say when you talk to yourself.... The more you think about anything in a certain way, the more you will feel that belief accurately mirrors reality.

Such negative self-talk stifles your wealth-building possibility thinking. As to investing, do any of these excuses sound familiar to you:

- I should have invested earlier; interest rates are heading back up.
- I'll never be able to come up with the cash necessary to invest.
- There's no way we can cut our spending. We're going without now.
- Property is no longer a good investment.
- There's not anything out there I like that I can afford.
- My credit score is too low.
- My debts are too high.
- Our generation has it tougher than those who came before us.
- It's too late. People who bought years ago were lucky.
- Sure, I would like to own property, but I don't have the money.
- I would like to invest *someday*.

This list could go on and on. You might add a few possibility-stifling excuses of your own. It's all too easy to loop about in a self-defeating circle. To a certain extent, negative reporting by much of the media programs us to block action with negative beliefs. Such negative beliefs begin to screen out positive facts or information. Only the negative comes through. Seeing only the negative, you begin to hold your negative beliefs more tightly. They comfort you. Eventually, you might see only what you have come to falsely believe.

Negative Self-Talk Blocks Positive Fact-Finding

People who get caught up in this vicious circle of self-defeat cannot see their possibilities because they screen out facts that don't agree with their hapless beliefs. Even worse, they close their minds to potential. To break this cycle, consciously examine each negative thought or belief that cuts you off from the future you want. Hook up an electrode to your mind. Give yourself a jolt every time you let negative thoughts short-circuit your problem-solving abilities.

Whenever such thoughts occur, grab your mental channel selector. Switch to a different program. Although negative self-talk may contain an element of fact, or a bit of truth, none reflects all of the facts or the whole truth.

> **Every time a negative thought comes to you, zap it. Replace it with a positive thought. This requires mental energy, but the result will be stamina—positive stamina, an ingredient that sustains your efforts towards success.**

When you switch to clearer channels, you bring in a new picture, a picture that directs other facts and knowledge to your attention. When you switch channels and search for positive pictures, you realize that you control your own destiny. You may not control the events and conditions of the world, but you do control how you respond to them.

Reprogram Your Self-Talk Tapes

How do you gain control and respond effectively? By reprogramming. First, erase all negative self-talk tapes that you keep playing. Rerecord positive self-talk. When you erase your self-constructed limits, you replace them with possibilities. To illustrate: Closely think through the following questions. What are *your* possibilities? Don't worry if you can't answer all these questions now. You will be able to by the end of this book. But I do want you to get out of cruise control and start shifting into overdrive. Ask yourself:

- What are six ways I can save more?
- What are six ways I can cut spending?
- What are six ways we can increase our income?
- What are four ways we can overcome credit issues?
- Who can serve as role models or mentors for us?

- What economic indicators are positive?
- What types of finance plans permit lower down payments or lower monthly payments?
- Where are the favorably priced up-and-coming cities and/or neighborhoods?
- What techniques are available to make investing easier?
- Who could I get to partner with me: parents, family, friends, investor, employer, co-owner, Donald Trump?
- What are 10 ways I could create value for this property or neighborhood?
- How can I use today's market conditions to plant acorns that will grow into oak trees?

To solve problems, answer these and similar questions. When you embrace the idea of possibilities, you can come up with the inquiries necessary to move you forward. When you uncritically accept preprogrammed conclusions, you not only won't ask questions, you look past the choices that could solve your specific problems. That's why achieving wealth and financial freedom forces you to jolt yourself out of false, limiting beliefs. Once you erase these beliefs, your positive attitude alerts the mind to hunt down and lasso facts, knowledge, and experiences that lead to opportunity. Josh Billings, the celebrated nineteenth-century American humorist, used to wisely remark, "I fear not the things I don't know, but rather the things I think I know that just ain't so."

As you read the following chapters, search, explore, discover, apply. Engage your mind. Make notes. Highlight ideas that might work for you. Reflect on your entrepreneurial possibilities. Review choices. Create alternatives. You can build wealth with property. Our years of real estate experience affirm your possibilities. Your journey to personal freedom begins when you throw away negative, self-limiting beliefs. Through positive attitude and education, you can gain entrepreneurial altitude with a "can do—will do" list of possibilities.

Dig Your Well Before You're Thirsty

No one makes it alone in real estate (or life). To succeed, build a network of relationships with loan reps, real estate agents, title companies, property inspectors, lawyers, zoning/building regulators, handymen, contractors, and, of course, sellers, tenants, and, at some point, buyers.

When should you begin to develop your network, get to know them, and let them know you? Now! In the words of Harvey McKay, "Dig your well before you're thirsty."

Right now: Join your local real estate investment club. Go out and call on a variety of loan reps and loan brokers. Learn the types of deals they're doing today. Learn what types of deals they would like to do. Ask for names of dependable, competent, and reasonably priced service providers. It's never too early to start filling up your Rolodex or Blackberry with the names of people who might assist you—and, of course, think, too, of how you might help each one of them.

Don't become a parasite—taking, never giving. Reciprocity is the name of the game. Think: How can you help the other person? People in real estate (and related services) appreciate referrals. When you know someone who's about to buy, sell, borrow, or renovate, give him or her the name of a service provider with whom you would like to grow a relationship. Tell that service provider that you referred someone to him or her and that he or she might even initiate contact with the person you know (with his or her permission, of course).

I once referred an investor friend to a real estate broker I had previously done business with in Dallas. I didn't think much more about it until six months later, when I opened my mail to find a thank-you note from the broker and a check for $10,000. It seems my friend (whom I had not recently talked with) had just closed on a $2.7 million neighborhood shopping center. Now that's reciprocity. To build and nurture relationships, live those three very big words: quid pro quo.

Cease Your Destructive Spending and Borrowing

The late night real estate infomercials entice with grand displays of luxury. They know their customers, and these customers do not include many high-achieving entrepreneurs. Infomercial customers who look for easy ways to make money consist chiefly of people who spend and borrow beyond their means. Why else emphasize the "no cash, no credit, no problem" sales pitch?

If you were to believe this sales pitch, you might conclude that real estate can quickly lift you from indebted spendthrift to multi-millionaire without extracting time, effort, or financial discipline. Just what the gullible seek: All gain, no pain.

Entrepreneurs know differently. To achieve wealth and financial freedom, ration your spending and eliminate debt that destroys your future. If you earn $60,000 a year, live on $40,000 (or less). If you earn $100,000, live on $60,000 (or less). Never borrow to finance new cars, clothes, jewelry, travel, entertainment, or other affectations of the "good life." Rely on your credit cards for convenience only. Never abuse your credit to finance spending that you otherwise cannot afford.

The larger your discretionary income and the less your destructive debt (debt that finances a depreciating asset or impecunious lifestyle), the faster you build wealth and personal freedom. Study *The Millionaire Next Door* by Thomas Stanley. You will see that the majority of self-made millionaires strictly discipline their personal spending and borrowing. Not one of Professor Stanley's millionaires borrowed or spent lavishly during the years of their serious wealth building.

Impress your bankers or property sellers with your strong credit score and financial statement, not a new Mercedes, a prestigious home address, a Rolex watch, or an Armani suit. For wealth-building entrepreneurs, conspicuous consumption hurts much more than it helps. Extravagance destroys your power to invest and borrow constructively. It gives you a "big hat, no cattle" reputation.

Plan Your Time, Shape Your Life

If you have time to be petty, it indicates you're not productive enough with your work.

Right now, list and describe your important lifetime goals: health, fitness, wealth, freedom, love, philanthropy? What else? How much of your time and effort advances you toward each of your goals?

If you're like most people, a yawning gap separates how you actually live from how you would like to live. Why? Because you fail to bring the future you want into the present. You spend too much time on small tasks and trivial pleasures. You invest too little time mapping out the route you must travel to your better life. Weeks, months, and years pass by, and still, major goals remain as distant as ever.

Your Three "Budgets"

Everyone faces a mental budget, a money budget, and a time/activity budget. Your mental budget refers to how you allocate your thoughts, attitudes, and beliefs. Do you program your mind with negative self-talk, self-imposed limits, and puny aspirations? Or do you affirm and explore expansive ideas and creative possibilities? As to money, do you favor consumption over investment? Or do you discipline your spending and borrowing to secure a prosperous future?

After you've identified and entrepreneurially programmed your attitudes and beliefs and also figured out how to allocate your finances more profitably, inventory your hours. Surely, you've asked this question, "Where does my time go?" Accept the challenge: Answer it.

Record the Use of Your Time (i.e., Your Life)

You rank wealth and personal freedom among your lifetime goals. Does the way you allocate your time match this goal? You will live

168 hours this week, next week, and each week thereafter. How many of those hours will you look at properties, build business relationships, read thoughtful and informative books and articles, and complete other activities that advance you closer to your goals?

I love people who get to the point when they call or come by. If they don't waste my time, I will talk with people.

To succeed as an entrepreneur, forget "wishing and hoping," forget "someday," forget "if I only had the time." Make the time. Erase low-priority, low-significance activities from your schedule. Bring the future you want into view. What actions will you pursue today, this week, and in the weeks that follow that will banish "woulda, coulda, shoulda" from your self-talk? Want to change your life for the better? Change the way you think and behave today.

Honor Your Appointments, Promises, and Agreements

To nurture productive, quid pro quo relationships, to obtain insightful information, referrals, and recommendations, first provide others with information, referrals, and recommendations. Yet, your successful career requires something more: Dependability. When you agree to perform, exceed expectations.

Real estate attracts more than its share of fakes, pretenders, wannabes, sharks, shirkers, and weasels. In one way or another, such disreputable folks feel no need to honor their appointments, promises, and agreements. They show up late or not at all. They overpromise and underdeliver. They push for concessions long after a deal is struck. They refuse to close contracts for slight or illegitimate reasons.

Although surprisingly some such folks hang around the business for years, their shortsighted "I win—You lose" one-upmanship costs them far more than they would gain through more respectable behavior.

At the start of my career, I needed sellers to finance my property investments. In the beginning, banks would only say no. As a middle-class college student, I possessed neither bank credit nor significant bank balances. Nevertheless, owners of rental properties soon began to call me to present unsolicited offers. I benefited from referrals because early on I established myself as a young, ambitious entrepreneur who followed through on my promises, contracts, and commitments.

The lesson: Distinguish yourself from the weasels, sharks, and pretenders. Distinguish yourself from the "tall hat, no cattle" crowd who never follow through. Establish your dependability. If you set an appointment for 9:00, show up at 8:55. If you shake hands on an agreement, don't try to weasel a later concession. Think/act quid pro quo. If a situation deteriorates and you must amend or default for good and unavoidable reasons, draft a revised plan of commitment that you can honor. Prove to others that they can count on you without worry or suspicion. The good deals will find you.

Learn Continuously, Improve Continuously

Every day brings something new. Vacancy rates go up. Interest rates go down. Condo conversions fade. Lofts become popular. New types of financing appear. Revised zoning, tax, or landlord–tenant laws are enacted. Foreclosures increase, credit standards tighten, Market conditions, demographics, lifestyles, and cultural preferences never stand still.

For some would-be investors, change presents only problems. For entrepreneurs, change alerts them to profitable opportunities.

Opportunity or Despair?

Say the year is 2002. You live in San Diego. Property prices have accelerated so fast that you can't locate reasonably priced properties in any of the neighborhoods where you would like to invest. What do you do? Complain? Tell yourself that you missed your chance for big profits? Indict yourself with "woulda, coulda, shoulda" recriminations? No, you would choose none of these responses.

As a possibility-driven entrepreneur, you would ask questions. You would explore other neighborhoods (National City?) and other cities (Las Vegas? Phoenix? Peoria?). You would investigate whether all types of San Diego properties had experienced the same fast rates of appreciation. You would evaluate the potential for converting apartments to condos. You would talk with members of southern California real estate investment clubs to learn where the smart money is flowing. You would buy and read books on foreclosures, fixer-uppers, condominiums, small-income properties, tax liens, and creative financing.

When most people see the door close to one opportunity, they give up. They resort to self-defeating self-talk. Entrepreneurs know that for every door that closes, another one opens.

Case in point: During 2004 and 2005, I spoke on the programs at Robert Kyosaki's Los Angeles, San Jose, and San Francisco Rich Dad events. There, I talked with dozens of Californians who were actively looking for new investment ideas. They weren't depressed by high property prices or media babble about the bubble. These resourceful folks knew they could earn money in real estate somehow, somewhere. Their job was to learn all they could and then act on that knowledge.

No one could make 40 Wall Street (now home to Trump University) work. They artificially limited their possibility thinking.

Today, markets present different opportunities than they did in 2002 or 2006. But nevertheless, I still hear so many complaints about why this is not a good time to invest. When markets boom, "Oh no, prices are too high," When markets cycle down, "Oh no, the market looks bad." For many people, the time is never right, the price is never right, and the place is never right. But, you know what, it's their thinking that's really not right.

No matter where you are, possibilities abound—if not in your own backyard (as advocated in the book and speech *Acres of Diamonds* made famous by Richard Conwell, founder of Temple University), then perhaps in the next neighborhood over or even in another community, state, or country. If you want excuses to stay out of the game, you can always invent them. If you really want to build wealth, you will abandon your excuse-making and turn your thoughts to solutions.

You're on Your Way

You're reading this book. Good for you. You desire to learn. But go further. Continue to develop your information and knowledge. Read, listen to CDs, attend seminars and conferences, enroll in technique-driven courses (such as those offered by Trump University or other reputable providers), look at properties, and talk with anyone and everyone. Learning encourages continuous searching. Learn wherever you are, whatever you're doing. The facts, knowledge, and insights you develop today will pay back in multiples tomorrow.

Everyone you know or meet has at one time or another bought, sold, rented, financed, remodeled, or invested in property. Learn from their experiences. Use that knowledge to generate ideas and perform more profitably.

With your entrepreneurial mind-set in place, we now turn to the eighth and perhaps most critical entrepreneurial skill: Make great decisions.

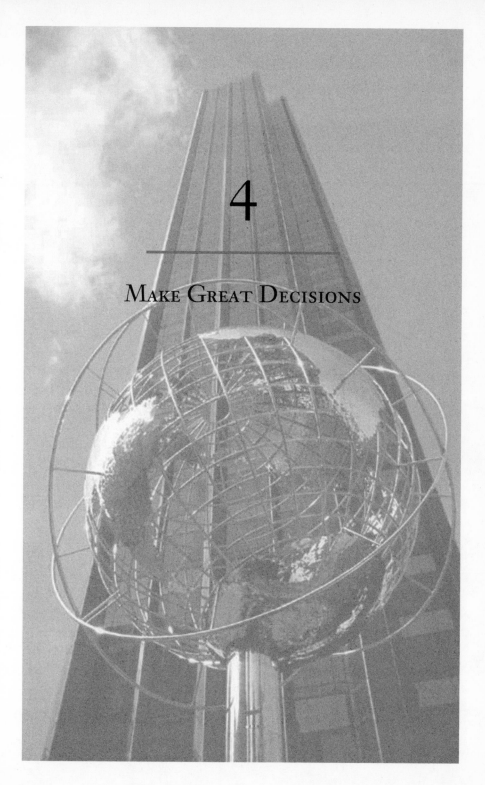

4

MAKE GREAT DECISIONS

CONSULT EXPERTS, RELY ON YOURSELF

"Too many people hire financial advisers and other experts," says Mr. Trump, "without realizing that those advisers can wreck their lives." Although Mr. Trump regularly consults with and relies on world-class experts, such as golf course designer Tom Fazio and architects Helmut Jahn and I. M. Pei, he never abandons his responsibility to make the final decision after multiple rounds of questions and research.

On one project, for example, Mr. Trump replaced Helmut Jahn because of Jahn's recurring conflicts with the New York City planning staff. (Unless you want trouble with your permitting, interact with the zoning and permit folks as cordially as possible.)

When it comes to market research, Mr. Trump decides. He doesn't employ a big staff of number crunchers to tell him where to build or what features to include. He knows his intended customers first hand.

I asked Jill Cremer, the Trump Organization's vice president of development and marketing, what techniques the company uses to find locations to build. She laughed and said, "We ask Mr. Trump, that's our research." She went on to say that he also chooses the carpeting, finishes, and many other building exterior and interior details.

In one instance, when Mr. Trump completely delegated a major property management task, he regretted his lack of attention when trouble hit. "Unfortunately," he lamented, "I made a critical mistake. I should have become involved myself in the beginning."

Naturally, someone who runs a company the size of the Trump Organization can't do everything himself. But Mr. Trump is no hands-off manager. If something happens, Mr. Trump is there to take responsibility. "I want to get the opinions of others before I decide," says Mr. Trump, "but I've gained more knowledge by asking questions than I ever have by commissioning a consulting report."

Consult experts, but never abandon your critical thought processes. Ask penetrating questions of everyone and anyone. Frank McKinney, the iconic Florida builder of $50 million spec homes tells this anecdote about Mr. Trump. "When I first met Mr. Trump," says McKinney, "he zipped right past the small talk. For the next 30 minutes, he fired questions at me to learn how I achieved so much in the luxury market. I've never met anyone so inquisitive."

Most people fear success. They fear commitment. They fear decisions. That gives people like me who know how to make great decisions an unbeatable advantage.

D O YOU ENDLESSLY mull over "What should I do" types of questions? Do you second-guess and rehash the decisions you've made? Do you regret past decisions? Have your past decisions sometimes failed to produce the results you wanted? Would you like to make better decisions in the future? If you answer yes to any of these questions (and who wouldn't?), here's how to open your life to a brighter future: Revise your decision-making *process* as it applies to your investing and your life.

Your life depends on the process you use to make investment decisions.

You can elevate your attitude, eliminate negative self-talk, plan your schedule, connect with other people, and learn everything about everything. But to become a top-gun property entrepreneur, you also have to figure out how to adjust your sights, where to aim, and when to pull the trigger.

Sometimes we go on for hours in the boardroom to get all of the information we need to make a knowledgeable decision.

In matters of real estate, as in matters of life, nothing substitutes for your ability to execute great decisions—decisions that move you quickly toward where you need to go. Yet, few (if any) of the courses that universities and colleges offer provide much help. They're long on problem solving but short on how to translate those "solutions" into profit-making action.

Contrary to dogma, "knowledge alone does not yield power." To power your life, put that knowledge to work. "I *knew* I should have ..." doesn't get the job done.

How do you increase the odds that your decisions will pay off the way you want them to? Easy. Do not focus on the decisions you need to make. Yes, you read that right—do not focus on the decisions you need to make.

First, engineer a fail-safe decision-making system. Hundreds of times, I've heard people complain, "Man, I screwed that up. I really made a bad decision when I ..." Yet rarely does anyone say, "Gee, all too often my decisions turn out badly because I've got a lousy decision-making process." However, more than likely, the fault does lie with your process.

So let's talk system. Let's work to improve the quality of your investment decision-making process. Here are five pointers that will help:

1. Rank priorities, explore possibilities.
2. Get your facts straight.
3. Use rules of thumb cautiously.
4. Question advice and recommendations (expert or otherwise).
5. Organize your thinking.

RANK PRIORITIES, EXPLORE POSSIBILITIES

"What *was I* thinking?" Surely—after you've made a mistake—you've asked yourself that question. It pops into your mind when you realize that your decision seems to have set you back from what you would like to achieve. To avoid this lapse, get in touch with your feelings, values, and priorities. Think through multiple ways to reach your investment objectives.

Set Priorities

Know yourself. Know what you want. Know which goals and activities you would like to pursue. Rank your priorities in importance. Without ranked priorities to guide your decisions, either you drift without aim or your life reflects the chaos of a Marx brothers comedy. You perpetually scurry in multiple directions—but never end up where you want to be.

Expand Your Possibilities

You may know where you want to go but not how to get there. Often people fail to make the decisions that best fit their goals and priorities because they narrowly limit their menu of choices. As I previously pointed out, I met many renters at my "Stop Renting Now!" events who truly valued home ownership but blocked themselves from this goal. They had not learned their real-life possibilities.

The reason I can move quickly is that I've done the background work first, which no one really notices.

Likewise, I often discover motivated sellers who want to dump their troubled properties. Yet, myself and other investors buy these "losers" and turn them into moneymakers. That's why savvy entrepreneurs persistently build their stock of ideas and knowledge. When you command a diverse and extensive repertoire of possibilities, you spot opportunity where others have suffered defeat. In later chapters, you'll see scores of issues from which you can draw ideas to estimate and create value or, just as important, spot risk (danger). Naturally, you won't apply each possibility in every situation. But your multitalented repertoire will definitely boost your power of possibility thinking: What can go right? What can go wrong? Great decisions anticipate both types of outcomes.

GET YOUR FACTS STRAIGHT

Quality decisions require accurate facts and data. *Fortunately*, such facts don't come easy. Why fortunately? Because when other investors fall for slipshod data and firehouse chatter, your thoughtful approach will give you a competitive advantage to deal with reality, not illusion. Before you accept a so-called fact, you think, analyze, and verify.

When I started out, I spent a lot of time researching every detail pertinent to the deal. I still do the same today.

Say that someone warns you, "Vacancy rates in the area have jumped up to 9 percent. This isn't a good time for you to invest in rental properties." How should you interpret this information?

Facts versus Opinion

To get your facts straight, distinguish *fact* from opinion. Opinions often *masquerade* as truth. Realize the difference. Even if—in some sense—the 9 percent vacancy figure is correct, the fear-mongering that follows represents a view that may or may not prove reasonable. So, beware! Much of the information you seek will be delivered to you as part fact, part opinion. Distinguish between the two.

Think of a *fact* as a data point that you can reasonably incorporate into your analysis and decisions. For example, you can generally obtain reliable facts about interest rates, apartment rent levels, real estate listings, property sales prices, time on market, population growth, and the number of properties for sale that remain unsold (inventories).

What about vacancy rates? These figures more frequently reflect "fact" or fancy. By "fact," I mean a figure that displays some truth but that is of limited use in its raw form. When reported by market research and commercial/investment brokerage firms, vacancy rates usually fall into this iffy category—informative but in need of a closer look.

Before you rely on such a number, answer questions such as:

- What geographic boundaries specifically delineate the area studied?
- How did the researchers gather their data? What sampling errors could distort the data?
- How does this 9 percent market vacancy rate differ among properties according to building size, unit mix, price ranges, amenities, features, condition, location, and so on? (Maybe one large 400-unit low-income HUD Section 8 property accounts for 40 percent of the vacancies in the total area under study. Maybe studio apartments enjoy waiting lists; three-bedroom, one-baths remain tough to fill.) When you speak of vacancy rates (as just one example), market segments and market niches matter greatly.
- Where are vacancy rates headed? Snapshots rarely provide a full, dynamic view. You want trend lines from the past and reasoned forecasts that look to the future.

Sometimes "facts" are better characterized as fancy. For any number of reasons, the people you talk with (or read) may not know what they are talking about. Obviously, we all inadvertently make mistakes. On other occasions, property sales agents give answers without facts so as not to appear ignorant. In some instances, people purposely steer you off track. Will an apartment manager truthfully disclose to a market researcher that her building's rent roll turns over twice a year and that her building's vacancies have climbed above 25 percent? I don't think so.

Think, Analyze, Verify

Savvy entrepreneurs search beyond conventional wisdom, "facts," opinions, and fanciful dodges or assertions. They know that quality facts provide the ingredients for quality decisions. As you move forward in real estate (and life), use multiple data points, multiple sources of information, and multiple valuation metrics (see Chapters 13, 14, and 15). Before you decide: Interpret, think, analyze, and verify. Avoid a rush to judgment. The world overflows with garbage in, garbage out (GIGO) decisions. But with facts, you can outsmart and outperform the crowd that uncritically accepts "facts," fancy, or ill-formed, distorted, or biased opinions.

> **Napoleon said, "A leader may rightly face defeat but should never suffer loss from surprise."**

USE RULES OF THUMB CAUTIOUSLY

Recently, I bought a property from an out-of-town owner. This owner didn't want to sell, nor had he placed his property on the market. Nevertheless, I persuaded him to consider my "generous" offer of $90 psf (dollars per square foot represents a rule-of-thumb value metric).

Given that this owner had bought this property years ago, my offer provided him a large gain. He responded to my offer with casual interest. Still, because he lived out of town and lacked up-to-date information on local property prices, he told me that before going further with discussions, he wanted to test my offer against the advice of a sales agent.

"No," the sales agent reported, "$90 psf is too low. The going price is around $100 psf."

The seller called back and told me he would sell at $100 psf. I objected, "That price is too high. The property needs a lot of work. You're taking advantage of me because you know I want the property."

Alas, my objections fell on deaf ears. I gave in. "Okay," I responded, "against my better judgment, I guess I can go to $100 psf. You just got my top dollar."

Loan Appraisal for This Property

"Holy cow!" the mortgage loan appraiser said to me as I showed him around the property. "Considering the low price you paid, I thought this place would be wrecked. I'm going to report a market value figure at the low end of the value range for this property, but that's still 20 percent more than your contract price. How did you find such a steal?"

Errors of the Agent and Seller

When the sales agent gave the seller her rule-of-thumb valuation of $100 psf, she recited a "fact," not a *fact*. True, on average, properties in the area *had sold* for the price she quoted. But the owner should not have relied on that rule-of-thumb figure for two reasons:

1. *Out of Date:* At that time, properties in that market were appreciating quickly. The rule-of-thumb figure of $100 psf reflected past closed sales, not pending contracts. More recently, current buyers had bid prices up another 10 to 15 percent. The agent lacked first-hand, up-to-the-minute knowledge of that specific neighborhood.
2. *Unique Features:* As a second factor, this subject property differed favorably from the average. Units displayed open floor plans, garden views, and bright/light interiors (because of skylights and many large windows). The units were also smaller than average. (All other things equal, and within the same neighborhood, smaller units tend to sell for higher price-per-square-foot figures than larger units.)

Go Beyond Rules of Thumb

In real estate (as with the stock market, too), you will run across many rules of thumb (discussed in later chapters). You will find measures (valuation metrics) such as gross rent multiplier, capitalization rate, price psf construction costs, energy costs, remodeling costs, maintenance expense ratios, rental rates, vacancy rates, and so on. Never accept any of these rules of thumb as *fact*.

Investigate further. Each market, each property, shows unique features and conditions. Before you apply any facts or rules of thumb, verify their relevance to your property or problem. (Of course, when you negotiate to buy or sell, you can rely on various rules of thumb that favor your position to persuade the other party that your offer is reasonable and justified.)

Question advice and recommendations (expert and otherwise).

Real estate authors and speakers often advise you to establish a team of individuals to whom you can turn for advice and recommendations. In our complex world, no one person can know everything. Good advice.

I go over every detail with my experts. They're on my team, but I'm the General.

Yet, heed this warning: Never delegate critical decisions to your advisers—regardless of whether they're trusted friends and family or world-class experts. Recall the out-of-town owner from whom I bought a property. He carelessly relied on his "expert" real estate agent. In doing so, he gave up $130,000 of potential gain.

The people you turn to for advice can fail you for a variety of reasons, some benign, some not so. Either way, your decision (and bank account) suffers. When dealing with advisers, guard against these five pitfalls:

1. Advice or approval?
2. Knowledge or ignorance?
3. Your preferences or theirs?
4. Conflict of interest?
5. Public soothsayers or media molls?

Advice or Approval?

Ask yourself, "Do I really want critical counsel?" We all know people who ask for advice but really want approval. In response, we approve. Why start an argument? The advisee then uses the approval to further justify what he wanted to do all along. Preconceived often means predecided.

To gain most from advice, insist on "no holds barred" counsel. Then question, listen, weigh, interpret, and apply as you deem wise. If you do not really want additional perspective, insight, or critique, don't burden your advisers with pretense. Don't seek advice for the same reason that a drunk seeks a lamppost—that is, for support, not illumination.

When undiluted support for your preconceived ideas is what you want, your friends, family, or consultants will probably oblige. But if that's the case, recognize their advice for what it is—"go along to get along," not disinterested critique.

Knowledge or Ignorance?

Do those you ask for advice possess the information, experience, and expertise necessary to advise you intelligently? Unless your friends or relatives have recently been shopping for property in the same city and neighborhood where you've been looking, they can't tell you whether you're getting a good buy. If your lawyer sister hasn't seen a real estate contract since her Real Property 101 course in law school, chances are she's not the one who should review your purchase agreement.

You may work with one of the best and brightest real estate agents in town, but if your property search takes you into neighborhoods or communities where your agent can't find her way without studying a map, it's time to bring in an agent who's more familiar with the area. Whether friend, relative, lawyer, or sales agent, just because someone offers an opinion does not mean he or she actually knows enough about your problem and goals to provide the counsel you need.

Beware: General Rule or Exception

Several years ago, I consulted a certified public accountant (CPA) to complete my federal income tax returns. During the years in question, I had served as a visiting professor at the University of Illinois, 1,000 miles distant from my permanent home in Florida. I told this tax professional that I wanted to deduct the living expenses I incurred while working in Champaign–Urbana.

"No, you can't do that," he emphatically declared. "Regardless of where you own a house, your tax home is located where your job is located."

Fortunately, I knew this law better than the tax specialist. As a general tax rule, the CPA was correct. He erred with his advice because tax law specifically states that employees may deduct their job-related living expenses when working temporarily away from home. (We need not go into the technical issues here.)

My point is that experts may know general rules and practices very well. But every subject, from accounting to zoning, involves specialized details. You may, for example, assume that conversations with your lawyer are private and privileged. As a general rule, you're right. Sue your lawyer for malpractice, and you'll be rudely surprised. That lawsuit voids the lawyer's previously inviolable pledge of confidentiality.

When you seek advice and recommendations, verify that your counselor actually knows the exceptions as well as the general rules. Had I followed that CPA's advice instead of the *exceptional* temporary work rule, my tax bill would have increased $8,000. Beware of generalists when you need a specialist.

Up to Date?

On one occasion when I sought legal advice on a property transaction, the lawyer informed me of the relevant law. On the basis of his analysis, I proceeded through the transaction. All too late, I learned that the lawyer had erred. The law in question had actually changed six months prior to the date I talked with the lawyer. That lawyer had failed to stay current. His error cost me more than $100,000. (Malpractice? I'll save that story for another time.)

When dealing with experts, do not assume that their advice reflects the latest developments. Question the date of their data, information, and knowledge. As with milk and eggs, the use-by date for legal/financial advice may have expired.

Age of Discontinuities

Real estate investors frequently look at past trend lines before they buy, renovate, or sell a property. They want to learn where the market has been moving. The real question, though, becomes more difficult to answer: Will current trends continue, or will discontinuities intervene? Here's an example.

Back in the 1990s, single-family houses appreciated faster than condominiums. In some cities, in fact, condominiums barely appreciated at all. So, after this dismal decade of little or no capital gains for most condominiums, many media commentators (circa 2001) provided this advice: "If you want a good investment, don't buy a condominium. Choose a condo only for lifestyle and affordability. Condominiums make lousy investments."

I differed from this prevailing negative forecast for condominiums. I believed that the slow-growth condo price trend of the past decade would not repeat itself. To explain my reasoning, in 2002, I wrote a book, *Make Money with Condominiums and Townhouses*.

In that book, I urged property investors (and homebuyers) to ignore the past and look to the future. Market conditions had changed in the following eight ways:

1. *Demographics I:* An increasing number of baby boomers were becoming empty nesters. They no longer wanted the big house and its time and expense of upkeep.

2. *Demographics II:* As of the early 2000s, the echo boomers were coming of age. Condos appeal not only to their empty nester parents but also to younger people who are buying their first home.

3. *Urban Living:* Throughout the 1990s, many cities reduced crime, revitalized downtown areas, and in general made city living more appealing. In addition, traffic congestion stuck commuters in intolerable delays. In-town condo living permitted escape from traffic hassles.

4. *Price Differences:* When one type (or location) of property appreciates faster than another, sooner or later many would-be buyers switch their preferences to the lower-priced alternatives.

5. *Lock and Leave:* People today travel more for both business and pleasure. They increasingly like the lock-and-leave lifestyle that condominiums make possible.

6. *Second (and Third) Homes:* Beginning in the late 1990s, demand for second homes grew substantially. (See my book, *How to Buy Second Homes for Vacation, Retirement, and Investment*). As often as not, second homebuyers choose condos and townhouses.

7. *Rent vs. Own:* The low interest rates of the early 2000s changed the rent–buy equation. With mortgage rates at 6 percent or less, tenants who preferred apartment living began to realize that they could own their own apartment for less than they were paying in rent.

8. *Investor Demand:* After stocks crashed in 2000, millions of investors began looking for good investment alternatives.

Even without appreciation, condo investments in many areas yielded great returns just from cash flows and mortgage payoff (amortization of the loan).

In addition to these eight reasons, my close study of the then current market (2000–2002) revealed that condo sales had picked up, prices had begun to increase, time on market for listings was falling, and condo/townhouse "for sale" inventories were shrinking. While most media articles were stuck in the past, my emphasis on the latest facts and market conditions (demand and supply) convinced me that conventional advice erred. Condos and townhouses would soon generously reward their investors.

Was I right? Yes. "Condo Price Increases Again Outpace Houses," headlined a 2005 article in the *New York Times*. In my Florida hometown, condos and townhouses that had sold for $125,000 in 2000 would quickly sell at $250,000 in 2005.

Yet, by late 2005, I expressed caution toward those cities where condo prices had shot up far faster than rents. Even more troubling, builders were bringing thousands of newly built units to market.

Follow emerging changes in supply and demand. Neither booms nor corrections last forever. Contrary to the way most people think and invest, a continuing boom always signals a slowdown or worse. Unthinking investors forecast boom times into the future as far as the mind can see. They follow the prevailing commentary that "this time it's different," or maybe "we are entering a new era where old rules of investing no longer apply."

On the other hand, when the boom ends, prevailing commentary advises against investing. People who want to sell greatly outnumber those who are shopping to buy. Those who thoughtlessly surfed the boom often become distressed sellers. Bargains are yours for the asking. (Well, actually you have to do more than ask.) Most people will not look beyond today's news to recognize the profits that the value investors of today are sure to reap tomorrow.

Your Preferences or Theirs?

Do your advisers truly understand your needs and goals? Or do they merely advise you to judge the world as they see it? When you ask for advice, fully explain your needs, goals, or the most important things you're trying to achieve. Likewise, when you offer counsel, you probably tend to shade recommendations toward your own biases. Indeed, most find it difficult to focus and accept the other person's perspective.

If you ask your brother to tell you what he thinks of that foreclosed, fixer-upper, three-bedroom ranch in Windsor Heights, he could answer, "No way! I wouldn't even think about buying that property." Has your brother actually answered according to your needs? Or does he express some bias against foreclosures, fixer-uppers, or the Windsor Heights location? What if a real estate agent tells you Windsor Heights is not a good area? Should you accept that advice without further inquiry? Of course not. Ask why the agent holds that view. Maybe this agent doesn't like Windsor Heights because he doesn't think much of its schools.

What Does Your Target Market Want?

Yet, if your targeted households of renters or buyers do not consist of families with children, perhaps schools won't matter much to them. Alternatively, maybe the neighborhood includes a nearby, reasonably priced private school. Or maybe the poor-school issue has so beaten down property prices in that district that the neighborhood now fits your investment strategy: Find relatively low-priced areas that offer strong promise for turnaround. As an ambitious neighborhood entrepreneur, you could spearhead a campaign for community revitalization and school improvement.

Sometimes advisers parrot approval of your ideas as a "go along to get along" tactic. More often, they paint their advice with colors that match their own picture of the world. Before you ask for advice or recommendations, explain the goals that you want your decision to accomplish.

Personal Reflection

Here's another personal reflection on this point: Dozens of times each year, I meet people who take a minute or so to describe a property to me. Then they ask, "What do you think? Does it sound like a good investment?"

I like to help aspiring investors. But with such sketchy data, I cannot provide useful input about the merits of the property.

A quick recitation of facts (or maybe "facts") hardly builds a solid base on which to hang my recommendation. Second, no property represents a "good" investment apart from the risks, rewards, and goals that remain personal to the investor. Rather than respond something like, "Yeah, seems like a good deal. I'd encourage you to go for it" (which I suspect most want me to say)—remember most people seek approval even though they feign to seek advice—I answer, "What are your goals, talents, inclinations, and plans? Have you performed your due diligence on the property's features, condition, rent levels, and expenses? Do your answers to these questions blend together well?"

Do not shift your decisions to experts—me or anyone else. Even if I am convinced that your deal looks great, it still might not work as the right deal for you.

That's why I qualify the advice that tells investors to "deal only with motivated sellers." Regardless of its potential to yield profits, this technique does not match the strategies and goals that many people prefer to adopt. Many investors who try it abandon the approach in disappointment—and regrettably give up on real estate without exploring the other sources of profit property that investing offers.

Conflict of Interest?

Do your advisers' interests conflict with your interests? When you rely on the advice of other people, detail how their advice may steer you into poor decisions. Some unethical real estate agents may try to talk you into a property or mortgage finance plan that doesn't meet your needs just so they can gain a commission or kickback. Your friends or parents may talk against an outlying neighborhood because they'd rather you live closer to where they live. Your friends could advise you not to invest in real estate because they're jealous, or maybe they think that you will drift apart as friends as you pursue new activities and responsibilities.

People often hide their own reasons for the advice they offer. Maybe they want to help you make a better decision. Maybe they are pursuing their own agenda. When someone says, "This is what you ought to do," "Here's what I recommend," or something similar, first reflect and critique. Think through the knowledge (ignorance), perspectives, biases, and *motives* that support such advice.

Read Intelligently and Critically

Have you ever wondered why the personal finance magazines heavily promote the idea, "Over the long run, stocks have outperformed all other investments"? Because it's true? Hardly. Look at the magazine's advertisers—mutual funds, stockbrokers, and life insurers, all of whom sell Wall Street-based retirement, investment, and insurance plans.

In like manner, few local newspapers run articles that criticize real estate brokers (or automobile dealers). These types of businesses often provide more than 30 percent of newspaper advertising revenues.

Public Soothsayers or Media Molls?

Many schooled professionals believe themselves experts even though they have never demonstrated practical competence in the areas for which they routinely offer advice to the public. Indeed, the media promote this misplaced conceit.

I never accept anything I read or hear from brokers, sellers, buyers, tenants, experts, or television, generally. I want to dig in and verify the data, interpretations, and conclusions.

Economic Forecasts Rarely Forecast Correctly

Newspapers, magazines, and cable news broadcasts, for example, refer to their quoted economic forecasters as experts. But for the most part, the expertise (if any) of these commentators lies in their intricate knowledge of theoretical economic models. Few consistently forecast accurately. For instance, recall that back in 1989, Harvard economist Gregory Mankiw (later to become chairman of President George W. Bush's Council of Economic Advisers), predicted that between 1989 and 2005, home prices would steadily fall by 40 percent. Rather than fall, most properties during that period doubled or tripled in value.

When Alan Greenspan appeared before Congress to testify about his competency to become chairman of the Federal Reserve, a senator asked, "Mr. Greenspan, we have reviewed your forecasts about the U.S. economy during the past decade. It seems that your predictions have erred far more often than they have proved correct."

Greenspan responded, "Yes sir, my forecasts often have missed the mark. However, I can say that fortunately, other aspects of my career have achieved a higher rate of success."

After 18 years as head of the Federal Reserve, Greenspan's monetary and regulatory policies are seen by some as leading causes for the recent credit crises and foreclosure morass.

Financial Planners: Technocratic Expertise or Investment Savvy?

Although few financial planners display out-of-the-ordinary investment savvy, the press promotes them as financial experts and routinely quotes their investment recommendations and asset allocations. Such expertise remains questionable. In the late 1990s, I never read one quoted financial planner who advised investors to sell stocks and buy property—even though such advice would have proved enormously profitable both in terms of achieving property gains and avoiding stock market losses.

Quite the opposite. Then and now, most quoted financial planners claim, "If you own your own home, you've got all of the exposure to real estate you need. Over the long run, count on stocks to outperform all other asset classes."

As to actual expertise, financial planners should know the technical rules of tax-deferred retirement planning, the investment styles of various mutual funds, and the source of low-cost annuities. They certainly know the conventional wisdom of investing and asset allocation as propagated by the theoretical finance professors and Wall Street purveyors of financial products. But few practicing financial planners (as opposed to media molls) even claim to know how to earn extraordinary returns on investments.

Moreover, the coursework leading to the certified financial planner (CFP) certificate devotes only three hours to the topic of real estate investing—the world's largest asset class. Contrary to their media-promoted image, most financial planners do not excel as investors any more than most economists excel as forecasters.

Uncharitable Critique

In stating this less-than-charitable critique of economists, financial planners, and other experts who serve as media molls, I do not intend wholesale indictment. The majority of professionals who do not regularly step onto the media stage tend to define themselves as technocrats, not soothsayers. They competently deal with the technical and theoretical issues of economics, investment selection, and portfolio diversification. I challenge as suspect primarily those investment commentators (often economists and financial planners, but they are not the only members of this species) who publicly advise investors about swings in interest rates, the direction of housing prices, which stocks to pick, currency exchange rate movements, and other topics on which these so-called experts have shown no superior forecasting skills.

Experience proves that media "experts" err with their investment forecasts and opinions more often than they get things right. Never *uncritically* base your investment decisions on such advice—even if it represents a so-called expert consensus.

Advice and Counsel Redux

Early in my career, I erred egregiously because I wrongly assumed that my lawyer possessed expertise in areas (negotiation and litigation) when he clearly did not. Such early experiences (now witnessed multiple times over) have warned me not to abdicate my investment decisions to experts or advisers.

Learn from my experience. Never assume that your lawyer, CPA, real estate agent, mortgage broker, financial planner, medical doctor, dentist, or other reputed expert knows enough to advise you in all the areas for which you seek advice. Be wary of media stage hounds who show little or no record of success in the areas where they offer advice. Question, probe, and explore issues. Only when you are satisfied with an expert's verified counsel should you incorporate that advice into your decision making.

In business and life, take off your blindfold.

Develop Your Ability to Question

I hear you object: "But, I don't know anything about . . . How can I ask my experts pointed, intelligent questions? How can I explore issues when I don't even know the relevant issues?"

You can develop this skill to question and probe through practice and education. How many laypeople know anything about cancer, heart problems, or other illnesses? Nevertheless, they are learning. Throughout the United States, an increasing number of patients no longer accept without question the diagnoses and prescriptions of the medical establishment.

Medical specialists told the famous writer and editor, Norman Cousins, that he needed to get his personal and business affairs in order because he had six months to live. Modern medicine offered no hope. Cousins refused to accept this death sentence. He studied his illness. He explored alternatives that lay outside the diagnostic and prescriptive models of medical conventions. He developed his own treatment plan. He lived another 10 years. (Cousins tells his story in his book *Anatomy of an Illness*.)

Sometimes experts know the answers we're seeking. Sometimes they don't. Thus, savvy entrepreneurs and investors (as do savvy medical patients) probe, question, and challenge their experts before they make a decision on the basis of such advice or recommendations.

Memorialize Advice in Writing

When you do choose to rely on professional advice, memorialize it in writing. During conversations, take detailed notes. Then follow up: Write the adviser (lawyer, accountant, appraiser, consultant, real estate agent, loan rep, contractor, and so on) a thank-you letter or e-mail. In that correspondence, express appreciation for his or her advice. Accent the adviser's expertise, restate your understanding of the issues, and discuss what decision you plan to make that flows from the information the adviser provided.

This follow-up letter achieves three purposes: (1) It helps build your relationship (everyone likes a letter of appreciation); (2) it gives the adviser a chance to correct errors on his or her part or misinterpretations from your end; and (3) if the advice subsequently proves faulty, your written note confirms the substance of the advice. Such evidence promotes peaceful remedy or, if necessary, supports a claim through lawsuit or regulatory complaint.

When you memorialize advice in writing, you not only reduce the chance of error but also increase the chance of a satisfactory informal settlement or legal recovery. With written evidence, you reduce or eliminate "I said, you said" quarrels that will not bring back the opportunities you've missed or the damages you have suffered due to the sub-par counsel.

Organize Your Thinking

To make decisions intelligently, you must sort through *facts* about property features, zoning laws, building regulations, target markets, vacancy rates, new construction, contracts, promotion, financing, economic conditions, and thousands of other details. This task raises two questions: How can you possibly make sense out of all this information? How can you even know what information you need to collect?

If you can't organize your thoughts quickly and come to a decision, that good deal you were looking at will have been snapped up by someone else.

In the pages that follow, I provide you answers to these two questions. Just as aircraft pilots rely on preflight checklists to prepare for takeoff, you need a takeoff plan to guide your real estate entrepreneuring. Instead of a checklist, however, we'll call this takeoff guide, the DUST framework. (We explain what the acronym stands for in the next chapter.) This entrepreneurial flight plan spells out the details to consider when you decide whether to buy and, if so, how much to pay for properties (or other opportunities, such as options, leases, air rights, or mortgages). Just as important, DUST shows you how to create the right market strategy and tactics that will create value for your tenants, your buyers, and yourself.

Thus far, in Chapters 3 and 4, you have learned a good set of questions and guidelines to refine and advance the process you employ to make investment decisions. Next, you will discover how to ask questions, collect facts, identify possibilities, and reason through your decision process to estimate, forecast, and create property values. To achieve your goals, you need: (1) a systematic and thorough thinking process, and (2) an entrepreneurial vision that can recognize opportunities to create value for others and yourself.

Winners solve problems as a great way to prove themselves.

5

Sharpen Your Entrepreneurial Thinking

Organize your information for quick retrieval and thorough understanding.

E VER SINCE WILLIAM NICKERSON wrote his now classic *How I Turned $1,000 into a Million in My Spare Time* (1959), best-selling real estate authors have been revealing "the secrets of my success." "Just follow these six steps," they say. "I'll give you everything you need to know." Sounds easy.

But here's the catch: If you adopt an investment approach that was developed by someone else in another place and time, you may end up losing your bank account. And, most certainly, you will miss the best opportunities that actually present themselves to you (albeit often unannounced). Why? Because real estate markets experience continuous change.

PROBLEMS OR OPPORTUNITIES?

Nothing remains the same: interest rates; existing properties for sale; vacancy rates; property prices; rent levels; number of foreclosures; employment; population demographics; consumer tastes, preferences, attitudes, and lifestyles; the cost and supply of new construction; government zoning rules, regulations, and restrictions. Every change presents problems and opportunities.

Fuse knowledge with imagination. In no time, you'll create something great to put in your "think big" tank.

That's why the same business plan that blessed you with profits last year could turn into a curse next year. Just look at the brand-name companies (such as Lehman Brothers, Merrill Lynch, Countrywide, Polaroid, Kodak, Sears, General Motors, Ford, Conseco, AIG, Kmart) who once excelled with well-crafted business models but subsequently suffered fatal or near-fatal losses because they failed to revise their entrepreneurial strategies in response to changes in financial markets, technology, competition, consumer preferences, and/or emerging lifestyles.

Look at the dozens of homebuilding and mortgage lenders who were racking up record profits during the boom years, yet now face record losses, a salvage-value stock price, or maybe bankruptcy, merger, or liquidation. Look at those many condo speculators in Miami, Las Vegas, Dubai, and Mumbai who failed to monitor adverse market signals and now are desperate to sell—even if it means they lose big.

It All Depends

No one can tell you the easy way to real estate riches. It's natural for people to believe that someone else can tell them exactly what they need to do to make a fortune in real estate. Most of us would like a simple five-step system that automatically loads our bank account with cash—better yet, a system that pretends, "no cash, no credit, no problem." But real estate's not simple. Learn from the experiences of others. Borrow ideas and adapt them to today's circumstances. Do read everything you can find that might lead to improved performance.

Setbacks are a part of life. Don't let them knock you off your feet.

Yet, before you follow a well-publicized investment technique or real estate guru, remember that your answer to the question "Will it work?" remains, "It all depends." Near the peak of the recent property boom, a well-known author wrote a book titled *52 Houses in 52 Weeks*. The subject: How to flip houses in Las Vegas. Any reader who jumped in to follow this author's system would have shortly thereafter gone broke.

A Strategy of Your Own

In this book, neither I nor Mr. Trump misleads you with "five magic paths" or "seven easy steps" to real estate riches. We won't pretend that you can profitably buy, improve, and manage properties without effort, time, intelligence, and at least a workable amount of seed capital.[1]

However, we do promise to provide the knowledge and techniques necessary for you to reason through a profitable, wealth-building strategy of your own. In the real world, you will conquer the challenges and vicissitudes of property markets only when you know how to discover and adapt as problems arise and opportunities unfold. In other words, from this book—as with no other—you will learn to think like an entrepreneur.

MVP: THE ONE CONSTANT RULE

To think like an entrepreneur, adopt one central rule: I call this unifying rule (or principle) the MVP (most *valued* property). When tenants (or buyers) search for a place to live or operate their business, they compare features, amenities, location, rent levels, lease terms, and dozens of other details that add to (or detract from) the benefits they expect that property to bring to them. They compare, contrast, weigh, and consider. In the end, which property do they eventually choose to rent (or buy)? The cheapest? Not necessarily. The best? Probably not. The biggest? Perhaps, but don't count the money just yet.

Create your business plan before you buy. You want to have Plan A, Plan B, and Plan C for adding value to the property.

---

[1] This money does not necessarily have to come from your pocket. Partners or relatives quite frequently provide seed capital and credit for both beginning and experienced real estate investors.

At the moment of truth, prospective tenants (buyers) will choose the property that offers the best value relative to all the other properties that they have considered. Hence, your entrepreneurial thinking should guide you to provide the MVP for your intended customers. From your perspective, MVP also means the property designs, features, and use that will add the most value to your net worth (i.e., the most *valuable* property). In other words, the MVP principle urges you to give your target customers their best value, while also maximizing the economic value of the property to you.

FEW OWNERS ACHIEVE MVP

During the past 20 years, I have looked at thousands of for-rent or for-sale properties. At least 90 percent of these fell short of MVP status for both their customers and their investors.

The property's owner, manager, or sales agent had not fully answered the question that MVP poses: "How can we enhance our total value proposition in ways that would better satisfy (wow) our customers (tenants, buyers) and at the same time pull more dollars into our bank accounts?"

**Every building that carries my name promises the
highest quality available.**

Make MVP Your Goal

To improve your life, you must want to improve. You must make the effort. You must believe that the effort will pay off. You reprogram your mental tapes with positive self-talk and possibility thinking. In sum, you develop an entrepreneurial attitude (which will elevate your altitude). Let's discuss the Demand, Utility, Scarcity, Transfer (DUST) process guide that will help you formulate your entrepreneurial flight plan.

The DUST Entrepreneurial Framework

Without education and using your brains, your ignorance will cost you a fortune.

Study Figure 5.1 from top to bottom. Use this analytical framework to guide your strategic reasoning process. It will guide all future discussions throughout this book. I use it to perform my own property analyses. It will help you estimate, forecast, and create property value.

You create MVP (most *valued* property, most *valuable* property) when you design your property features to meet demand and differentiate from supply competitors. Then you formulate your transfer process (promote, negotiate, and contract) to lease or sell. DUST addresses your six decision points:

I. Explore your entrepreneurial objectives (personal and financial).

II. Set up your due diligence investigation.

III. Advance your market strategy (DUST) through data collection, analysis, and discovery of opportunities.

IV. Value the tactical and strategic possibilities from the perspective of customers and your financial goals.

V. Synthesize, interpret, and decide.

VI. Execute, monitor, and revise your tactics and strategy to create and enhance the property's MVP.

Entrepreneurial Objectives

Who are you? What goals do you want to achieve? Take stock of your personal and financial resources, your talents, and your risk tolerance. Then choose an investment program and market strategy that will serve your purposes and desired style of life. Let your priorities and values guide your decision process. "I want to

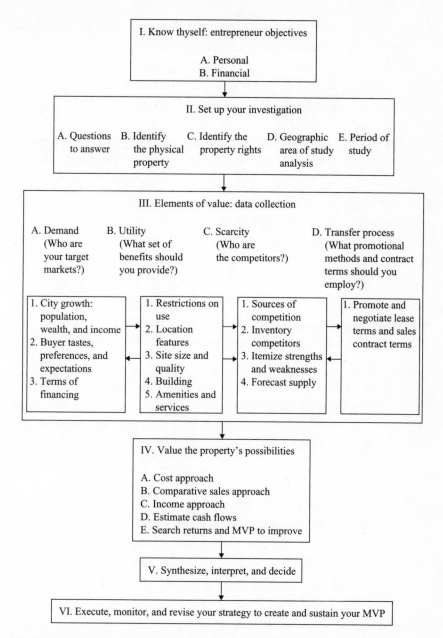

Figure 5.1 DUST Entrepreneurial Decision Framework for Creating Wealth through Real Estate. Copyright © Gary W. Eldred. Reprinted with permission.

make a lot of money" may reflect your base desire. But to achieve that goal, align your efforts, feelings, and resources.

Talents, Inclinations, Resources, Priorities

When I began buying and renovating properties, I not only lacked a clear entrepreneurial plan but also failed to inventory my talents and inclinations. Only after trial and error did I manage to create an investment program that worked personally and financially. Many would-be real estate investors (speculators) choose without thinking. They fail. Then they give up without ever realizing their true potential and possibilities.

Assess your interests. What do you love? Create a blueprint for your life. Without goals, no momentum. Without momentum, you are daydreaming.

Become proactive. Design your investing to align with your personal values, abilities, resources, likes, dislikes, and priorities. "No pain, no gain" still rules. As you deliberate choices, envision the life of freedom and financial security you want. But, to realize your dreams, sacrifice and trade-offs must also play a role:

1. *Time and Money:* How many hours per week or per month are you willing to invest? What does your financial profile look like (credit, cash, earnings, borrowing power)?
2. *Trade Skills:* What types of manual fix-up or renovation skills do you possess? Do you enjoy working with hammers, saws, and paint brushes?
3. *Creativity and Design:* Do you enjoy the search for new ideas? Are you willing to learn and adapt the ideas of others? Do you like to look at properties, attend trade shows, and browse through magazines and journals on property management, creative improvements, and related topics?

4. *Partners:* Do you prefer to play as a one-man band? Or would you like to join with others to share equity financing, work, responsibilities, and decision making?

5. *Tenants:* What types of people would you like to attract as tenants?

6. *Real Estate Agents:* Do you want to search, buy, and sell on your own? Or will you enlist the help of real estate agents?

7. *Numbers:* Can you learn to work with income statements, cash flows, rate-of-return calculations, cost estimates, budgets, and tight rehab and renovation budgets and schedules?

8. *Personal Achievement:* What types of real estate would give you the greatest sense of personal achievement and pride of accomplishment?

To succeed as a real estate entrepreneur, anticipate and prepare. Match your expectations to reality. Some property owners try to "do it all." They burn out. Others buy with "little or nothing down" and then find they lack the cash or credit necessary to handle repairs or cover losses from vacancies or bad debts. (Today, many such investors or homeowners have become distressed sellers who must sell at bargain prices—"just to get rid of this financial headache." Their failures have now become your opportunities.)

Passion conquers fear. Take a tip from Nike—"Just do it."

Review Your Spending and Borrowing

The promoters of nothing-down real estate have pulled too many starry-eyed investor wannabes down the path to financial ruin with their mantra of "no cash, no credit, no problem." Although you can buy real estate without cash or credit, that fact begs the question. If that's your situation, why do you lack cash or credit? Indeed, the foreclosure auctions now brim with properties once owned by the "no cash, no credit" buyers. Sad to say it, but their pain now sets the opportunity for your gain.

So, respect yourself, and exercise financial discipline and responsibility. "No cash, no credit" can create big problems and big risks for those whose empty wallets result from destructive spending and borrowing. Investing in real estate steers you onto the road to financial freedom only when you borrow *constructively* and spend miserly (or at least, conservatively).[2]

Review your credit score and constructive borrowing power, your available cash, and your monthly cash flow. How much money can you come up with to acquire real estate and pay for fix-up work—while you still maintain a reserve to meet contingencies and unanticipated setbacks? Because you run some chance of mistake, stay well within your limits. Use your first properties to gain experience. Fine-tune your abilities and strategy without overextending yourself.

What is your credit score? In their efforts to judge your creditworthiness, mortgage lenders (and many owner-will-carry sellers) will check your credit score. Although a variety of credit-scoring systems exist, among the most widely used scores are those calculated by the Fair Isaac Corporation (FICO). To learn your FICO scores, go to www.myfico.com. For around $40, FICO will provide three scores (as calculated from your credit data on file with Experian, TransUnion, and Equifax), suggest ways you can improve your scores, and let you know how your scores compare to the general population. On the basis of your credit profile, FICO estimates the interest rate that lenders will charge you. (However, note that your credit score *influences* the cost and availability of mortgage money—but other factors also contribute to the approval and interest cost equation.)

What is your net worth? Your financial net worth consists of the total value of what you own less the total amount you owe

---

[2] Again, I'll mention the insightful book that describes the personal discipline necessary to become wealthy: *The Millionaire Next Door* by Thomas Stanley.

to others. (If you've previously completed a mortgage application, you're probably familiar with this form, which is called a personal balance sheet.)

How liquid are you? Mortgage lenders tally up your assets, liabilities, and net worth, but they also examine your cash position. The more cash in your accounts, the easier you can weather setbacks. You (or your partners) will also need cash to close your purchase (down payment, loan costs, property repairs, escrow payments, and perhaps property improvements). If your balance sheet shows little cash (including near cash such as stocks, bonds, or certificate of deposits), sell some assets (cars, boats, vacation home, jewelry, and so on) to beef up your cash account. Liquidity adds to your borrowing power and it gives you the ready money to jump on good deals when you spot them.

How much free cash flow do you generate each month? Some people spend and borrow so heavily that there's little if any money left at the end of the month. People who struggle payday to payday rarely build wealth.

So increase your free cash flow. What spending can you slash? What debts can you eliminate? What luxuries (frivolities) can you do without? As financial planners emphasize, to build wealth while you're still young enough to enjoy it, spend conservatively and never borrow to make ends meet. Live *below* your means. Each $1,000 you invest today can easily pay you back $10,000 or more within a decade (or less).

Financial Goals

Okay, you've reviewed your financial wherewithal and personal talents and inclinations. It's now time to set goals. How much wealth would you like to create during the next 5, 10, or 20 years? How many properties would you like to acquire? In what price range? Do you plan to fix and flip, fix and hold, or passively buy and hold? Write out the numbers. Explore possibilities. Think big. Once you set a goal, draft a business plan. Attach a timetable. Schedule deadlines. Without a written business plan, goals, and a timetable, you procrastinate, you drift. You eventually settle into "woulda, coulda, shoulda." Navigate away from this trap. Commit yourself to a plan and *specific* action steps.

Though we haven't yet itemized the full variety of financial returns that you (entrepreneurial) investors can earn, when you have read through later chapter discussions on "running the numbers," you can revisit this issue. For now, think about setting your goals. Then, as you read through later chapters, note the ideas that might work for you. Apply ideas and relate them to your own possibilities.

SET UP YOUR DUE DILIGENCE INVESTIGATION

With goals in place, it's time to investigate markets and properties. Before you randomly look at potential investments, investigate these issues:

- Explore the investment questions you must answer.
- Identify the physical property.
- Identify the relevant property rights.
- Identify the area(s) from which you will draw customers (tenants, buyers) and identify the location and sources of potential competitors.
- What period of time defines your investment horizon (your holding period)?

Explore the Questions You Want to Answer

As a real estate entrepreneur, you face many types of questions that require intelligent and informed answers. What's the market value of a specific property? Where's the competition headed? What cities or neighborhoods offer good opportunities for growth? What cities or neighborhoods offer good cash flows? What tenant segments offer great potential? What features would advance your MVP strategy? What lease terms would enhance your MVP strategy? How might a property's value go up if its zoning were changed?

Throughout your investing career, you'll answer questions such as these as well as many others. But you can't address all of them at the same time. Instead, focus. Each question requires its own data and methods. Market value questions, for example, differ from market forecasts. Cash flow questions differ from those that forecast appreciation potential.

You'll discover other essential questions as you read later chapters. For now, focus on these three points:

1. Begin every investment decision with questions. Probe for details.
2. Never decide to buy, improve, or sell without looking at the property from multiple perspectives. (For example, although that bargain price may appeal to you, maybe the property yields weak cash flows or holds little potential for price growth—maybe this property's a flipper, not a keeper.)
3. The greater your ability to identify and ask questions, the greater your profit potential. Questions alert you to opportunities that ordinary investors, property owners, and managers overlook. ("Could I get zoning changed?" "Could I split the lot?" "Could I go after the corporate (serviced apartment) rental market?" "Could I split the building into multiple units?" "Could I create a view?" (Questions alert you to possibilities.)

Identify and Describe the Physical Property

It might surprise you to learn that when some people buy property, they really do not know what they are getting. Why? Because they do not closely inspect the details of the property. To prevent this mistake, verify these features:

- Number and mix of the rental units.
- Square footages of the total building and each rental unit.
- Site size and features.
- Type of construction, architectural style, and overall condition.
- Personal property and fixtures.

As you look at a property, list defects and deficiencies. But look, too, for opportunities to create value. So, first, put on your Sherlock Holmes hat, grab your magnifying glass, and ferret out potential costly repairs, tenant turnover, or high energy bills. Next, to form an opportunity perspective, put on your rose-colored glasses. Imagine how the property could perform after you work your magic.

Number and Mix of Rooms and Rental Units

As with square footage (see the next section), sellers and their agents sometimes generously describe the number and mix of rental units within a building. I have seen so-called two-bedroom apartments that lacked closets, efficiencies that were nothing more than a sleeping room with a hot plate and a dorm fridge, and damp, musty basement suites with no natural light. (To technically qualify as a bedroom, a room must include a closet.)

Before you buy a building, inspect each unit in the property. Sometimes agents (or sellers) will say, "The units are all *basically* alike; you don't want to look at all of them, do you?"

You should answer, "Yes, I think I do. You don't mind, do you?"

Square Footages of the Total Building and Each Rental Unit

Agents and owners may quote two types of square-footage figures. One figure applies to the total size of the building. The other applies to the sizes of the individual units. The naive investor accepts these square-footage figures at face value. The smart investor questions the figures closely.

What areas are counted within the square footage figures? Apartment buildings, for example, devote space to hallways; basements; balconies; laundry facilities; heating, ventilating, and air-conditioning equipment; as well as the actual living units. Break down square-footage totals and allocate them across the various uses within the building. Carefully investigate square footage for two reasons:

1. No consistent standard applies to square-footage measurements. Some sellers or agents may count basements and balconies. Others may not. Precise space measurements enable you to uniformly compare buildings.
2. Count *rentable* square footage. Some buildings waste square footage because of inefficient design. A building of 13,500 square feet might actually include more *rentable* square feet than another property that measures 15,000 square feet. (This principle of rentable/usable square footage applies to single-family houses, office buildings, shopping centers, and industrial uses.)

Owners and agents sometimes promote their properties as a "great buy" because such properties compare favorably to the asking/sales prices of other properties when calculated as price-per-square-foot. However, when the quality of a seller's square footage stands inferior to peer properties, then that property deserves to sell at a discounted price per square foot. Its lower asking price does not signal the great buy that the seller claims. All square footages are not worth the same price.

Are the square footage figures accurate? Even though sellers and their agents avoid warranting their estimates of square footage, beginning investors often rely on such figures—only to learn too late that the figures erred. In instances where price per square foot counts heavily in your property comparisons and evaluations, pull out your tape measure. Measure the dimensions. Guard against the shock of fewer square feet than you bargained for—and thus a higher price per square foot than you thought you were paying.

Site Size and Features

In many cities, the value of the lot on which a building sits can account for 30 to 70 percent of the property's total value. Even small differences in site size or features can add (or subtract) tens of thousands of dollars compared with other, seemingly similar properties.

Consider two similarly sized triplexes. Both properties brought in about the same amount of net rental income. Yet one triplex was listed at $289,000. The other was listed at $309,000. If you compare the buildings alone, the $289,000 property looks like the better buy. But, the $309,000 property offered "hidden value" in the site. It turns out that this property's *site* size (and zoning) would permit its owner to build a fourth rental unit.

Additional site size might permit you to add on to a building, expand parking or storage space, create a view, or provide better privacy. To evaluate a site, note the quality of its landscaping, its ingress and egress (how easily cars can pull in and out of the property), and amenities such as swimming pool, tennis courts, workshop, or storage shed. When comparing size and features, itemize all those differences that can make a difference.

Personal Property and Fixtures

When you buy real estate, you pay for the land and the buildings, which are called *real property*. A seller's asking price might also include *personal property*, which refers to washers and dryers, refrigerators, stoves, furniture, curtains, blinds, window air-conditioning units, wall mirrors, and similar items not attached permanently to the land or building.

The list price for a property will include items that have been so adapted for use with the building that the law classifies these items as *fixtures*. Fixtures may include ceiling fans, lighting, chandeliers, garage door openers, garbage disposals, built-in cabinets and book-shelves, and built-in dishwashers. All other things equal, a property that includes a washer, dryer, ceiling fans, range, dishwasher, and refrigerator is worth more than one that omits such items. To value a property, itemize the personal property and fixtures that the trans-action includes. (Sometimes, after a sale, sellers remove fixtures even though legally these fixtures should remain with the property. For that reason and others, perform a final walk-through just before closing or taking possession.)

Avoid confusion and disappointment. Negotiate "what stays with property, what goes with the sellers." Identify and list these items in your sales contract or attach via an addendum.

Understand Rights and Restrictions

"This is *my* property! I'll do with it whatever I want." In times that predate zoning restrictions, building codes, tenants' rights, mort-gages, leases, and a multitude of other laws, ordinances, and con-tracts, your uncompromised claim to freedom may have carried weight. Not today.

Today, restrictions of one sort or another govern your rights to design, build, occupy, use, lease, mortgage, renovate, add on, or enjoy a property. Verify that your entrepreneurial plans for the properties you buy, manage, renovate, lease out, and sell comply with the legal rights that you actually possess (or can obtain).

On the other hand, zoning laws, contracts, ordinances, rules, covenants, and regulations do not merely restrict in a negative sense. Entrepreneurs rely on rules and restrictions to help fashion their target market strategy. Given the importance of legal restrictions, Chapter 8 provides you more guidelines. To value a property and craft your MVP, review the legal limits as well as the legal possibil-ities that govern the property.

What Geographic Area(s)?

Most investors limit their search for properties to a geographic area that falls within say, a 60-minute drive from their homes. These investors prefer to live near their properties so that they can easily deal with day-to-day issues (showing the property, making repairs, attending to tenants, and so on). Although their preference for proximity makes sense in some ways, it fails in others.

What if prices in your area have climbed beyond your reach? What if you can't find properties that yield positive cash flows or good potential for appreciation? What if your local economy looks shaky? In other words, what if your area seems to lack good investment alternatives that you are willing and able to buy? Maybe you are right. Or, maybe, you feel this way because you have not fully explored the possibilities in your locale. Maybe you've accepted conventional wisdom and negative self-talk without a detailed look at the facts.

Regardless of whether your locale offers good possibilities or not, we advise you to open your mind to other geographic areas. During the next decade or two, real estate investors in some neighborhoods, cities, and countries will enjoy a doubling or tripling of their property values and rent levels. Property investors in other locales may do well to keep up with inflation. Or you might prefer to invest for cash flow more than for appreciation. Here again, different locales offer different potential. As to my own investment objectives, I look for areas where I can achieve at least four good sources of return: (1) cash flow, (2) market appreciation, (3) opportunities to add value, and (4) amortization (mortgage payoff).

In recent years, I have bought properties in North Carolina and Florida. All of my recently acquired properties yield positive cash flows and are worth today substantially more than I paid. I did not buy property in Dubai—even though I was working there throughout its boom years. Why? Because my personal investment strategy prohibits me from buying properties in locales where speculators dominate the market. Nor did I buy in Las

Vegas, Phoenix, or Miami during their boom (i.e., speculative) years.

My point here is not to recommend a specific market area. That's up to you to decide for yourself according to your goals (with help from Chapter 6). However, I encourage you explore and compare a variety of locales. If you decide to invest close to home, do it by design, not default.

Time Period

As part of your investment decision-making process, think about the length of time you plan to hold your properties. If you plan to fix and flip, your economic and market study need not forecast further out than say, 24 months. As a buy, improve, and hold investor, you would adopt a mid- to long-range perspective of, say, 5 to 20 years.

Different time perspectives lead to different investment choices. Many lower-priced neighborhoods and communities are primed for turnaround and attractive property appreciation. But such areas require a patient investor. To earn quick cash, find bargain-priced properties/foreclosures/REOs that you can fix up and immediately resell (or exchange). In any case, don't choose your locations or your properties until you think through the timing of your entrance and exit strategy.

As many naive investors, homebuyers, and speculators have re-cently learned, property prices and rent levels rarely follow a neatly drawn, upward-sloping trend line. Indeed, the faster and longer prices increase, the more likely and severe their fall. Include timing in your entrepreneurial strategy. The MVP for a two-year horizon (or less) could vary greatly from an MVP strategy that extends over 5 to 10 years. Plan both your entry and exit with well-reasoned research and assumptions.

Now, let's look at the types of data and investigations that you can use to forecast the demand and supply trends in the area(s) where you see possibilities.

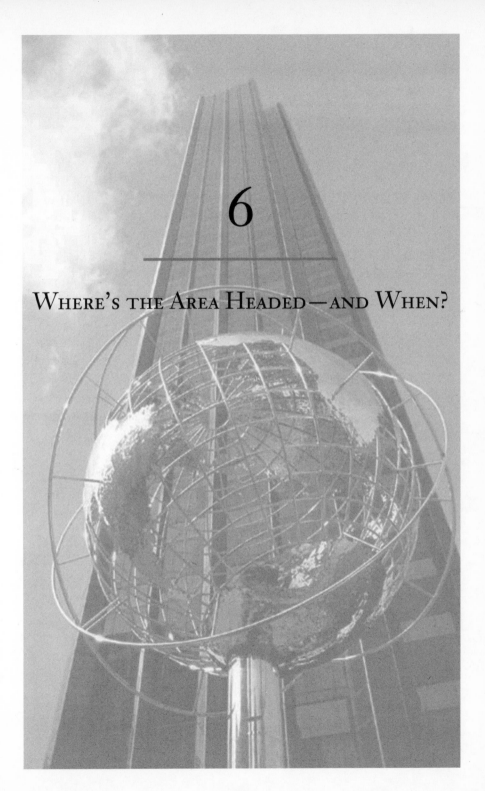

6

Where's the Area Headed—and When?

LOOK BEYOND
YOUR OWN BACKYARD

When Donald Trump began his career, he had his eye on Manhattan, not his native New York borough of Brooklyn. He wanted to build in Manhattan because that's where he saw the greatest long-term opportunity to accomplish both his personal goals and financial objectives.

Today, the Trump Organization has been partners in U.S.-based projects in Miami, Tampa, Chicago, Phoenix, Las Vegas, Los Angeles, Palm Springs, and Atlantic City. Trump has even partnered on a project in Dubai, UAE.

What's the lesson? Avoid that tired cliché, "Never invest more than an hour's drive from your home." Throughout the United States, throughout the world, opportunities await those who will explore, investigate, and, yes, take a little risk. As Mr. Trump says, "Get out of your comfort zone, climb out to the edge."

Somewhere, real estate offers exciting possibilities for profit. You may find acres of diamonds in your own backyard. But there's no need to only dig there. As Mr. Trump perpetually advises, "Think big. Multiply your possibilities."

Perhaps, like Mr. Trump, you, too, can develop a system that works superbly for a special niche of tenants or buyers. Perhaps, you, too, can find partners to work with elsewhere. Challenge yourself to explore beyond your own backyard.

Location, location, location. That cliché is preached by know-nothings who fail to think. You're looking for the most profitable deal that might exist in any location. Plus, do what I do. Use your property to boost the value of the location.

"THE AUTHOR DID IT—and so can you!" So opens the blurb page of the real estate classic *How I Turned $1,000 into a Million in My Spare Time* by William Nickerson. With these words of encouragement, I devoured the contents of this book. And at age 21, I began to immediately put Nickerson's advice into practice. I soon found (what I thought were) super bargains. According to Nickerson's formula, the price of rental property should equal 10 times that property's net operating income (NOI). Using this formula, I couldn't believe the terrific deals that were coming my way. I routinely bought small apartment buildings for five to seven times NOI. In other words, I bought income properties that—according to Nickerson's advice—should have sold for $100,000. Yet I paid only $50,000 to $70,000.[1] Back then I thought, "These sellers are crazy. They don't know what they're doing."

Alamo, California (Fast Growth Area) versus Terre Haute, Indiana

As it turned out, it was me (not my sellers) who failed to understand. I did not realize Nickerson's pricing standards did not apply to my hometown. Unlike the high-growth, high-demand San Francisco Bay Area (where Nickerson lived), my hometown of Terre Haute suffered a frail economic base and a no-growth, low- to moderate-income population. Whereas Nickerson's properties typically doubled in value over a period of 10 years, mine struggled to keep pace with inflation.

Fortunately, my properties did yield huge amounts of positive cash flow, and because these beginning investment experiences predated the 1986 Tax Reform Act (TRA), my properties gave me huge tax write-offs for depreciation. Using this tax shelter, I enjoyed tax-free income from both my rent collections and most of my professional earnings.

This comparison of locales shows that to profit most, weigh the pros and cons, the risks and rewards of an area's growth and appreciation potential against that area's property prices and cash flows.

---

[1] These figures reflect proportionality, not the actual numbers.

In other words, look for increasing *D*emand (remember DUST) where you can acquire properties at a reasonable price relative to rent levels.

RECOGNIZE TWO COMMON MISTAKES

Some investors (both beginning and seasoned) search for properties to buy in an area (region, city, neighborhood) without much thought about how that area might compare to other areas 3, 5, 10, or maybe 15 years into the future. Typically, these investors only want to buy properties that look like a below-market deal here and now. I call this practice the Mr. Magoo mistake. It's too nearsighted.

In contrast to Mr. Magoo, others (such as recent Las Vegas investors) buy properties located in high-growth, high-demand areas—especially areas where properties have shown strong recent rates of appreciation. These investors (speculators) seem to care little about today's negative cash flows (low rents relative to purchase price) because they (unreasonably) assumed that high rates of appreciation would continue. I call this practice the wishful thinker mistake. It omits the cyclical reality of property markets—especially those that experience extended speculative booms.

Today, I favor an approach (first referred to in Chapter 1) called *right place, right time, right price* investing.

VALUE INVESTING: RIGHT PLACE, RIGHT TIME, RIGHT PRICE

You might recognize right place, right time, right price investing as similar to the value investing approach used to select stocks (see my book *Value Investing in Real Estate*, Wiley, 2002). A value investor in stocks never buys a company's shares simply because it's a great company. Nor will he buy just any company even if its stock price is low relative to its earnings and dividends (annual cash flow). For the value investor to buy, he or she needs the right company, at the right time, at the right price.

Value Investing in Real Estate

As a value investor in real estate, you search for areas (right places) that are positioned for growth, turnaround, gentrification, or revitalization. You next ask, "Is this the right time?" Harlem was positioned for turnaround as far back as the early 1980s. But its renaissance did not begin to take off for another 10 to 12 years. Throughout the 1980s, Harlem suffered from drugs, crime, and further deterioration—even though it was located just minutes away from Manhattan's elite Upper East Side and other high-income employment, shopping, and residential districts. (In fact, Trump Tower sits no more than a six-minute subway ride from Harlem.)

In 1990, San Diego was the right place to invest, but like Harlem of the 1980s, the timing for investment wasn't right. As one of the most desirable places to live in the world, no one could deny the solid long-term prospects for "America's number one city."

The short term, though, raised troubling issues. As a major center for defense-related jobs, San Diego was about to suffer a steep increase in unemployment because the fall of the Soviet threat foreshadowed a rollback of military spending in the U.S. budget. The San Diego property market would drop before it would regain its predictably strong long-term future.

In 2000, Phoenix and Las Vegas represented great "right place, right time, right price" locations. By 2006 though, that opportunity had passed. Speculative buyers had pushed prices up far beyond the level that rent revenues would support. Plus, builders had flooded these cities with new subdivisions and condo complexes (Supply).

To profit most in real estate, look for areas (countries, regions, cities, neighborhoods) that are both positioned and *poised* for growth, turnaround, gentrification, or revitalization. Look for able and *ready*. The right time matters.

What about Price?

In my right place, right time, right price trilogy, you can think about right price in four ways:

1. *Market Value:* Never pay a price that exceeds market value *except* when you know precisely why the deal justifies your price premium.
2. *Premium Value:* On occasion, you might reasonably (if you have to) pay a premium above market value to acquire a property loaded with potential. Such reasons might include favorable terms or costs of financing, conversion possibilities, special use potential, upzoning imminent, or other value-added potential.
3. *Price Trends:* An area can stand positioned and poised for growth, but current market prices could tumble over the short run (e.g., Miami, Las Vegas, Orlando, Dubai, and Beijing). Any or all types of variables—unfavorable changes in the cost and availability of credit, a surfeit of new construction, a shift upward in the number of foreclosures, excess amounts of conversions, or positive or negative legislative changes, such as the 1986 TRA—might bring about a temporary stall (or fall) in property prices.
4. *Price to Earnings:* As of the mid-2000s, many properties (especially in much-sought-after locations) failed to yield positive cash flows when financed with a 30-year fixed-rate loan and a 20 percent down payment. For this reason, value investors avoided such areas as "wrong price"—no matter how otherwise desirable the area appeared for the long term.

Look for properties in marginal areas that are located near more appealing areas. These properties will surely appreciate as they improve.

Summing Up: Right Place, Right Time, Right Price

Mr. Magoo focuses on the specific property deal. For this type of investor, a "good buy" is nearly any property that's priced at a discount to its current market value. As a result of his nearsightedness, Mr. Magoo frequently misses properties in areas positioned and poised for growth. In addition, because Mr. Magoo pays slight attention to economic and market outlooks, he can fail to notice market data that signal imminent price declines.

I'll ask the people who live nearby about an area—schools, crime, shopping, whatever. I ask cabdrivers, postmen, FedEx guys. I ask, ask, ask, until I hone my analytics as well as my instincts. Then, I decide.

Wishful thinkers *assume*—but do not thoroughly research—prospects for property prices in the areas where they invest. But (like Magoos), they can drown in the whirlpool of a down cycle. Or waiting for future rescue, wishful thinkers get eaten by alligators. Their negative cash flows consume most (or all) of the profits they had counted on from property appreciation.

Although no one can perfectly predict the future, value (entrepreneurial) investors typically make the best forecasts and most profitable decisions. Rather than merely assume the short- or long-term future of an area, rather than choose their areas or properties by naive criteria (close to home; strong, *recent* rate of appreciation; below-market price), value investors research these three questions:

1. Where's the right place (country, region, city, neighborhood) to invest?
2. When's the right time to invest?
3. What price offers low risk (a margin of safety) and strong potential for future reward?

DEMAND

Unlike the media molls who often offer up little more than shallow conventional wisdom, you can reason with a deeper, more analytical view of the facts. You *can* accurately forecast the prospects for an area. Before you invest, review these big-picture (macro) indicators of demand (the **D** of DUST):

I. **D**emand.
   a. Population growth.
   b. Employment, wage levels, and household incomes.
   c. Costs of doing business.
   d. Quality of life.
   e. Wealth.
   f. Community attitudes toward growth and economic development.
   g. Entrepreneurial spirit and the creative class.

Strong growing demand pushes up price and rent levels only if supply lags—rather than runs ahead of—demand. Also review indicators of supply (the **S** in DUST), such as the following:

II. **S**upply: Review the quantity, quality, and pricing of potential competitors.
   a. New construction.
   b. Existing homes for sale.
   c. Existing homes for rent.
   d. Condominiums for sale.
   e. Condominiums for rent.
   f. Apartment vacancy rates.
   g. Apartment rent levels.
   h. Available buildable land.
   i. Zoning and land use restrictions that inhibit new building.
   j. Mortgage delinquencies and foreclosures.

You will discover ways to assess supply (competitors) in a later chapter. Now, on with a look at an area's Demand (current and future).

Technical talk about economic base, market signals, demand, and supply might not sound exciting. You might simply want to say, "Just tell me what I need to know to earn a lot of money." But until you research the economic facts about your local area (or the local area where you plan to invest), you are accepting unknown risks. You may get lucky, but, then again, you may not. Even when you score gains, don't become smug or self-assured about your successes (as we all are apt to do). While you're enjoying the sunshine, thunder clouds may be moving in quickly.

Donald Trump admits to such a mistake in the late 1980s. He lost focus, jumping from deal to deal; he borrowed too much; he played too much; he just assumed the good times would continue to roll. Then trouble hit. As he tells the story, he had "fun, fun, fun, until the banks took the Gulfstream away."

Property markets cycle up and down (and as nearly everyone now knows) the most recent down cycle has taken its toll on many of those who failed to prepare. So use this down cycle to profit from the mistakes of others. And as you invest, monitor demand and competition (supply). As markets change, stay on top of current conditions. Adjust your most valued property (MVP) strategy—and your debt loads.

Let's discuss the macro factors that can spell opportunity (or danger) for property investors.

Will the Area's Population Grow?

Population growth (or decline) results from three sources: (1) births, (2) mortality, and (3) people moving into or out of an area. What's happening in your chosen area? Are more people moving in or out of the area? How is the age distribution of the population changing? For example, some people think of Florida as God's waiting room. But the number of children in the state is growing fast. If the number of seniors flooding into the state should stop (which will not happen), playgrounds full of today's children will provide tomorrow's demand for apartments, houses, retail sites, and office buildings.

Pockets of Existing and Potential Growth

Population growth seldom spreads itself evenly across countries, states, cities, or neighborhoods. Geographic areas develop pockets or corridors of growth. Determine where the heaviest growth has occurred. Is this area reaching its limit? Are the roads and freeways choking with traffic? Have rents and housing prices shot upward? Where will the next burst of population increase occur? Look for the emerging areas that now attract people who are now seeking to avoid the high prices, traffic congestion, and other problems that rapid growth can generate.

Find Out the Actual Population Figures

Sometimes the media report that the population growth *rate* of an area is slowing. Most people interpret this news to mean that growth *itself* is slowing. Often that's not the case. Rather, as the population of an area gets larger, the percentage increase can fall even though the number of people moving in continues to increase.

Say that during the past decade the population of a county jumped from 300,000 to 400,000—an overall growth of 33 percent. During the coming decade, this overall growth rate is expected to fall to 25 percent. Nevertheless, even with this lower growth rate, the county population will increase by 100,000 people—exactly the same *number* of people as in the previous decade. It is the *number* of people who create demand, not the percentage growth rate per se. Track the growth trends by the actual numbers of people moving in (or out).

Beware of False Negatives

If you examine the population growth figures within the city limits of Highland Park, Texas; San Francisco; Washington, DC; or New York City; you would note little upward change in numbers during the past 30 years. Yet housing prices and rent levels in each of these cities have climbed to rank among the highest in the United States. Why? Because these cities—as do most cities throughout the world—draw their demand from their larger metro areas, the country, and even the world. To judge the total demand for housing in a specific city or neighborhood, study the projected population growth figures for the entire metro area. Evaluate big-picture (macro) influences on smaller areas—especially when that area limits new construction below the levels actually needed.

Are the Number of Basic Jobs Increasing or Decreasing?

To prosper, most (but not all) areas need to grow their *basic* employment. *Basic* employers are those that generate income from outside the local areas. (As an exception, for example, property prices in Aspen, Colorado, have increased 10 times over without significant gains in basic employment. Wealthy out-of-area buyers account for most of the demand.) But for a majority of cities, you should identify the major basic employers, their predominant types of businesses, and their potential for growth. As for risks, research whether any economic declines, layoffs, plant closings, or business relocations appear on the horizon.

More specifically, basic employers conduct activities that bring outside money into an area. When these businesses decline, so do all the nonbasic locally oriented businesses and government employers who feed off the revenues generated by these core employers. Basic employment typically includes the following:

1. *Manufacturers:* To see the critical role that manufacturers play, watch the Michael Moore movie *Roger and Me*.

This documentary catalogs the economic downfall of Flint, Michigan, after General Motors closed the local Buick plant. Of course, more generally, you now can see manufacturing decline—and the falling property prices that such decline creates—throughout much of the state of Michigan.

2. *Professional Service Firms:* Most low- and mid-level architects, lawyers, accountants, consultants, and advertising agencies count only as town fillers (nonbasic), not town builders (basic). Real estate agents, stockbrokers, and insurance agencies also fit into the nonbasic service category. However, some professional and financial service firms sell to a regional, statewide, national, or even global clientele. The billings of these firms may bring tens of millions of dollars into a local economy. Think of Chicago's Skidmore Owens Merrill (SOM), the internationally respected architectural and engineering firm that designed the Burj Dubai tower, which is scheduled to become the world's tallest building (Dubai, UAE).

3. *Medical Services:* Health care has become the second largest business (behind real estate) in the United States and will become much larger as the baby boomers hit their 60s. Many local areas now provide hospitals, clinics, and testing labs that bring in patients from hundreds (or even thousands) of miles away. Think Mayo Clinic in Minneapolis, Minnesota.

4. *Travel and Tourism:* Nearly every city, state, and country now wants to capture part of the $1 trillion worldwide market for travel, tourism, conventions, and other leisure-related activities. Think Chicago's McCormick Place; Hong Kong's Convention and Exhibition Center; Disneyworld; and the sun, surf, sand, and festivities of Penang, Malaysia.

5. *Colleges and Universities:* Many towns and cities are home to colleges or universities that bring millions (or billions) into the local area. (Boston, for example, is home to 62 colleges.) College-related spending in the small town of Bloomington, Indiana, tops $2 billion a year.

6. *Retailing and Distribution:* The Omni shopping center and the Sawgrass discount mall in Miami, Florida, attracts shoppers who live in Mexico, Brazil, and Argentina. Honey Creek Mall in Terre Haute, Indiana, draws shoppers from the surrounding rural areas and small towns up to 60 miles away. Bangkok, Thailand, attracts shoppers from throughout Asia, Europe, the Middle East, and North America.

   A local grocery store does not support an area's economic base. But large shopping malls, catalog centers, and warehousing operations (e.g., Amazon. com, L.L. Bean) can provide wage/salary income for hundreds (or even thousands) of local residents that originate from sales revenues generated throughout the region, the country, or the world.

7. *Centers of Government:* National, state, and provincial capital cities generate revenues from throughout their respective jurisdictions. Washington, DC; Ottawa; and London draw in tax dollars from throughout the United States, Canada, and the United Kingdom, respectively. Other cities bring in revenues from state and federal agencies, military bases, defense contractors, and government hospitals that are located in the area. Think how important NASA is to the small town of Titusville, Florida (site of the space shuttle launches and other space missions and research facilities).

Most individual investors do not pay enough attention to their area's basic employment—unless their local economy has already turned into recession (or extended decline). When the Southern California economy boomed in the late 1980s, wishful thinkers and irrationally exuberant homebuyers imagined that property appreciation rates of 10 to 20 percent a year would last forever. When the Berlin Wall fell in 1989, few San Diego buyers or investors anticipated any effects on Southern California property prices and apartment rents.

What Connected San Diego to the Berlin Wall?

Spending by the U.S. Department of Defense supported thousands of basic jobs in southern California. After the Berlin Wall fell and the Soviet Union began to break apart, Congress (predictably) cut back defense budgets. Military contractors, in turn, slashed tens of thousands of jobs. Congress also eliminated thousands of military personnel who had been stationed at the San Diego Naval Base.

With unemployment increasing, demand for homes and apartments fell. Nearly everyone who worked in home building and home selling began to feel the effects. Home builders shut down their construction sites. Most real estate agents, mortgage loan reps, home inspectors, property lawyers, title insurers, and apartment managers experienced cuts in income. These depressing effects further rippled through the local economy. Furniture retailers, interior designers, and auto dealers all lost business.

In 2009, Greenwich, Connecticut, felt a severe downturn in property prices. Many of the basic jobs for that city were provided by hedge funds based there. As the assets of the funds have evaporated, so too have many high-paying jobs for fund analysts and managers. Those that have survived are bringing in far less earnings from fees and commissions.

Recovery Provides Large Profits to Those Who Brave Forward

At the time of that early 1990s downturn in Southern California, I was living in Berkeley, California, and frequently flew down to La Jolla (near San Diego) for weekend excursions. I kept my eye on market signals firsthand. By the mid-1990s, everything was in place. The market had hit bottom. Both population and job growth were turning from negative to positive. Mortgage lenders were making it easier to borrow. Inventories of unsold homes had shrunk. Weekend open houses were attracting dozens of prospective homebuyers. New construction of houses and apartments was at a near standstill.

That's why, in 1996, I wrote, "By the year 2001, many renters throughout Southern California will sorely regret the housing bargains they missed during the mid-1990s" (*Stop Renting Now*, p. 161). Yet, at the time, a so-called real estate expert for the *San Francisco Examiner* wrote, "A home is where the bad investment is" (November 17, 1996). And another California expert wrote, "The quick buck profits [in real estate] are long gone. . . . Buying a property in excellent condition and hoping somehow to earn a profit is a no-win situation" (*San Diego Union-Tribune*, September 8, 1996).

Why could I see what others missed? Because I know how to read and weigh market signals. I tracked indicators of emerging *D*emand against indicators of diminished *S*upply. Whereas, most observers merely forecast the recent past into the future.

Businesses Seek Lower-Priced Areas with a Qualified Work Force

Why did the old-time New England textile manufacturers move their factories to the South? Why did many Silicon Valley technology firms move all or part of their operations to Austin, Texas? Why did my publisher, John Wiley & Sons, Inc., give up its longtime world headquarters at 605 Third Avenue, Manhattan, New York City, in favor of a new office complex just across the Hudson River in Hoboken, New Jersey? Why do savvy real estate entrepreneurs forecast huge growth in warehousing and distribution employment along the I-4 corridor that links Daytona Beach, Orlando, and Tampa–St. Petersburg, Florida? Costs. Lower costs of running a business.

Businesses and Employment Migrate to Lower-Cost Cities, States, and Countries

In the highly competitive national and global marketplace, major firms persistently scout for business locations that will reduce their costs of labor, transportation, real estate, energy, and taxes. In addition, they look to see what kinds of incentives government(s) might provide, such as worker training, low-interest financing, and tax credits and incentives.

This company search for lower costs at times may simply encourage a move from the central business core to the suburbs or perhaps across state lines to a more tax-friendly environment. On other occasions, the move may take the firm's jobs to a different state or country.

Size up the relative cost competitiveness of the area(s) where you plan to invest. Do you think that its cost structure (on balance) will encourage employers to move in—or push them to move out? Because of its low manufacturing costs, Shenzen, China, grew from a population of 500,000 to 5,000,000 within a period of 10 to 15 years. Property prices escalated 10-fold. Now, though, Shenzen has lost some of its cost competitiveness. Hundreds of factories have closed. Within the past two years, property prices have been shaved 30 to 40 percent.

Cost of Living for Employees

Basic employers also factor in an area's costs of living for their employees. The quip in Silicon Valley for the past several years has been, "What do you call an engineer who earns $150,000 a year?" Answer: A renter. Given the outrageously high living costs (not only housing prices but also California state income taxes, traffic congestion, and auto and homeowners insurance), many Silicon Valley firms will need to find alternative locations that provide a more affordable lifestyle for employees.

In the past, Seattle and Austin attracted high-tech firms that wanted to offer their employees an area with a lower cost of living. While still cheaper than Silicon Valley, these cities no longer offer the clear-cut cost advantages they displayed at the start of the 1990s. So the question now becomes: Where are the next hot spots for high-tech (or other types of) employment that will grow strongly in the future? Salt Lake City? Pittsburgh? Chapel Hill? Atlanta?

Champaign–Urbana? Where does your knowledge or research lead you to look?

How about Lenoir, North Carolina? Google has recently opened a $600 million facility in this small North Carolina town that was once a prosperous center for furniture manufacturers—but then fell on hard times as companies closed their facilities. Currently, property prices still sit well below their earlier highs. With economic turnaround nearly certain to occur, Lenoir might represent a solid growth opportunity. As another plus, the quality of life of the surrounding area rates quite high.

Quality of Life

Today, people choose places to live and work according to the quality of life (QOL) available in the area. Executives evaluate new locations on the basis of climate, recreational activities, school systems, cultural facilities, municipal services, crime rates, housing affordability, the costs of doing business, and traffic congestion. Before you buy, ask, "Will this area improve with time? Will the area become more desirable, or less?"

Many communities that seek growth try to build their QOL images. A passage from an Edmonton, Alberta, economic brochure reads as follows:

> The distinct seasons enjoyed by Edmontonians are indicative of the recreational activities available. Summers are warm, with daytime temperatures averaging 22°C (72°F) and evening temperatures cooling to a pleasant 15°C (60°F). Summer is complemented by a mild spring and autumn, as well as plenty of sunshine, making much of the year enjoyable for hiking, cycling, trail riding, golf, tennis and camping. Trails for bicycles and hiking in Capital City Park are linked by four pedestrian footbridges across the North Saskatchewan River. Along this river valley are adjacent golf courses, boat launches, picnic sites and a beautiful network of trails. . . .

To complement the pleasant summers and invigorating winters, Edmonton offers virtually pollution-free and pollen-free air. Edmonton is a city to be enjoyed by all, for all seasons.

Have the city boosters aroused your desire to seek a job or start a business in Edmonton? Increasingly, cities that achieve economic growth will also be able to sell their advantages as a good place to raise a family and enjoy life. How does QOL rate in the areas that attract your interest? What efforts are aimed at making the area a better place to live, work, and play? Are people relocating to the area for reasons of QOL; or are people leaving in search of better weather, more scenic land (or sea) scapes, or a more culturally vibrant life?

Quality of Life Also Attracts Wealth

Who buys property in Aspen, Colorado; Jackson Hole, Wyoming; Longboat Key, Florida; Banner Elk, North Carolina; Ashland, Oregon; or Sedona, Arizona? They're not primarily the people who currently hold jobs in those areas. They're people with high incomes or wealth who choose where they want to live (or own a second home). Increasingly, too, free agents (writers, artists, consultants, inventors, programmers, entrepreneurs) enjoy the money and occupational freedom to set up their lifestyle wherever it suits them.

Cities, towns, and even rural (rustic) communities that appeal to the footloose and financially mobile will experience increasing demand for their residential properties. This trend definitely shows staying power. Boomers heading into retirement as well as Internet/Intranet technology permits increasing numbers of people to work from home—no matter where that home is located—people will abandon high-cost, low-quality-of-life areas in favor of those areas where they would rather live. What areas do you know that will attract these prosperous sojourners?

Community Attitudes and Actions

Another factor that boosts demand and explains why some areas grow faster than others is community attitudes. Do the city leaders promote economic growth?

Not All Areas Seek Growth

Some cities answer this question "no." On occasion, to protect vested interests, local business or government leaders discourage new firms from locating in an area. Politicians develop a power base that they do not want outsiders to challenge. The citizenry may prefer to preserve local culture.[2] Placing pressure on elected and appointed officials, no-growth advocates make it difficult for new firms to obtain permits, licenses, and zoning approvals.[3] In the past—and especially in towns dominated by one or several major employers—powerful owners of existing firms have successfully kept new industry out of an area. These power brokers try to avoid additional bidders for available workers and thereby maintain low wage rates for their own employees.

Growth Sought

In cities that promote economic growth, firms, private organizations, and various government officials actively recruit investment and new employers. For example, the Jacksonville Chamber of Commerce hired a national consulting firm to prepare a

---

[2] During the late 1970s, Oregon opposed economic growth vigorously, even to the extent of advertising Oregon as a state where newcomers were not welcome. By 1984, tough political leaders and citizens had changed their tune. Badly hurt by the recession of 1981–1982 and still slow to recover, Oregon went out to recruit new industry. Since those days, Oregon's population has grown at an above-average rate—and likewise, so has the value of its properties.

[3] For example, the city fathers in Terre Haute turned away 400 high-paying jobs because local power brokers opposed the company (an internationally prominent chemical manufacturer).

comprehensive economic analysis of that city. The study sought to identify the types of employers whose needs would best match Jacksonville's strengths. In addition, the consultant recommended ways for Jacksonville community leaders to improve the marketing of the city to targeted employers.

Two rapidly growing cities in Canada have been Calgary and Edmonton. Although their economies benefited from the well-endowed resource base of Alberta (especially oil and farmland), a contributing factor has also been the probusiness, progrowth attitude of the provincial and city governments. In Canada, a country where left-leaning political attitudes gain substantial support, Alberta positions itself more closely toward free enterprise.

(An aside that illustrates my point: During the early- to mid-2000s, as oil prices climbed to nearly $150 a barrel, Calgary gained billions of dollars of investment and thousands of basic jobs as oil companies ramped up their production from the oil sands generously deposited in Alberta. Property prices in Calgary tripled. But as oil prices have settled down—around $40 a barrel as I write—layoffs and reduced spending by oil companies is cutting deeply into the local Calgary economy. Property sales have nose-dived, and home prices are now coming back to earth—though they are still way above the levels that prevailed before 2003. Anticipate a local economic boom and you will profit—but beware and prepare. Booms rarely last forever.)

Entrepreneurial Spirit

Professor Jeanne C. Biggar traced the shifts in population that the United States has experienced since 1970. She noted that 15 Sunbelt states had accounted for nearly two-thirds of America's population growth. Biggar pointed out, however, that such disproportionate growth among a minority of states held meaning well beyond the population figures themselves. More critically, the *quality* of those who migrated spelled decline for the older cities. "The industrial North," Professor Biggar found, "is losing the able young who might be most likely to provide the creative ideas and enthusiastic leadership needed to tackle the problems associated with deteriorating cities"—in other words, those who approach life with what I call an *entrepreneurial attitude* have migrated and continue to migrate away from the "rust belt"—those once prosperous, now struggling industrial states and cities.

In other words, cities do *not* decline because they lose their economic base; rather, they lose their economic base because they lose the individuals who could breathe new economic life into their ability to compete nationally and internationally. No city, state, emirate, province, or country can create or sustain prosperity unless it nourishes entrepreneurs who remain alert to changing markets; who can discover and execute opportunities; and who can combine resources in new and better ways to create value for others.

Regardless of an area's natural resources, the drive of its people will determine its prosperity. Do the people who live (or are moving into the area) display the entrepreneurial spirit? Look for areas that attract entrepreneurial talent.

Summing Up

When I first bought properties in my hometown, I knew nothing about my city's economic base. (Although I did realize the city's QOL left much to be desired, I never realized the links between economic base, QOL, and property appreciation potential.) Quite likely, I couldn't have told you what the term *economic base* meant. But since then, I have witnessed booms and corrections in Dallas, San Diego, Miami, Atlanta, Las Vegas, Vancouver, London, Hong Kong, Singapore, and Dubai—to name just a few. I know that a strong local economy can help turn real estate investors into multimillionaires and that a slide (even when temporary) can turn unprepared investors upside down and shake their pockets empty.

Even if you're a short-term flipper, or even a fix and flipper, monitor the area's basic sources of jobs, income, wealth, and quality of life (and of course, *S*upply). When economic signals flash yellow, pay attention. Don't think you can speed through blindly without risk.

Use your knowledge of economic base to help you select geographic areas and communities that show long-run promise. Discover those cities, suburbs, or even neighborhoods that will experience high rates of growing demand over the next 5, 10, or 15 years. Had I understood the basics of *D*emand—the explanations that I have laid out for you in this chapter—at the start of my career, I would have chosen to invest somewhere other than Terre Haute. Or perhaps I would have targeted a more promising area of Terre Haute than those neighborhoods where I actually did buy. At the least, I would have recognized that my properties were unlikely to achieve the same rates of appreciation as those properties in San Francisco, California, or Aspen, Colorado. Properties across the world, the United States—or even throughout the same metro area—seldom increase in value at a uniform pace. Those properties appreciate fastest where future demand will push against a constrained supply of competitors.

Put this knowledge to work. Basic employers, tourists, government, professional services, QOL, and other determinants of *D*emand can shift—sometimes within a short time frame. When you evaluate these determinants—and act accordingly—you reduce your risks and enhance your opportunities. In the words of Donald Trump, "Before you invest, you've got to know your territory."

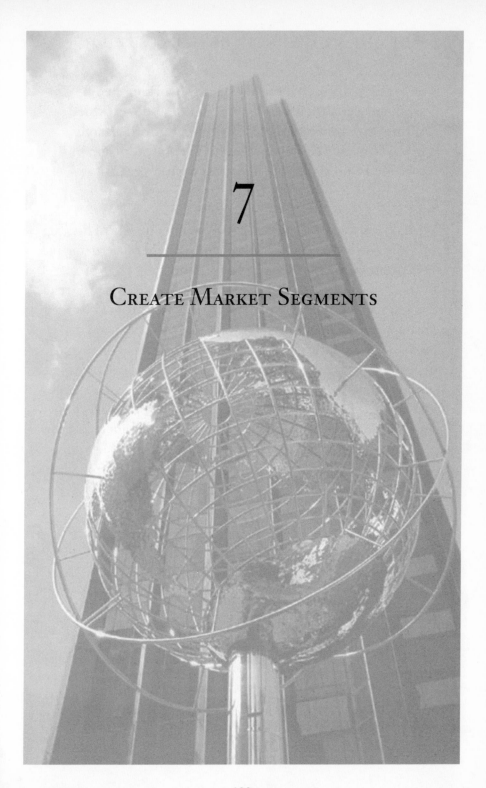

7

CREATE MARKET SEGMENTS

My father offered a top product to working people who had lived their whole lives in cramped, crowded rental apartments: modestly priced, suburban-style brick houses. His buyers bought them faster than he could build them. He knew his customers just as well as I know mine.

POPULATION GROWTH, JOBS, incomes, wealth, quality of life, supply of competitive properties—these and other macro (big picture) demand factors (Chapter 6) begin your study of an area. Yet, in today's world of real estate, population diversity (micro trends and market segments) also plays a critical part in your strategy to create a most valued property (MVP). To maximize your entrepreneurial profits, explore and create niche market segments of renters and buyers. What features and services can you provide to achieve a competitive advantage for tenants or buyers who express similar—yet difficult-to-fulfill—needs, wants, desires, and preferences? In a world filled with choices, your tenants must not only possess the income necessary to pay rent, they also must be willing to choose your property over those units offered by your competitors.

DIVERSITY RULES

True diversity in micro *D*emand includes a panorama of demographics and psychographics (feelings, lifestyles, and attitudes). The features of a property I like may not appeal to you. The features you like may not appeal to someone else. When you notice how people differ in their likes and dislikes—as well as what they're *willing* and able to pay for, you can zero in on a bull's-eye of tenants or buyers.

Even if your customers don't make as much money as mine do, still make your property seem special to them. That's what my father and I did with Swifton Village.

Demographic Differences

Think how you might use one or more of the following characteristics to segment a market. With such attributes in mind, craft a strategy to meet a motivating need, want, or problem of these people. What properties have you noticed that cater to certain types of buyers or tenants? What ideas can you generate? Study these demographic characteristics:

- Young professional.
- College student.
- Female/male.
- Occupation/employer.
- Retiree.
- Nonsmokers/smokers.
- Disability.
- Neighborhood.
- Household size (number of persons).
- Household composition (characteristics of household members).
- Income/credit score.
- Wealth/cash savings.
- Stage of life.
- Religion/ethnicity.
- Credit score.
- Homeowner/renter.
- Marital status.

Here are several examples from my experience. (*Note:* Before you develop your market segmentation strategy, learn the rules of the fair housing laws that apply to your rental or sales practices.)

Share-a-Home (Age and Health)

Among my properties, I formerly owned a 3,200-square-foot, five-bedroom, four-bath, single-family house that rented back then for

$850 a month to a married couple with children. In talking with another property owner in the neighborhood (always searching for ideas), I discovered a more profitable use for that house, that is, a better MVP strategy.

It turned out that this neighborhood investor owned four large houses and rented individual rooms in each of these properties to individual seniors. Typically, these people were age 70 or older. They were healthy enough to care for their own basic everyday living but not up to maintaining their own private residence. The investor essentially operated these properties as upscale boardinghouses. He called these houses "share-a-homes." At that time, I had not heard of this type of tenant segmentation/property differentiation strategy.

Following up on this idea, I learned that good fortune favored me. Not only was my large house located within a share-a-home zoning district, but also, with no changes whatsoever, the property met the strict regulatory housing codes that applied for this use (e.g., size of bedrooms, number of bathrooms, number and location of exits, window locks, kitchen facilities). Although I had no interest in personally managing a share-a-home, I did lease the house to the operator down the street. My new rent: $1,350 per month. He then leased out four bedrooms at around $600 a month each for a total rent collection of $2,400.

Share-a-Home Update: Sunset Village, Inc.

Along these same lines, a development project called Sunset Village has modernized the share-a-home market segmentation/property differentiation strategy. Here's an excerpt from one of its promotional letters:

> There is no other product in the rental market within our rent range that offers the amenities [fitness center, heated swimming pool, beauty salon, card and Super Bowl room, putting green, shuffleboard, maid service] that we are offering. Our

target market for rental is the senior that cannot quite handle the daily upkeep of a home or apartment, yet they are healthy and are not ready for the assisted living type of care. . . . Seniors can keep their independence longer.

Sunset Village provides a value proposition that many seniors prefer. Given the success of their previous share-a-home developments, they have clearly achieved a competitive advantage over more generic rental properties.

OTHER MARKET SEGMENT POSSIBILITIES

You can slice and dice demographics in thousands of combinations. Moreover, because you're renting out (or selling) one property at a time, you can pinpoint the needs of a quite narrow type of person, family, or household. Unlike Procter & Gamble that typically needs millions of consumers for its variously segmented product lines, you can tailor property to a market segment as small as a single person or household.

Donald Trump's MVP appeals to the wealthy (often new money) who value image and status. One renovator I knew designed and remodeled apartments and houses to better accommodate roommate living, families with young children, or families with teenage children. Wheelchair-friendly units also seem to be in short supply relative to demand. Some property owners target the financially responsible yet cash- or credit-impaired renter. One of my previous properties was located two blocks from a hospital. I fixed up the property and drafted a rental agreement that made these units especially appealing to single nurses.

Psychographic Differences

Most large developers, home builders, and apartment complexes combine demographics with psychographics to create their target

113

markets. In this sense, I'm using the term *psychographics* to refer to all types of mental predispositions, such as likes, dislikes, tastes, preferences, attitudes, values, and lifestyle. Again quoting from a Sunset Village promotional letter:

> Our goal is to offer safe and affordable housing to the healthy, active senior. Many seniors have a major problem with loneliness and lack of interaction with other people.... [Therefore] seniors like this shared living concept ... and generally form little family-type groups.... We are able to sponsor a program of activities for our residents.

From this passage, you can see how Sunset Village blends demographic characteristics, such as age and health, with psychographic characteristics, such as active lifestyle, social interaction, and safety. Notice how the firm understands the needs and wants of its target audience and crafts its apartment units, amenities, and services to meet those needs.

I know my customers. I'm not going for the old wealth that dates back to the Rockefellers and Du Ponts. My target is the rich Italian with the beautiful wife and the red Ferrari. That's the audience that Trump Tower was designed for.

MYRTLE BEACH CONDOMINIUMS

Some years back, I was called in as a marketing research consultant by a developer in Myrtle Beach, South Carolina, who was trying to obtain development financing to build a condominium project. Unfortunately for this developer, mortgage construction lenders thought he was nuts. At that time, the national economy was mired in recession. Gasoline prices were shooting up, and, of no small concern, the Myrtle Beach market was littered with partially built, unsold, see-through, mid-rise, beachfront condo projects.[1]

But this developer wasn't crazy. He had studied his market segment. He knew that as one of the premier golfing centers in the United States, Myrtle Beach attracted hundreds of thousands of visitors each year who cared nothing about a beachfront location or ocean-oriented activities such as boating or swimming. These visitors come to play golf all day and dine on seafood, drink, and share camaraderie with friends all evening. These golfing buddies didn't need or want an expensive beachfront condo (or hotel). They wanted comfortable, private, and spacious accommodations at an affordable price.

So, this developer created a uniquely attractive value proposition (MVP): A 1,350-square-foot, townhouse style, two-bedroom, two-bath condo, located 14 blocks west of the beach yet within 15 minutes of most popular golf courses. Because of this supposedly "off-the-beaten-path" site, the developer could price the units for 60 percent less than the condos that had created the beachfront bust. Yet that wasn't the end of the story.

The developer knew that many golfing buddies circulate within a group of 6 to 10 friends. To make his condo value proposition more affordable, he promoted shared ownership among perhaps 4, 6, or even 10 partners. With this type of purchase plan, he significantly increased the number of potential buyers for his units. The golfing buddies were able to secure accommodations that surpassed the quality of hotels or motels in the market. But when figured on a per-person, nightly use basis, the townhouse unit costs much less than a Holiday Inn.

Within 18 months, the developer had sold out the first two phases of his project and was already planning a third phase. Savvy target marketing and product development created huge profits for this

---

[1] A "see-through" building is a partially built, abandoned project. Since only the skeleton (frame) of the building has been put up, you can see right through it.

astute entrepreneur—when most other condo builders were going broke. This builder realized that even "oversupply" doesn't necessarily foreclose opportunity. When macro fundamentals look poor, your micro strategy can still create a profitable MVP—when you choose the right market niche to aim at.

AVOID STANDARD LABELS, PICTURE YOUR ACTUAL RENTERS (OR BUYERS)

You may have heard people refer to broadly based housing segments such as empty nesters, yuppies, burpies, first-time homebuyers, move-up buyers, the age 55+ market, and, more recently, the Hispanic market, the Asian market, and the Islamic market. Similarly, SRI (formerly known as the Stanford Research Institute, a Menlo Park market research firm) developed a generic market segment classification system known as VALS (an acronym for values and lifestyles) that was naively used by some apartment complex owners and homebuilders. VALS classified much of United States' population into the following simplistic segments:

- Survivors.
- Sustainers.
- Achievers.
- Belongers.
- Emulators.
- Societally conscious.

As catalysts to stimulate thought, such labels might provoke brainstorming sessions. But never let mere labels shape your market segmentation strategy. One book for real estate investors tells its readers to sell their renovated properties to first-time homebuyers. But that label (as do all generic segmentation labels) lacks precision. I learned that fact during the 1990s, when I offered "Stop Renting Now!" seminars throughout the USA. My audience of first-time buyers fit no single demographic. They included a range of ages, income, wealth, and family size:

- Age (25 to 55).
- Income ($20,000 to $120,000).
- Cash down available (0 to $100,000).
- Credit record, from excellent to lousy.
- Family status (single, divorced, separated, married, married with children, unmarried partners).
- Race (all races).
- Lifestyles (all the values, attitudes, and life situations that anyone could imagine).

Their financial ability and knowledge differed. Their tastes and preferences in home features differed. Their motivations differed (e.g., better schools for their kids, more space, location, investment, close to nightlife, time horizon).

When you create a target market of tenants or buyers, imagine the actual person. "First-time buyer" cuts across too wide a segment. Picture the characteristics (demographics, psychographics, lifestyles, preferences, turn-ons, and turnoffs) of the people for whom you would like to create an MVP. Then design the features of your property and leasing (purchase) program to motivate your specific customers to act (rent or buy).

COLLEGE STUDENTS

Owners of rental houses and apartment buildings often remark that they avoid renting to "college students." But similar to the first-time homebuyer market segment, college student segments come in all types. I once renovated a 16-unit apartment building specifically for a target market of college students. That building proved quite profitable—and the students appreciated the way management operated the property to serve tenant preferences.

But we didn't rent to just any college students. We targeted top students who did not smoke, possessed above-average financial resources, and were mature in demeanor, quiet, and clean. In return, we offered a pleasant place to live at a fair rent level. We achieved extraordinary profits through lower costs for repairs, marketing, and management as well as near zero vacancies and bad debts. We achieved MVP status for our tenants and ourselves.

HIT THE BULL'S-EYE

You can think about target marketing with broad-brush labels such as sustainers, achievers, college students, first-time buyers, active seniors, empty-nesters, young marrieds, roommates, singles, moderate income, or even that once ubiquitous segment known as yuppies (who are now referred to as aging boomers).

Broad-brush labels such as first-time buyers or college students might point you toward market segments that share some similar characteristics. But the hearts and minds within each of these generalized categories show differences that make a difference. To hit that most profitable bull's-eye within a broadly based market segment, search for the unique and intense needs that best motivate select types of people. What features and benefits would really motivate your prospects?

FIND UNIQUE AND INTENSE NEEDS

To create an MVP, discover or create those intense (motivating) needs and wants that other competing property owners miss. Identify your tenants' (buyers') hot buttons. I found that the nurses I rented to were worried about their personal safety. So I increased the amount of outdoor lighting at the property, installed double-deadbolt door locks, and placed heavy-gauge wire mesh screens on the building's first-story windows.

These nurses also wanted more closet space than the other apartments in the neighborhood provided. Luckily, the bedrooms in my property measured approximately 16 by 18 feet. That feature allowed me to set off two feet of room length and add a full-wall closet in each bedroom. As a special touch, I installed full-length mirrors on the new closet doors. These mirrors gave the bedrooms a brighter, more spacious appearance.

Individual Leases

In taking a cue from Doreen Brierbrier (*Managing Your Rental Property for More Income*), I rented to the nurses individually rather than as a group. I also permitted any nurse to end her lease at any time if she would find a substitute tenant who proved acceptable to me and the other existing residents of the house. These (primarily younger) women appreciated that flexibility—although few exercised this option. In fact, the low tenant turnover at that property actually surprised me.

Throw Away Standard Operating Procedures

Most owners of small rental properties operate their buildings according to some combination of standard operating procedure, the detailed, how-to directions offered by authors of their favorite real estate books, or maybe the owner's own insights and idiosyncratic prejudices, unguided by a customer (tenant) profile. I encourage you to practice a more profitable approach. Understand your intended customer. My experiences and the experiences of other entrepreneurs prove that the more closely you attend to the motivating needs (hot buttons) of potential tenants, the more they will reward you with a higher and more dependable stream of rental income (MVP applies to you, too).

Contrary to the principles of maximizing rewards relative to risks, owners who merely offer a generic rental property to a generic tenant earn (at best) generic returns. When you follow their example, you (at best) receive so-called market rent levels because that's what market implies: The average rent for a standard, look-alike product in an open and competitive marketplace. No MVP entrepreneur competes with a "me-too" generic product.

How Do You Identify the Wow (MVP) Features for Your Tenants?

Since you can't read minds, you must discover those elements of your value proposition that will motivate your customers to act now. Here are several methods that have worked for me and other entrepreneurial property investors:

- Talk informally with people; discover their problems.
- Pay attention, eavesdrop, read, watch.
- Talk with insiders and experts.
- Conduct (informal) focus groups.

Informal Conversations

I'm an inquisitor. I strike up conversations with people to learn their thoughts, problems, likes, and dislikes. In fact, I discovered the housing opportunity for nurses while visiting one of my parents in the hospital. In casual conversation, I asked a nurse where she lived. That opened the door to one of those "Don't get me started on that" comments.

That backhanded invitation intensified my inquiry and led to further conversation with the nurse. She then went on to describe how much difficulty she and her workmates encountered when looking for a decent and affordable place to live near the hospital—which is where they preferred to live given their odd-hour work schedules.

People know what they want, so ask them.

Similarly, because I've taught from time to time at various universities, I talk with students to learn about their housing problems, preferences, likes, and dislikes. Such conversations led me to develop an MVP strategy for the 16-unit income property I mentioned previously.

How many people do you know (or know of) who have shopped to buy or rent in the past year or two? Question them. Learn their reactions to the properties they looked at. Why did they eventually choose their current home? What was the difference that made *the* difference for these people? What features would they have liked yet found rare or unavailable? Talk with people. Probe. You'll surprise yourself at how much valuable information you can pick up.

Pay Attention

Read the neighborhood and community sections of the local newspaper(s). Follow those human interest stories and question-and-answer columns where people talk about their house-hunting and rental problems. Go to the library or onto the Internet to read the articles in the Sunday Real Estate or Homes sections of the *Los Angeles Times*, the *San Diego Union-Tribune*, the *San Francisco Examiner*, the *Chicago Tribune*, or the *Orlando Sentinel*, or the Saturday edition of the *Washington Post*. These newspapers not only feature stories on the latest real estate trends but also carry various nationally syndicated real estate columnists.

You can find other idea-provoking articles in magazines such as *American Demographics*, *Journal of Property Management*, and state *Realtor* magazines. Eavesdrop. Turn your ears toward people when they talk about buying, selling, renting, or investing in real estate. Visit real estate chat rooms and blogs on the Internet. When you discover something new or interesting, mull it over. Think whether this fact, trend, or problem could help you better tailor a property toward a market segment of renters (buyers). Is there some feature or benefit that you could offer that establishes a competitive advantage for your property or properties?

Talk with Insiders and Experts

People who work in a dozen or more occupations and professions gain firsthand state-of-the-moment information by talking directly with homebuyers and renters. Talk with people who work in these types of jobs:

- Real estate agents.
- Property managers.
- Mortgage loan reps.
- Property inspectors.
- Credit counselors.
- Remodeling contractors.
- Real estate investors.
- Newspaper reporters who cover housing and real estate.
- Existing tenants.
- Social service agency personnel.
- City planners, building permit inspectors, zoning personnel.
- Professors (architecture, consumer sciences, planning, real estate, housing).
- Staff who work at the city and state housing finance agencies.
- Apartment finder services.
- Roommate finder services.
- Building and zoning code enforcers.
- Home builders.
- Government landlord/tenant agencies.
- HUD Section 8 administrators.

Discover demographic and psychographic trends, personal problems, shortages, and surpluses. Ask who's renting, who's buying, where, and why? What's hot, what's not? When homeowners remodel, what features do they prefer? Are increasing (decreasing) numbers of people feeling financial pain? Trend analysis shows you how to profitably adapt to change.

Focus Groups

During the past 20 years, focus groups have emerged as one of the most popular ways to get into the minds of potential tenants and homebuyers. Focus groups bring together 6 to 15 people from your proposed target market. Then, through give-and-take conversations, you probe their beliefs and feelings.

Most major home and apartment builders in the country now run focus groups to learn the preferences of their intended customers. I ran my "Stop Renting Now!" seminars as quasi focus groups. Often real estate firms and mortgage lenders paid my fees. In return, I provided these clients the names of prospects along with the comments and concerns that I had elicited from my seminar's question-and-answer sessions.

To create its share-a-home property, Sunset Village employed the Osceola County Council on Aging to hold 15 focus groups (200 total participants). The insights gained helped Sunset Village formulate its marketing theme as well as the specific property features, amenities, and services that the firm blended into its triplexes and total value proposition.

To take advantage of this research technique, you need not conduct a formal focus group. That may go beyond the time, effort, and money that you want to put into your investment research—at least during your beginning stages. Nevertheless, if you find yourself (or can place yourself) in a group setting, try to get the group members to discuss topics that alert you to rental (sales) market opportunities. Scout for profitable ideas any where you can find them—which means practically everywhere you might find yourself.

ANTICIPATE AND ADAPT TO CHANGE

Anticipate change. Discover how trends will affect future demand for specific types of homes, apartments, neighborhoods, and communities. If you look at the writing on the wall, it reads, "Profit."

The Age Wave

Everybody knows that the population of the United States, Canada, Europe, China, and Japan are getting older. During the next 20 years, at least 60 million people in the United States will celebrate their sixtieth birthday.[2] Sixty million new retirees are on the horizon. Where will these people prefer to live? What kinds of housing units will they want (Sunset Village type share-a-homes)? What features amenities, services, and benefits will press their hot buttons?

The real estate investors who jump on the front end of this freight train to opportunity will certainly ride to glory. Yet, as I have emphasized, "over 60" itself doesn't define a target market. It merely flashes the signal to stop, look, and listen. What bull's-eye segments within this over-60 market will remain underserved until some entrepreneur senses their need and creates a way to fill it? Here are some of the trends that demographers are beginning to detect:

1. *Downsizing:* A shift away from the McMansions that became so popular during the recent property boom years.
2. *College Towns:* Retirees like the combination of education, sports, arts, theater, health facilities, and diversity without the big-city costs and aggravation.
3. *Rural/Small Towns:* Especially those towns that combine abundant outdoor recreation with a degree of upscale culture (such as Ashland, Oregon).
4. *Single-Floor Housing Units:* Post-60-year-olds often prefer to avoid stairs.
5. *Doorways and Door Levers:* Wider doorways to accommodate wheelchairs and walkers. Door levers are easier to manage than doorknobs.

---

[2] The media frequently report a figure of around 75 million baby boomers. But that figure overstates the actual number because millions of boomers will die prior to age 65. However, we must add immigrants to the total number, thus the actual number at least reaches 60 million, but possibly as high as 70 million.

6. *Mild Four-Season Climate:* While Florida will remain the most popular state for retirees, mild four-season states, such as Tennessee, Georgia, the Carolinas, Virginia, New Mexico, and Colorado, will become increasingly popular. In fact, the entire South will grow the number of migrant retirees.

7. *High-Cost to Low-Cost Areas:* Why live in a prewar Brooklyn bungalow when you can rent or own a large new house or apartment just outside sunny Orlando or Tampa for less than half the housing costs in Brooklyn?

8. *Security and Low Maintenance:* Lock and leave without worry. With extensive travel on the agenda, retirees won't want to concern themselves with the safety and security of their home while they're away.

This list just samples a few emerging trends. Talk to the people you know. What plans are they making? What features and benefits will motivate their next purchase or rental?

ECHO BOOMERS

Each year, many nationally published articles discuss how the baby boomers might impact the housing market. To date, though, the media have not spent much time on another perfectly predictable demographic trend.

The birth years for baby boomers were from 1946 to 1964. The birth years for the baby bust were from 1965 to 1977. Then, beginning in 1979, annual births again shot up into the range of 4 million per year and continued at or near that pace for more than 15 years.

The first wave of these echo boomers turned age 30 in 2008. Reminiscent of the 1970s, once again, near record numbers of young people will be flooding into the entry-level homebuying and rental markets. What types of houses and apartments, what features, and what locations will appeal to the diverse segments of the echo generation? Put up your early detection antennae. What signals are the echo boomers sending as to how their preferences will evolve in the areas where you are buying?

Local Trends and Changes

The age wave and the echo boomers represent two definite and profound demographic changes that will hit full stride during the coming decade. How will these trends play out in the areas where you plan to invest? Or, vice versa, can you discover areas (neighborhoods, communities) that stand to benefit from the broadened growth of these two age groups?

What other demographic and psychographic trends are occurring in your investment area? When you talk with housing experts and insiders, explore their views about population and community change. Track shifts in tastes, age distribution, incomes, job growth, and neighborhood popularity. Find a trend and ride it to profits.

As the trend grows, so will your knowledge and ability. You will learn from your tenants. You will refine and expand your property purchase, property improvement, and rental strategy. Your MVP will stand out from your competitors.

8

CREATE *UTILITY* (BENEFITS) WITH AND
WITHIN THE RULES

TO UNLOCK POTENTIAL PROFITS, WORK THE LAND-USE LAWS TO YOUR ADVANTAGE

"The addition of this luxury structure to Jersey City's Gold Coast," announced Jersey City's Mayor Jerramiah T. Healy, "testifies as to why our city attracts people to live, work, and raise families. We are pleased to welcome Mr. Trump and Mr. Geibel as codevelopers of this project whose shared vision contributes to the continued growth and success of our downtown revitalization.

"We are honored to be working with Donald Trump to create a world-class living experience in Jersey City, with its incomparable views of the world's most famous skyline, outstanding amenities, and convenient transportation links. I also want to thank Mayor Healy for his efforts to create an environment where Trump Plaza is possible," said Geibel, whose Hoboken-based Metro Homes LLC is the codeveloper of the project.

In Tampa, Florida, the Trump project gained similar acclaim. "This is an exciting development for Tampa in many ways," said Mark Huey, the city's economic development administrator, on behalf of Mayor Pam Iorio. "When this project was announced, the focus and attention on the vibrancy and viability of downtown Tampa as a wonderful place to live, work, and play was taken to a new level. We're delighted with how Trump Tower Tampa incorporates and celebrates the Tampa Riverwalk and how this level of investment and commitment to quality reflects on our city."

"The entire development team is mindful of the significance and impact this project will have on the City of Tampa and the downtown area," stated Jill Cremer, vice president of development and marketing for The Trump Organization. "To that end, we took all the time and steps necessary to make sure that every aspect of this development would be executed to the highest standards which Mr. Trump and his partners at SimDag share."

What attributes do each of these projects share? What attributes do all Trump Organization projects share in common? The ability of the Trump team to work with government officials to secure zoning and building approvals.

When working with government, of course, nothing is guaranteed. Mr. Trump's well-publicized battles with then-New York City Mayor Ed Koch illustrate that fact. Nevertheless, more than a small part of Mr. Trump's success lies in his ability to work the zoning and land-use laws to his benefit. When preparing to buy a site or building, Mr. Trump reviews all building regulations as well as the sentiments of the city officials and community residents. In every case, he's trying to identify opportunities to use the property in a way that maximizes value to his target market and himself.

Most famously, perhaps, was his coup to build 80 stories on a site originally zoned for less than half of that amount of space. The secret: Buy air rights from the surrounding property owners—at the time a little recognized loophole in the zoning law. Today, Trump World Tower at United Nations Plaza stands as one of the tallest residential buildings in the world.

Use enthusiasm to capture and excite the people you need to get your deals permitted, financed, leased, and sold. Enthusiasm runs contagious.

A FRIEND OF the popular 1930s and 1940s curmudgeon comedian-actor, W. C. Fields, once spied Fields reading the Bible. "Bill," the friend said, "why are you reading the Bible? That doesn't seem like you."

"Looking for loopholes," Fields answered, "looking for loopholes."

You need to read the rules, regulations, and laws that govern property and land use for the same reason that W. C. Fields read the Bible: To look for loopholes. As you design the *U*tility (benefits) that you will offer tenants to accomplish your most valued property (MVP) strategy, you will encounter a web of restrictions. The question then becomes: Will you get stuck and entangled within this web? Or, like the agile spider, will you learn to use this web to benefit you and your market segment of tenants or buyers?

Without the agility to navigate this web of rules, you can make these mistakes:

1. *Missed Advantages:* Without detailed knowledge of what you can and cannot legally do in creating your MVP, you can miss profitable possibilities. If Trump had not ferreted out the loopholes within the NYC zoning rules, Trump World Tower would stand a mere 40 stories tall.
2. *Purchase Errors:* Prior to purchase, learn whether the property fits within all applicable laws. If not, at some point, the regulators might require you (the new owner) to make costly renovations to make the property comply with code. If, say, that enclosed porch or converted attic doesn't fit within the regulations, you may have to tear out those illegal features and rebuild according to applicable rules and regulations.
3. *Mistakes in Use:* Land-use rules create zoning districts (commercial, residential, industrial), and they also govern occupancy, signs, parking, home businesses, noise, yard care, and even whether you can put up a basketball hoop or hang clothes on an outdoor clothesline. Without knowledge, you could design an MVP strategy that the government authorities shoot down.
4. *Mismanagement of Rentals:* Federal, state, and local laws govern every issue from security deposits to discrimination to eviction. Failure to follow lawful rules and procedures can subject you to large fines or serious liability claims and court judgments.

To profit from property ownership, follow the rules, lobby for change, or seek a lawful exception. I've heard investors rail against the rules of government or the rules of their homeowners' associations. Yet these rules were in effect at the time the investors bought. These disgruntled folks had failed to investigate before they invested.

Study the government, private, and contractual rules that govern your property (or the property that you're negotiating to buy). Your superior knowledge will pay off in two ways: (1) You will capitalize on profitable opportunities that others miss, and (2) you will steer around those entanglements that ensnare others. Here are the main sources of rules, regulations, and laws that govern your properties:

- Homeowners' associations.
- Private contracts, such as mortgages, leases, insurance policies, and easements.
- Governments (federal, state, county, city).

Restrictions, of course, do not govern only *your* property. They also govern your neighbors and your tenants. You can use the rules to stop others from acting in ways that run down the value of your property. Government and homeowner association (HOA) rules can help control the neighborhood riffraff or to straighten up troublesome tenants.

Homeowner Associations

In addition to city, state, and national governments, private HOAs also issue rules, regulations, and laws that courts will enforce. These essentially private governments tax, assess, fine, and collect fees from their "citizens." As with rules and regulations, courts do enforce payment of HOA demands. Absent payment, these private HOAs can foreclose on their delinquent property owners.

Today, more than 35 percent of all houses and condominiums in the United States and Canada are governed by some type of homeowner association. Although, generally, HOAs perform reasonably well, never assume that peace, responsibility, and fiscal discipline prevail within such a community of owners and residents.

Obtain a Copy of the Resale Package

Before you invest in a property that's governed by an HOA, obtain and read a copy of its so-called resale package. This package of documents includes the HOA's constitution, bylaws (declarations), rules and regulations, budget, reserves for repairs and replacement, and other operating policies and procedures.

As you read these documents, verify that the condo rules will allow you to carry out the entrepreneurial MVP strategy that you would like to design for the property. In addition, inquire about the monthly fees, special assessments, and periodic maintenance charges that the HOA will require you (and all other owners) to pay.

Rules and Regulations

Some HOAs govern lightly. Others detail personal conduct, property upkeep, property improvements, and occupancy down to the last minutiae. The HOAs can govern parking, musical instruments, cooking odors, grilling, moving in, moving out, lease terms, pets, and the types, numbers, and ages of tenants—plus virtually anything else you can think of.

I stress this "need to know" about the HOA because many investors buy properties and then learn they can't renovate or lease out their units as they intended. Or they're hit with large, unexpected fees or assessments. (In this book, we won't be able to detail HOA operations, but my book *Make Money with Condominiums and Townhouses* addresses all of these topics.)

CONTRACTS RESTRICT PROPERTY USE AND IMPROVEMENTS

HOAs, as well as local, state, and federal governments, can limit your right to do with your property as you please. Mortgage and insurance contracts also set rules and restrictions relative to occupancy, use, and maintenance.

For example, mortgage contracts often include clauses that require you to:

1. Maintain the property in good repair.
2. Obtain the lender's written permission before you remodel or make other substantive changes to the property.

3. Obtain the lender's written permission before you change the use of the property (converting it, say, from residential to office or retail). Usually, you will need to arrange new financing.
4. Live in the property for at least 12 months—unless you've financed it with higher-cost investor (non-owner occupied) financing.

Your property insurance policy includes clauses that apply to use, occupancy, vacancies, materials and repairs, and major renovations. If you materially breach the mortgage agreement, the lender can (after notice to cure) call the loan due immediately. If you materially breach the insurance agreement, the insurer may refuse to pay any claim you file. Play it safe. Before you unknowingly breach a contract requirement, read your mortgage and insurance agreements.

Zoning and Related Ordinances

Since the 1920s, zoning and other property ordinances have steadily increased their depth and breadth. Almost nothing escapes their attention.

To learn how zoning affects a property, consult your area's zoning map. Find out the type of zoning district and the relevant governing rules and regulations. Or locate neighborhoods on the map that are zoned in a way consistent with your entrepreneurial intent. Then look for specific properties whose features fit your requirements.

The District Concept

To set up zoning laws, planners design zoning maps that lay out multiple districts that may range in size from one small parcel of land up to several square miles or more. Sometimes, small zoning districts lie within larger districts—as when a small office complex or convenience retail center is surrounded by houses and apartments.

Elite cities may even zone out nearly all multifamily, commercial and industrial land uses.

As you can see from Figure 8.1, planners designate a variety of zoning districts. This listing in Figure 8.1 samples only a few district categories. A full listing of categories could number into the hundreds.

Article IV. Use Regulations

Division 1. Introduction to Districts

Sec. 30-41.	Establishment of zoning districts and categories
Sec. 30-42.	Designation of district boundaries
Sec. 30-43.	Rules for interpretation of district boundaries

Residential Zoning Districts

Sec. 30-51.	Single-family residential districts (RSF-1, RSF-2, RSF-2, and RSF-4)
Sec. 30-52.	Residential low-density districts (RMF-5, RC, and MH)
Sec. 30-53.	Multiple-family medium-density residential districts (RMF-6, RMF-7, and RMF-8)
Sec. 30-54.	Residential mixed-use district (RMU)
Sec. 30-55.	Residential high-density districts (RH-1 and RH-2)
Sec. 30-56.	General provisions for residential districts
Sec. 30-57.	Residential leases; teaching of the fine arts
Sec. 30-58.	Home occupation permits

Office Zoning Districts

Sec. 30-59.	Office districts (OR and OF)
Sec. 30-60.	General provisions for office districts

Business and Mixed-Use Zoning Districts

Sec. 30-61.	General business district (BUS)
Sec. 30-62.	Automotive-oriented business district (BA)
Sec. 30-63.	Tourist-oriented business district (BT)
Sec. 30-64.	Mixed-use low-intensity district (MU-1)
Sec. 30-65.	Mixed-use medium-intensity district (MU-2)
Sec. 30-66.	Central city district (CCD)
Sec. 30-67.	General provisions for business and mixed-use districts

---

Figure 8.1 Types of Zoning Districts.

If a property, for example, were located in a city's residential mixed use (RMU) district, you would turn to Section 30–54 of the city's zoning manual. If from the zoning map you see that the property is located in a RSF-4 district, you would consult Section 20–29. From the zoning manual, you would learn the specific rules that govern properties located within that district category.

Types of Restrictions

Zoning and other related ordinances can control about anything you do outside the privacy of your own bedroom, including:

- Type of property use
- Special uses/exceptions
- Setback dimensions (front and rear)
- Side-yard dimensions
- Floor area ratio (FAR)
- Lot coverage ratio
- Building height
- Parking
- Noise
- Light
- View
- Trees and shrubbery
- Accessory apartments
- Swimming pools
- Subdivision layout
- Animal control
- Party walls
- Obnoxious behavior
- Smoke, dust, pollution
- Aesthetics/Architectural Review Boards
- Occupancy
- Home occupations
- Home businesses

- Trespass
- Fences
- Crowds
- Historical districts
- Yard care, weeds
- Health and safety
- Solar panels
- Signage
- Environment and ecology

Some cities (such as Palm Beach, Florida, or Mill Valley, California) regulate everything that's possible as tightly as possible. Other cities (such as Orlando, Florida) adopt a more flexible and expansive policy. In Gilchrest County, Florida, it appears as if anyone can place a mobile home about anywhere without fear of legal challenge. In the neighboring county of Alachua, legal sites for mobile homes are tough to come by. With some governments, almost anything goes. With others, you need permission to put up a new mailbox.

Setbacks, Side Yards, and Height

Zoning ordinances tell property owners that they can't site their buildings too close to the street, their adjacent neighbors, or the neighboring site in the rear. What's too close? What buildings? It all depends. For example:

1. *Dimensions:* Look at Table 8.1. Notice the requirements for four different residential single-family (RSF) classifications in one town. Except for the maximum height requirements of 35 feet, the other dimensional standards *do not* represent "typical." In fact, no typical exists. Until the zoning law was changed, Vancouver, Canada, permitted houses to be built on some lots as small as 16 feet wide, side yards of 2 feet, and front setbacks of 10 feet. In Barrington Hills, Illinois, an exclusive suburb of Chicago, at one time, minimum lot sizes for houses required five acres. Some planned unit

Table 8.1 Dimensional Requirements for Residential Single-Family Districts

Principal Structures	RSF-1	RSF-2	RSF-3	RSF-4
Maximum density	3.5 du/a	4.6 du/a	5.8 du/a	8 du/a
Minimum lot area	8,500 sq. ft.	7,500 sq. ft.	6,000 sq. ft.	4,300 sq. ft.
Minimum lot width at minimum front-yard setback	85 ft.	75 ft.	60 ft.	50 ft.
Minimum lot depth	90 ft.	90 ft.	90 ft.	80 ft.
Minimum yard setbacks				
Front	20 ft.	20 ft.	20 ft.	20 ft.
Side (interior)	7.5 ft.	7.5 ft.	7.5 ft.	7.5 ft.
Side (street)	10 ft.	10 ft.	7.5 ft.	7.5 ft.
Rear	20 ft.	20 ft.	15 ft.	10 ft.
Maximum building height	35 ft.	35 ft.	35 ft.	35 ft.

Accessory Structures[a] (Excluding Fences and Walls)

Minimum front- and side-yard setbacks	Same requirements are for the principal structure.
Minimum yard setback, rear[b]	7.5 ft.
Maximum building height	25 ft.
Transmitter towers	80 ft.

du/a = Dwelling unit per acre; RSF = Residential single family.

[a]Accessory screened enclosure structures, whether attached to the principal structure or not, may be erected in the rear yard as long as the enclosure has a minimum yard setback of 3 feet from the rear property line. The maximum height of the enclosure at the setback line shall not exceed 8 feet. The roof and all sides of the enclosure not attached to the principal structure must be made of screening material.

[b]One preengineered or premanufactured structure of 100 square feet or less may be erected in the rear and side yards as long as the structure has a minimum yard setback of 3 feet from the rear or side property lines, is properly anchored to the ground, and is separated from neighboring properties by a fence or wall that is at least 75 percent opaque.

developments permit zero lot lines, as do some big-city townhouses and tenements.

2. *Buildings or Structures:* When you check the requirements for setbacks and side yards, notice what buildings or structures must comply. Zoning rules may permit screened porches, freestanding storage sheds, swimming pools, decks, garages, and driveways to sit closer to the property lines than setback and side-yard rules imply. With such exceptions common, you may enjoy more room for improvements than a casual glance at the requirements might

indicate. Setbacks do not limit all types of structures and improvements equally.

Floor Area and Lot Coverage Ratios

If you plan to add living or storage space to a primary structure, see whether the zoning code sets floor area ratio (FARs) or lot coverage ratios (LCRs) for the property. FARs define the square footage of a building as a percentage (or multiple) of the square footage of the lot. For example, the FAR for a single-family house might be set as follows:

$$FAR = \frac{2,400 \text{ sq. ft. (building size)}}{8,500 \text{ sq. ft. (lot size)}}$$
$$= 28.2\%$$

If a regulation limited the FAR to, say, 35 percent, you could add as much as an additional 575 square feet of building size:

$$\text{Maximum FAR} = 35\% \times 8,500$$
$$= 2,975 \text{ sq. ft.}$$

For a mid- to high-rise building, the FAR will typically be set as a multiple of the site size. For instance, in the previous example, if the FAR were 10, you could build a multistory structure with a total square footage of 85,000 square feet.

Your building construction (or addition) plans might also have to meet a lot coverage ratio (LCR). To permit enough room for parking and yard space, site planners may limit the footprint of the building to some specified percentage of the site size. Say that in the previous single-family house example, zoning set the maximum LCR at 30 percent. You would have to add your space as a second story rather than build a ground-floor addition:

$$30\% \text{ (LCR maximum)} \times 8,500 \text{ sq. ft. (lot size)}$$
$$= 2,550 \text{ sq. ft. (maximum footprint)}$$

Another complicating issue: What parts of the structure count within these ratios? Basements, decks, porches, garages, driveways? There's only one way to find out. Read the zoning (and other pertinent) rules. If the rules remain silent or ambiguous, talk with a land-use lawyer to see whether you might have found a profitable loophole. Maybe you can add some of these improvements even though the current structure seems to press against the FAR and/or LCR limits.

Occupancy Restrictions

On one occasion, I called about a single-family investment property that was up for sale. The seller told me that he was renting the house to five college students for $1,500 a month. "Sounds pretty good," I said. Then, trying to score some negotiating points, I mentioned that the city's occupancy code limited single-family rentals to three unrelated adults. Therefore, I couldn't pay what the seller was asking because I would risk a code enforcement that would subsequently reduce the amount of rent the property could yield.

"Not really," the seller countered. "This house is located within a commercial district. Five students do not violate the commercial district occupancy code."

Well, it turns out that, on this issue, the seller knew more about the code than I did—at least as it applied to his rental property. Smart seller. He had anticipated code questions and had prepared factual and accurate responses. A refreshing change from most run-of-the-mill sellers and real estate agents who don't bother to learn anything about the zoning and building codes—until a serious mistake teaches them a hard lesson. (Of course, such lack of knowledge works in your favor when it's the seller who fails to realize the real legal and market potential of his property.)

So, never *assume* that you know the zoning law. Quirks, quicksand, barricades, and loopholes are placed throughout the rules, laws, and regulations—as well as within the actual execution and enforcement process of same.

Parking

"No on-street parking between the hours of 2:00 AM and 6:00 AM." You might think that neighborhood parking ordinances relate to traffic control or perhaps even street cleaning hours. Sometimes they do. But sometimes restricted parking limits are intended to reduce the population density of a neighborhood. How can 8, 10, or 15 occupants of a single-family house find adequate on-site parking? Park in the front yard? The zoning (or other) rules probably outlaw that response because they typically regulate all types of on-street and off-street parking. (If the tenants do not own cars, then government might take other measures to reduce occupancy.)

Home Businesses/Home Occupations

Millions of people now work out of their homes. This trend will continue to grow. Renovating and remodeling houses to meet this home office need can present an entrepreneurial opportunity. But beware: Zoning rules often regulate or prohibit home offices and businesses. (HOAs frequently impose even stricter home business rules than zoning laws.)

Does the zoning district of the property permit work at home as a right? If not, does your property fit within a special exception category (see later discussion)? What rules apply to parking, the number of allowable customer visits, hours of operation, signage, business licenses, and the maximum number of square footage that a home office/business might occupy? To what extent could you legally modify the structure to accommodate a home office or business? Could you rent an office or business portion of the residence to someone who doesn't live within the property? What occupations or businesses will zoning permit?

Depending on the specific ordinance, you could target any of the following (often overlooked) market segments:

- Writers.
- Artists.

- Accountants.
- Lawyers.
- Insurance agents.
- Music instruction.
- Financial planner.
- Seamstress/tailor.
- Beauty shop.
- Network marketers.
- Child care.
- Answering service.

This list merely samples the variety of small, independent occupations and businesses that proliferate in a rapidly evolving free-agent world where flexibility reigns. Many people do not need to work in office buildings or on the premises of their employers. Learn what locations and property features work best for these free agents. You may find a lucrative niche of entrepreneurial opportunity. (Remember to talk to people. Ask them about their needs. Listen to remarks people make and the conversations that they engage in. Clues abound everywhere.)

Special Uses

Zoning districts typically permit certain uses as rights and other named uses as special exceptions. If designated a right, you can proceed with your plans. When you comply with setbacks, height, and other details, zoning administrators must approve your intentions (unless they find a loophole of their own to use against *you*—or your plans). If the use is classified within the special exception category, zoning officials could deny (or modify) your plans (see Table 8.2). They would have to object because your use would harm the public interest or create adverse effects for neighboring property owners.

Fortunately, owners can appeal the authority's objection. And (in the United States—but not necessarily in other countries) if you challenge the ruling in court, the judge will reverse the normal

Table 8.2   Uses by Right or Special Exception as per One City Zoning Ordinance for a Single-Family District (R-1-AA)

Uses by Right	Uses by Special Exception
1. Single-family houses	1. Public or private schools
2. Customary accessory uses	2. In-home professional offices
3. Boathouses and boat docks	3. Churches
4. Foster homes	4. Tennis clubs
5. Adult congregate living facilities	5. Guest cottages
	6. Golf courses
	7. Public swimming pools
	8. Shelter homes

legal presumption that government knows best. Instead, the officials must prove through the greater weight of the evidence that the court should uphold their opinion.

Note that a designated residential, commercial, or industrial district does not necessarily exclude other uses. Even districts zoned single family may permit churches, recreation clubs, home businesses/offices, childcare facilities, or other uses.

Noise Ordinances

In most cities, noise ordinances restrict the maximum decibel levels that are legally tolerated within various zoning districts. If a noisy neighbor makes it difficult for you to sell or rent one of your properties, don't launch a neighbor war. Instead, insist that the code enforcer order the offender to quiet down. Likewise, if your (or other building's) tenants party into the wee hours and stir up neighborhood complaints, use the noise ordinance to mute tenants' boisterous behavior.

Challenging the Zoning Rules

If you feel that zoning rules impact your property too harshly, use some combination of the following to gain more favorable treatment:

- Plead for a variance.
- Petition for rezoning.
- Sue for relief in court.

**Inform people how they will benefit
if the deal goes through.**

Ask for a Variance

As a matter of right, property owners may request a variance when a zoning rule creates undue hardship. However, if you merely tell the authorities, "I want to make more money," you won't get sympathy. From the planner's perspective, that "hardship" qualifies as tough luck.

When planners speak of hardship, they mean some unique feature of your property that makes it difficult to use in what would otherwise be a legal manner. Say that side-yard setbacks require 10 feet. Your lot line cuts at an angle. At the front part of your planned building addition, you've got 12 feet of width, more setback than necessary. But at the back part of the lot—only 8 feet of width. Absent some serious objection by the adjacent property owner, you would probably receive your variance.

**If the critics or the press harass you, turn their
negatives into positives. "The building's too tall."
"Doesn't New York deserve the
world's tallest building?"**

Petition for Rezoning

If your property is uniquely situated to benefit from a more profitable use, petition the planners to rezone your site. Say that because of a new nearby office development, increased traffic flows, and the evolving changes within the neighborhood, you could propose that your building deserves another zoning classification. Professional offices would now better fit this location.

When you work with the land-use and zoning personnel, wear kid gloves and handle with care. Unless all else fails, don't try to bulldoze your way through permissions. Human and political relations count as much as the rules and regulations that fill their manuals.

Unlike a variance, which according to zoning theory should require only adjusting a regulatory detail or two, rezoning puts you in another league with a different set of rules. As with a variance, planners won't rezone your property (or the neighborhood) unless you show that rezoning will not harm nearby properties or the tenor of the comprehensive community plan.

Go to Court

Nearly all zoning laws give property owners and citizens several levels of appeal within the regulatory system. If you strike out with frontline personnel, next go to the department head, then to a zoning board of adjustment, and eventually perhaps to a city or county council. Should you fail at these levels, you (or with other property owners who also endorse the change) can file suit.

You might sue to force government to treat you and your property in a way that better serves your interests. Or you might sue to block the rezoning or planned use of nearby land that will bear adversely on the value of your property as well as the health, safety, morals, or general welfare of the community. (Remember, when possible, work the community-needs angle into your presentation. Ayn Rand notwithstanding, neither planners nor judges typically appreciate the virtue of pure selfishness. Position your request in terms of the public interest.)

BUILDING CODES

We haven't yet distinguished zoning and other types of land-use codes from building codes. Partly that's because no clear distinction applies. A rule that falls under zoning in one locale may be covered under building codes in another locale. Sometimes rules and reviews are subject to multiple government agencies (e.g., fire safety, environmental, health, zoning, historical preservation).

Primarily, you will meet up with *building code* inspectors when you perform (or contract for) major plumbing, electrical, remodeling, or roofing work. Building codes may force you to use construction techniques, design, or materials that can add to your costs (generally for reasons of safety). But they will seldom seriously restrict basic plans for renovation and market strategy (as can zoning and other land-use ordinances). Remember, too, if you perform your own work, that work still must comply with permits and codes.

ENVIRONMENTAL LAWS

Property investors in urban areas may run into one or more of the following environmental issues:

1. Lead paint.
2. Asbestos.
3. Underground heating oil tanks (especially if a tank has been leaking).
4. Septic systems and wastewater disposal.
5. Tree ordinances.

Let's address the easiest first. Tree ordinances may prohibit you from cutting down a tree on your property. This tree could make a building addition more difficult or impossible. Or maybe you want to remove the tree to enhance a view of the mountains or bay. Views may add more benefits (to tenants or buyers) than the tree, but the tree law could block you from providing that benefit.

As to the costly issues of lead paint, asbestos, heating oil tanks, and waste disposal (if the property's not connected to a city or county sewer line), get copies of the pertinent brochures published by local, state, and federal environmental agencies. If you find a property that requires abatement of any of these problems (unless you have deep pockets and the property shows great potential), climb back into your car and look for another investment.

Beginning investors should not carry out an environmental cleanup. It usually involves too much risk for too little payback. Instead, focus on value-enhancing opportunities to create your MVP.

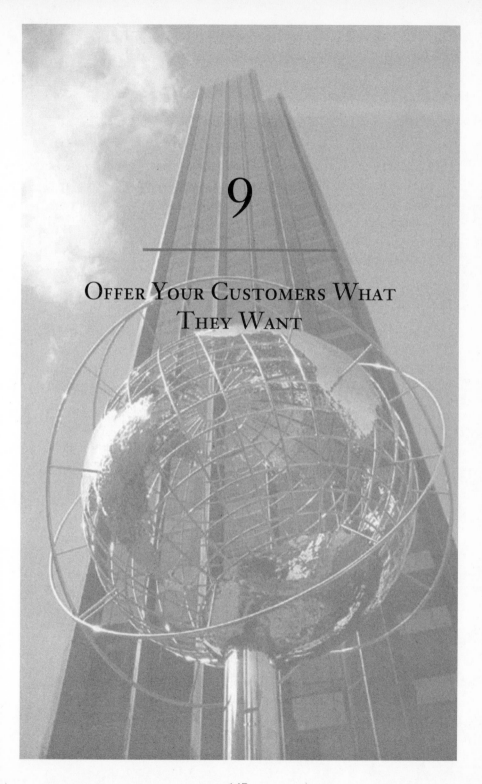

9

OFFER YOUR CUSTOMERS WHAT THEY WANT

Give Your Customers
What They Want

The public recognizes Donald Trump as a builder who offers his wealthy customers the best of breed in luxury hotels, condominiums, golf courses, and high-end shopping. But most people do not know that Mr. Trump's early real estate projects targeted blue-collar, moderate-to-middle-income homebuyers and tenants. Yet, even with these less well-to-do market segments, Mr. Trump still followed this principle: "Give your customers what they want."

Consider Swifton Village. While attending college, Mr. Trump continually thought and read about real estate. Football weekends or fraternity parties did not excite him nearly as much as a choice property loaded with profit potential. That's why and how he discovered Swifton Village. As he was reading the Federal Housing Administration's (FHA) list of foreclosed apartment buildings,[1] he spied a deeply troubled, 1,200-unit property. Always alert to opportunity, Mr. Trump investigated further.

He learned that the FHA badly wanted to rid itself of this property that suffered a near 70 percent vacancy rate. Having located a motivated seller (the FHA), Donald and his father negotiated a sweet deal and arranged favorable financing.

Nevertheless, no matter how low the price and how favorable the financing, they could not profitably operate a rental property that fails to attract rule-abiding, rent-paying tenants. And to attract and retain good rent-paying tenants, owners must offer tenants benefits (*Utility*) that look better than the value propositions offered by competitors (remember the most valued property or MVP goal). So, to provide these competitive benefits, the Trump team (among other things), initiated a new set of improved features and benefits:

1. *Eliminated Bad Tenants:* Bad tenants drive out good tenants. If you don't quickly deal with problem tenants (or the problems that tenants present), you'll soon find that your entire property

[1] You can find a link to FHA/HUD foreclosures at hud.gov.

has turned into a money pit with increasing vacancies and repair costs.

2. *Enhanced Safety and Security:* It's not just the rich who care about safety and security, all decent people want to live free of hooligans, ruffians, gangbangers, and drug dealers. The Trump team beefed up safety measures that included security patrols and community watch programs.

3. *Improved the Aesthetics:* Good tenants want to live in a *home* that shows pride of ownership. When renting to the less well off, many property owners ignore this market-differentiating advantage. Mr. Trump thought differently. So, he not only attended to big-ticket maintenance issues, he also added special touches such as white shutters, colonial white doors (to replace the ugly, cheap aluminum doors), and an impeccable cleaning program.

Know your customers. You've got to really get into the mind of the audience you're aiming at. I don't like hired gun, number-crunching market researchers. I do my own surveys and research. I draw my own conclusions.

G OVERNMENT, HOMEOWNER ASSOCIATIONS, and contracts set the rules for property use and improvements. Within those rules, you are free to design your entrepreneurial MVP benefits strategy to give your targeted customers the features and services they prefer—and those they're willing to pay for. From your customers' viewpoint, your MVP attitude distinguishes you from your competitors. Correspondingly, MVP adds to your cash flows and equity build up. You achieve the ideal match—a win-win outcome—a Most Valued Property (tenant perspective) and a Most Valuable Property (your perspective).

Search for Competitive Advantage (Create MVP)

Many owners of small to mid-sized investment properties still think of themselves as "landlords" (with an emphasis on "m' lord"), and they think of their residents merely as "renters" who do not deserve customer care. But just the opposite is true. Today (and in the future), increased returns require that investors treat their tenants as valued customers—not serfs.

I don't just build to a market. I create the market. I deliver to my customers more than they expect.

To create an MVP, intelligently survey and inspect competing properties. This market knowledge helps give you the insight to strategically customize your properties to make them stand out in the eyes of potential tenants. When you adopt this MVP approach, you add to your profits (and to the value of your properties) for two reasons:

1. *Better Resident Relations:* The residents (tenants) of your properties will reward you with lower turnover, fewer complaints, and higher rents.
2. *Alert to Opportunities:* With a customer-oriented, constant-improvement attitude, you will consistently look for and come up with ideas that add value to your property operations.

Inventory Competitors

If houses and apartments were like cans of Campbell's tomato soup or bottles of Coca-Cola, every similar-sized unit would rent (or sell) for the same price. You could calculate a true "market" rent or price level. But houses and apartments aren't like cans of soup. They differ in dozens of ways that potential tenants (buyers) find appealing or unappealing.

**You can create a prestige effect with any property.
Just make it the best of breed for your
market segment.**

You can use any (some, all) of these differences to set your property apart from the crowd. When you tour competing properties, what do you see? How do the properties rate with respect to the following features:

- ☐ Views.
- ☐ Energy usage/efficiency.
- ☐ Square footage (rentable, usable).
- ☐ Natural light.
- ☐ Ceiling height.
- ☐ Quiet/noisiness.
- ☐ Parking.
- ☐ Room count.
- ☐ Appliances (quality, quantity).
- ☐ Landscaping.
- ☐ Quality of finishes.
- ☐ Heat/air-conditioning.
- ☐ Decks/patios/balconies.
- ☐ Cleanliness.
- ☐ Carpeting/floor coverings.
- ☐ Electrical outlets.
- ☐ Emotional appeal.
- ☐ Color schemes/aesthetics.
- ☐ Living area floor plan.
- ☐ Closet space.
- ☐ Storage space.
- ☐ Kitchen functionality.
- ☐ Entryway convenience.
- ☐ Tenant demographics.
- ☐ Tenant lifestyles, attitudes.

- ☐ Lighting.
- ☐ Security.
- ☐ Laundry facilities.
- ☐ Fireplace.
- ☐ Physical condition.
- ☐ Window coverings.
- ☐ Types/style of windows.
- ☐ Image/reputation.
- ☐ Furniture.
- ☐ Kitchen and bath pizzazz.

This checklist doesn't mention other important tenant concerns, such as the amount of the security deposit (total move-in cash), the terms of the lease, the quality and attentiveness of the management, and, last but far from least, location. Only after you think through each of these possible differences can you intelligently conclude that your two-bedroom, two-bath units should rent for $975 a month. Compare and contrast your (prospective) property feature by feature to a selection of competing properties. Record every detail.

With accurate, market-researched information about competing property features and rent levels, you improve your ability to assess the pros and cons of your property. Plus, you sharpen your mind's eye to spot opportunities to lift MVP for your tenants and yourself.

Give Your Property a Donald Trump Makeover

After you have identified, visited, and inspected your competitors, walk slowly through your (prospective) property. Stimulate your thinking with the facts and ideas you found on your tour of competitors. Here are some suggested ways to create an MVP. But in practice, your improvements should flow from both the tenant (buyer) preferences you've discovered and the features/benefits offered by the competing properties.

> **We're spending $250 million on the building but taking nothing for granted. Every detail from marble patterns to the color of the window frames has got to work together to create the effect we want to achieve.**

What's Your Overall Impression?

As you enter the unit, what are your first impressions? Do you see faded paint, scuff marks, outdated color schemes, cheap hollow-core doors, nail holes in the walls, worn carpeting, torn linoleum, old-fashioned light fixtures, cracked wall switch plates, or stained sinks? If you answer yes to any or all of these questions, you've found an easy way to create value.

Pay Special Attention to Kitchens and Baths

To really wow your potential tenants, bring in the ideas of the Trump design team to redo the kitchens and bathrooms. Flip through the pages of kitchen and bath magazines. Look for that right combination of materials and colors that will create a light, bright, cheerful, and inviting look. Eliminate those harvest gold appliances, the chipped and stained sinks, and that cracked glass in the shower door. Do not waste money on granite countertops, but do create a "wow, isn't this beautiful" appearance.

As you inspect the kitchen and baths, focus for 30 seconds on each of the following:

- Floors.
- Ceilings.
- Sinks.
- Toilet bowl.
- Windows and windowsills.
- Electrical outlet plates.
- Lighting.

- Faucets.
- Walls.
- Cabinets.
- Cabinet and drawer handles.
- Appliances.
- Countertops.
- Mirrors.

When you focus for 30 seconds on each detail in these rooms, notice blemishes, cracks, stains, and so on that reflect unfavorably on the overall appeal. Focus accents your ability to see shortcomings that you would otherwise miss. Throughout the entire apartment unit (or house), details count. But they especially count in the kitchens and baths. Add the right pizzazz to the kitchens and bathrooms, and you transform a ho-hum rental unit into a showplace.

Cleanliness Generates Profits

Do you want to attract tenants who will care for your properties? Thoroughly clean the units as if you are the hired property manager and Donald Trump is about to perform a white-glove inspection. Do not think "rental property." Think "home." Clean units attract clean tenants.

Clean everywhere. Remove the dirt, dust, cobwebs, and dead bugs from all corners, baseboards, light fixtures, and shelving. Pull out all kitchen drawers and dump the bread crumbs and accumulated debris. Wipe all windows and mirrors to sparkle and shine. Look closely for grime and mold in the shower and shower door tracks. Scrape the rust out of the medicine cabinets and repaint where necessary. Eliminate odors—the unit should look and smell fresh and clean.

Natural Light and Views

If your units seem dark, brighten them up. Add bright colors, windows, or skylights. Remove light-blocking window coverings. If you're lucky, you might buy one of those older buildings with 10-foot ceilings—now artificially reduced to 8 feet via suspended acoustical tile. For a reason unknown to me (energy conservation?), dropped ceilings became popular several decades ago. Today, they're outdated. Rip them out. The rooms will seem larger and brighter. In rooms with high ceilings, install clerestory windows to bring in more light.

> **Add a view, add value. We built Trump Tower with a spectacular design to give commanding views that gave us commanding power to sell apartments at prices that towered over competitors.**

For first-floor units, enhance the view with landscaping or attractive fencing. To create views for upper-story units, think long term; plant trees. Although windows are expensive, weigh the costs and benefits of adding them. Ugly views turn off most tenants and buyers. Pleasant views provide good selling points. Give your tenants better views than dumpsters, parking lots, and the walls or rooftops of other buildings. In return, they will pay you more in rent (or purchase price).

Special Touches

For those special aesthetic touches, accent with chair railings, wallpaper borders, upgraded door handles, paneled doors, and wood stains (rather than paint). Upgraded light fixtures, too, can help you add pizzazz. Track lighting systems, for example, have retained popularity with some market segments. Visit a large lighting store and ask what trends in lighting are emerging. (Of course, various energy-efficient types of lighting will add appeal and reduce you and your tenants' costs.)

> **I always include special, unique features that dazzle my tenants or buyers and arouse their emotions.**

Develop ideas for special touches from home decorating and re-modeling magazines. Visit model homes and upscale apartment, townhouse, and condominium developments. Don't get carried away with special touches, or you will cut into your profitability. Still, a few "wow, look at this" features will help prospects differentiate and remember your units.

SAFETY, SECURITY, AND CONVENIENCE

Look for ways to combine safety and convenience. Increase the number and capacity of electrical outlets. Older buildings, especially, lack outlets and amperage to safely handle plug-in appliances, computers, printers, fax machines, and entertainment centers. Many renters don't notice this annoying inconvenience until after they move into a unit. Then they "solve" the problem with adapter plugs and roaming extension cords. If the unit lacks electrical capacity, upgrade.

Install peepholes for entry doors to enhance security and convenience. Many people like to see who's knocking before they open their door.

Other Issues of Safety and Security

Other safety issues of concern include smoke alarms, carbon monoxide detectors, fire escape routes, door locks, first-floor windows, and first-floor sliding glass doors. As security against break-ins, verify that all windows and doors lock tightly and cannot be jimmied with a credit card or even a screwdriver. Double-deadbolt locks are best.

Tenants and buyers want to feel safe in their homes. If doors, door locks, and windows seem flimsy or easily breached, some tenants won't rent the unit—regardless of its other oohs and aahs.

Environmental health hazards may exist because of lead paint, asbestos, or formaldehyde—any of which may be found in building materials used in construction (or remodeling) prior to 1978. Before you invest, obtain and review seller disclosures about these hazards. If the building is suspect, don't buy it without firm remedial cost figures from an abatement contractor. Even then, I would urge new investors to pass on buildings or sites that present anything more than minor environmental issues.

Stairs, Carpets, and Bathrooms

Repair steps or stair railings that may be loose or dangerous. Frayed carpets and bathtubs that lack no-slip bottoms and handrails can result in falls. Itemize and remedy each safety and security hazard within the property. Even when a repair doesn't add to your rent collections, it protects your tenants. It reduces the chance that you could sit on the wrong end of a tenant's lawsuit for damages. Unsafe conditions and features provide evidence of negligence—mostly civil but sometimes criminal.

RIGHTSIZE THE ROOMS

Have you ever walked into a house or apartment and found some rooms too large, others too small? In many houses, builders design a huge great room along with a huge master bedroom and bath. Then they add three or four dinky-sized bedrooms for kids, guests, or study. The house lacks a sense of proportion.

Create a Sense of Proportion

What sense of proportion should a house or an apartment unit display? The answer varies by tenant segment, price range, and timing. From decade to decade, tastes and preferences change. In turn, these changes present entrepreneurial opportunities for improvement. Buy an out-of-style building. Then redesign the internal floor plan to appeal to a contemporary market segment of renters or buyers.

Modernize Postwar Units

I once bought an eight-unit apartment building. It had been built in the late 1940s to meet the pressing demand for housing by returning veterans of World War II. The units still retained the three-bedroom, one-bath floor plan (common to that period)—one moderate-sized bedroom for the parents and two small bedrooms for those recently born baby boomers. In the early 1990s (when I bought the property), most of the potential tenants I wanted looked at the units and said, "Ugh, no way. We couldn't live here."

Because the seller had trouble keeping the units rented, I got a bargain price. To create value, in each of the units I divided one of the small bedrooms. I used half that space to enlarge the other small bedroom and the other half to add a second bathroom. I then rented the building to tenants looking to share their rentals with a roommate. Rent collections jumped by $175 per unit per month—a profitable return on my investment and renovations.

The MVP strategy worked. The benefits (*U*tility) created were much appreciated by the singles who found the units matched what they were looking for—but encountered difficulty finding elsewhere—at a similarly affordable rent level.

Create More Storage

Self-storage (miniwarehouses) represents one of the fastest-growing property uses in the United States and Europe. We've all become pack rats. "Throw it away? No way. I might need that some time." Talk with tenants. Talk with homeowners. Many will tell you the same thing: "I like my home, but we lack space for storage." To add appeal to your rental houses and apartments, add storage space. You can add storage space in two basic ways:

1. Bring dead space to life.
2. Increase the usefulness of existing space.

Bring Dead Space to Life

Here's an example that may seem trivial, yet it mildly amuses many prospective tenants. Look in the cabinet under your kitchen sink. You will see a small gap between the front panel of the cabinet above the door and the sink: dead space. How might you convert that small gap to usable space? Install a small pull-down compartment to stow away soap, sponge, and steel-wool pads. Eliminate sink clutter. Show this little innovation, and you'll receive a favorable response, such as, "Isn't that neat?"

Trivial? Yes. Still, it illustrates the point. All houses and apartments include opportunistic quantities of dead space that you can bring to life:

- Under stairs and stairwells.
- Bay windows with storage built under the window seat and under the outside the window.
- Garden windows.
- On top of kitchen cabinets.
- Dead-end cabinets.
- Walls suitable for shelving.
- Recessed storage between studs (as with an in-wall medicine chest).
- Kitchen hanging bars for pots and pans.

Such ideas only sample the possibilities. If you search through any house or apartment and persistently ask, "Where are the dead spaces that I can bring to life for storage?" you will find them.

Increase the Usefulness of Existing Space

To achieve "more benefits with less," follow the lead of the California Closet Company (CCC). As ideas from this innovative (and much imitated) firm have proven, you can double (or triple) your storage capacity without adding one square inch of new space. Redesign space that already exists. Although founded as a closet company, CCC now redesigns basements, garages, offices, workshops, and kitchens. Put these same organizing principles to work, and you'll wow your prospects. You will offer a sought-after, yet relatively scarce benefit.

In addition, create multipurpose spaces: For example, install a Murphy bed that folds up against (or into) a wall. A Murphy bed not only adds usable floor space but also creates possibilities for shelving alongside the bed. Use the existing wall cavity or create a larger cavity by bringing a new wall out even with the Murphy bed. Thoroughly inspect and note each opportunity a property offers to use space more effectively—both for storage and livability.

Abate Noise

No one likes noise. Before you invest, test the units for soundproofing. Will noise from a television or stereo carry throughout the house or apartment? When you inspect properties, bring along a portable radio. Test various rooms. Turn up the volume. Do the walls provide soundproofing? Families and roommate tenants want privacy and quiet. If your property fails to offer quiet, your units will lose appeal.

Listen for Neighborhood Noise

Just as important, will your tenants (buyers) hear neighbors or neighborhood noise from inside their units? People pay for quiet. They discount sharply for noise.

You'll typically hear more noise in neighborhoods filled with apartment buildings. But single-family neighborhoods can also suffer from loud stereos, barking dogs, and unmuffled car engines. Does the drum corps of the nearby high school practice outside three or four hours a day? Visit the property during periods of high traffic or peak noise. Verify noise levels at various times. Even some seemingly tranquil neighborhoods do not offer peace and quiet every hour of the day.

Ask for Written Disclosures

Seek written disclosures from the seller of the property. Talk with tenants and neighbors. Find out whether anyone has tried to enforce quiet by complaining to city government or a homeowners' association or by filing a nuisance suit. If you invest in the property, can you invoke noise ordinances against these noisy tenants (or homeowners) who show no respect for anyone else? Can you add features to the property (soundproof windows, heavy doors, more wall insulation, or tall, thickly growing hedges) to block noise from either outside or inside the building? Quiet the building and you strengthen your MVP.

OVERALL DESIRABILITY: SUMMING UP

> **To build a great brand, protect and bolster the image and the quality of the product. Trump Tower focused not only on location, but the quality of the building—the windows, floors, rooms, kitchens, the entire benefit package.**

To create an MVP set of benefits, provide people a *home*. As you inspect a property, decide whether the units will provide your target market these features and benefits (*U*tility):

- Do the units offer enough square footage?
- Are the units spotlessly clean, fresh, and bright? Do they smell clean and fresh?
- Do the room counts, sizes, and floor plans represent the most sensible and profitable allocation of space?
- Do the aesthetics of the units excite with emotional appeal?
- Does the unit bring in natural light?
- What views will the tenants see from inside the units looking out?

- Do the units offer generous amounts of closet and storage space?
- Are the units quiet?
- Will tenants feel safe and secure within the units?
- Do the kitchens and baths offer eye-pleasing pizzazz?

Experience proves that *homes* rent faster and yield higher occupancies than mere rental houses and rental apartments. *Homes* sell faster and command higher prices than mere houses. Offer your tenants and buyers special benefits. They will pay you higher rents, stay longer, and show more care for their units because they will regard those units as their home.

10

MORE IDEAS TO CREATE A MOST VALUED PROPERTY

CREATE MULTIPLE
STREAMS OF INCOME

Mr. Trump advises you to evaluate your properties to find multiple uses, multiple streams of income, or even multiple target markets. In the past, developers would construct an office building, a hotel, a condominium project, or perhaps a golf course. One idea, one use, one target market.

For Trump Tower, Mr. Trump thought more creatively. He saw this project as a prime location for upscale retailers who are willing to pay rents of $500 per square foot per year (or more). The high floors of the buildings, he knew, would appeal to the very rich who would value the 5th Avenue address and the expansive views of Central Park, the Hudson River, and the New York City skyline. As to the problematic middle floors, Mr. Trump envisioned offices but realized he would have to innovatively market them to command the rent levels he wanted.

His ideas succeeded. George Ross, a Trump adviser, recalls that, "In the late 1970s, Trump's vision of a three-tiered, multiuse condominium represented a very unusual combination of uses." Today, many other builders have tried to imitate this example.

Similarly, when they developed a renovation and leasing plan for the Trump Building (40 Wall Street, now home of Trump University and located almost across the street from the New York Stock Exchange), George Ross and Mr. Trump decided to pursue a multiuse approach. As George Ross told Mr. Trump, "The experts have been taking the wrong approach and they've reached the wrong conclusion. You don't have one office building, you have three. They just happen to be on top of each other."

So, that's how they renovated and marketed it—to three different market segments. They turned this 1929 building with its outdated configuration and floor plans into a modern masterpiece with each series of floors designed to appeal to specific types of tenants. In contrast to its near-vacant status at the time of purchase, today this property stands nearly 100 percent occupied.

> **Attend to the details. Just like my father did, I walk
> every project. It's my responsibility to make
> everything look exquisite.**

Y OU'RE ON THE WAY to creating a most valued property (MVP) set of benefits. You've designed great livable homes that sparkle with pizzazz and emotional appeal. These features and benefits (*Utility*) will keep your building full of tenants who will pay premium prices. Yet before tasteful, livable interiors can woo your prospective tenants (or buyers), you must get them to keep their appointments to inspect the homes that you offer. To accomplish this goal, enhance curb appeal.

And to add even more to your cash flows and property benefits, provide services to your tenants, create more rentable space, and revitalize the neighborhood. Any or all of these techniques will create value for tenants, buyers, and you—the very definition of MVP.

CREATE STRIKINGLY ATTRACTIVE CURB APPEAL

You can write an award-winning ad that will make your phone ring. But your Madison Avenue talents will fall flat when great tenants pull up in front of the building and immediately begin to ask themselves, "What are we doing here? This place is nothing like I imagined. Let's not even go in."

> **When prospects pull up to your property, make
> sure they immediately feel, "This looks like a nice
> place to live."**

"You're right, why waste time? This property looks like a dump. We don't want to even think about living here."

Your Building Is Your Best Advertisement

Hundreds (maybe thousands) of people pass by your property each week. What do they notice? Will the property become known as that run-down rental of the neighborhood? Or will it cause passersby to remark, "Isn't that building kept up well? Those flower gardens and brick walkways seem to reach out and invite us to take a look inside."

I'm always trying to figure out, "What can I do with this property to give it flair, pizzazz—something my customers can find nowhere else?"

To generate more rental income, create an inviting exterior. Create award-winning publicity with knockout curb appeal. Not only will an attractive, well-kept exterior appeal to a better class of tenants, but it will also increase tenant satisfaction and reduce turnover. To create strikingly attractive curb appeal, try these improvements:

1. *Clean Up the Grounds:* When you take over a property, meticulously clean up the grounds, parking area, and walkways. Cart away trash, accumulated leaves, and fallen tree branches. Build a fence to block that view of the dumpsters. Tell tenants to remove their inoperable cars from the parking lots, parking spaces, or driveways. If abandoned cars are parked along the street, ask the city government to post them and tow them.
2. *Yard Care and Landscaping:* Tenants and homebuyers alike love manicured lawns, flower-lined walkways, mulched shrubs, and flower gardens. With landscaping, you can turn an ugly-duckling building into a showcase property. With landscaping, you can create privacy, manufacture a pleasant view looking out from the inside of the units, or eliminate an ugly sight. Plant trees, shrubs, flower gardens, and hedges

now. When you sell, those mature plantings will easily earn you a return of $10 for each $1 the plantings cost you.

3. *Walkways and Parking Areas:* Replace or repair major cracks and buckling that may appear in your sidewalks and parking areas. Remove all grass or weeds that are growing through the cracks. Edge all the areas where the yard abuts concrete or asphalt. Neatness pays. Overgrown grass and weeds stain the curb appeal of a property—precisely because these types of blemishes often signal that the property is a rental.

4. *Fences, Lampposts, and Mailboxes:* For good looks, privacy, and security, install quality fencing. In contrast, a rusted, rotted, or half-falling-down fence scars the property. Likewise for rusty lampposts with broken glass fixtures. For a decorative touch, add a white picket fence or a low-level stone fence in the front of the building. If the building houses a cluster of mailboxes, keep the area clear of misdelivered letters, junk mail, and discarded advertising circulars.

5. *Exterior of the Building:* The building should signal to prospective tenants that you care for your property. Paint where a change of colors/design would enhance appeal and wherever you see a faded (or flaking) appearance. Repair wood rot. Clean roof and gutters.

   Improve the building's appearance with shutters, flower boxes, a dramatic front door and entryway, and new (or additional) windows. Add contrasting colors for trim or accent the building design with architectural details. How well does (or could) the property's exterior distinguish it from other comparably priced rental properties?

Think outside the lines of conventional thought.
Move out of your comfort zone and achieve
something unique.

Dazzle with Curb Appeal

Unless you're creatively gifted, you might not spontaneously generate *great* ideas for improving a property. I know. Creative design doesn't come easily to me. I rank high among the artistically challenged. Here's how to compensate for this dull artistic vision.

Carry a camera in the glove box of your car. When you see a building or yard that displays eye-catching features, snap a picture. Over time, put together a collection of photos. When you try to figure out how to give a property strikingly attractive curb appeal, pull out some of these photos and select model properties to compare feature to feature with your investment property. Compare and contrast to bring forth a rush of value-creating, MVP ideas.

Rely on the photos of others, too. Dozens of magazines and books fill the shelves of groceries and bookstores. Buy these publications. Their articles and photos will definitely extend your creative thinking and aesthetic sensibilities. Also, I have found good visual ideas by Googling images using the search term, "before and after" along with specifics such as kitchen, landscaping, living rooms, garages, and so on.

Collect More Than Rent

When you review a seller's income statements, you may see an entry called "other income." These amounts may include revenues received from laundry machines, parking fees, storage lockers, or other services and amenities. Savvy entrepreneurs think of ways to generate extra income from their properties:

1. *Laundry:* Rental units should include washer/dryer hookups. But if they don't, look for space somewhere else on the property where you can install coin-operated (actually electronic card-operated) washers and dryers. Without

on-premises laundry facilities, your building will suffer a serious competitive disadvantage. Most potential tenants do not want to carry their dirty clothes to a laundry or Laundromat.

2. *Parking Fees:* If parking spots are scarce in the neighborhood where you own properties, charge extra for parking (or perhaps a fee for a second car). Do not arbitrarily assign one parking space per rental unit. Some tenants may not have cars. Others may be willing to park on the street. When you price your scarce parking separately from the units, those tenants who want it most will pay more.

3. *Build Storage Lockers:* Back to the idea of adding storage space. You create value any time you squeeze some profitable use out of every nook and cranny within the building and within every square foot of the site. One such profitable use is storage lockers. Does the property include an attic, basement, or crawl space where you could carve out room for more storage? You can charge $20 to $50 per month for the lockers (maybe more, depending on size). Achieve payback in five years or less. If no existing space within the building can serve this purpose, erect one or more premanufactured storage buildings (such as those available at home improvement stores).

4. *Add Other Amenities or Services:* When you take over management of a property, list services or amenities that you could provide (preferably at a price) that would increase your revenue *and* strengthen your competitive benefits for your target market. Consider services such as cleaning, day care, or transportation. Would your target market appreciate (and pay for) a swimming pool, tennis courts, racquetball or squash courts, a fitness center, or a study room? As investor Craig Hall advises, "Keep an open and searching mind. Seek out things you can do to attract and satisfy the best tenants for each specific investment."

Convert a Garage, Attic, or Basement to Living Space

Look for properties with an attic, garage, or basement that you can convert to *quality* living space. Note the emphasis on *quality*. Amateurs often convert as cheaply as possible. Not only do their finished spaces look cheap, but they may lack natural light, the ceilings may hang too low, or the newly created internal traffic patterns or floor plans may seem convoluted or garbled. Add quality space, not space that invites a grimace or turned-up nose.

Savvy investors who design and finish their conversions to wow potential tenants or buyers can and do make serious money for their efforts. To establish an MVP set of benefits and features, your space conversion should achieve the following objectives:

- Satisfy the target market.
- Please aesthetically.
- Integrate the new within the overall plan and design of the property.

Satisfy the Target Market

When you remodel for personal use only, it's okay to convert your basement into a recreation room that mimics the look of your favorite tavern or billiards parlor. For MVP remodeling, aim to please your target market. What type of highly valued space can you offer that competing properties lack: a home office, a study, a playroom for the kids, a workout area, a library, an entertainment center, or a seductive master bedroom suite and bath? Open your mind's eye. What can you envision that your tenants will gladly pay for? Market research provides the answers you need.

Please Aesthetically

Basement conversions often fail because they lack windows and give off that damp, musty odor so common to belowground living areas. To overcome these problems, use window wells and carve outs to bring in natural light. To eliminate the musty smell and dampness, use high-quality sealants and fresh air ventilation. Follow the same general ideas for attic and garage conversions. To command a premium price, these finished areas must look, live, feel, and smell as good as the rest of the house. They must exude light, height, warmth, and color. Do not tack up cheap four- by eight-foot paneling, hang acoustical tile ceilings, or lay down a roll of indoor-outdoor carpeting. Romance the unit. Think pizzazz!

Integrate the New within the Overall Plan and Design of the Property

When you evaluate properties, think how you can integrate any newly added living space into a coherent floor plan. MVP conversions flow smoothly to and from the original living areas. Think access and flow. Blend the conversion into a natural traffic pattern.

MVP conversions do not immediately announce themselves as conversions as someone first approaches the space. Avoid signaling to your prospects, "Now entering a converted garage (basement or attic)." Or "Watch your head. The ceiling's low in here." A well-planned conversion can pay back $4 (or more) for every dollar you invest.

CREATE AN ACCESSORY APARTMENT

Variously called in-law suites, basement suites, garage apartments, mortgage helpers, or accessory apartments, these separate living units pay back their cost many times over. Depending on the city and neighborhood, an accessory apartment can bring in rents that range anywhere from $250 to $750 per month. And, unless you build from scratch, you can often create a desirable unit for as little as $5,000 and certainly no more than $15,000 or $20,000.

Your return on investment, say, $10,000 in renovation costs, can generate a rental income of $4,000 to $6,000 per year. You can search the world over and not find as much return for so little risk.

CREATE A SPECIAL PURPOSE USE

When you create a special purpose use, you might receive a premium price or rental rate. Many investors renovate generically. In return, they receive a generic profit. But when you renovate toward the specific needs of a bull's-eye segment such as seniors, the disabled, children, home businesses, college students, or any other specialized target of tenants (buyers), you favorably distinguish your product.

To discover a profitable niche, talk with people at social service agencies, hospitals, and local colleges. Imagine the uniquely intense needs of single parents, multigenerational households, hobbyists, roommates, group homes, and shelters. Look for improvements where *D*emand runs strong and *S*upply falls short. Run-of-the-mill investors know how to fix up a property; entrepreneurs search for a special niche of customers (tenants, buyers). Entrepreneurs tailor the features and benefits (*U*tility) of the property to match that target market's criteria for their MVP.

Change the Nature (*U*tility) of a Property

Rental apartments that sell as condominiums, gas stations that operate as convenience stores, homes converted to office space, rural acreage now covered by a shopping center—such properties provide examples of adaptive use of both land and buildings brought about by a locale's growth and change.

Adaptive use or reuse offers multiple opportunities for the entrepreneur. Office space sometimes rents at twice the rental rate of housing. The opposite also can occur. In London, during the mid-2000s, housing prices climbed so high that retail, warehouse, and offices were converted to apartments. To create your MVP, adapt the property to a more profitable use.

Convert Apartments to Condominiums

To plan a condo conversion, study the local market to learn what prices various types of condo units are selling for. Compare those condo unit prices to the price per unit that apartment buildings are generating. If you notice a gap in prices of $25,000 or more (sometimes less), you've probably discovered an opportunity to earn profits with an MVP apartment-to-condominium conversion.

Here's how to calculate the potential profits of converting rental units into individually owned condominiums as illustrated by a 16-unit apartment building:

> Assume you paid $480,000 ($30,000 per unit) to acquire this 16-unit rental property. After all costs of conversion, your to-tal investment increased to $770,000 ($48,125 per unit). But these figures haven't yet considered profits. If you want to net $10,000 per unit, you will need to sell the units at a price approaching $60,000 each ($30,000 more than your original per-unit purchase price).

To decide whether such a project makes sense, research rental properties, condo prices, and condo conversion laws. Run numbers through some feasibility calculations. If preliminary estimates look promising, talk with an investor, contractor, attorney, or real estate consultant experienced in the conversion process. With the knowledge gained from these talks (and perhaps some follow-up research), decide whether such an investment offers you enough profit potential to compensate for risks such as cost overruns, slow sales, and government permitting delays.

The condo conversion business runs in cycles. In the late 1990s, few conversions looked profitable. As condo prices jumped during the early to mid-2000s, conversions multiplied like dandelions after an April rain. Today, many condo markets seem woefully over-supplied with new construction and recent conversions. In many cities, opportunities to convert rental apartments to condominiums have become nearly impossible to find.

But cycles revolve. Stay alert for profits in new or future markets. Or look to cities that missed the recent speculative boom (and fall) and have not yet caught the entrepreneurial eye of condo converters.

Convert Apartments or Houses to Office Space

Sometimes you can profitably convert apartments or houses to office space. Think through this possibility and answer these questions:

1. Is the property in a commercial zone? If not, can you get the property rezoned (or maybe even a variance)?
2. What is the current vacancy rate for office space in the area of the subject property? Are any market segments under-supplied?
3. Does the site provide adequate parking for office space? The city may require one parking space for every 250 to 500 square feet of rentable office space.
4. How much will it cost to convert? Could you borrow the money to finance such a conversion? And, finally, will the cost, legal procedures, and time and effort be worth the profit you plan to earn?

Study the property, current and future *D*emand, and *S*upply (potential competitors). Figure the costs and rental revenues of the projected conversion. For more complex projects, partner with someone who is more experienced. Place the promising property under an option or purchase contract with contingencies. Then strike up an agreement with your partner(s) and proceed.

Cut Operating Expenses

Every dollar you slice from a property's operating expenses can add $10 or more to the building's value. With gains like that, detail all expenses. Then reduce, shift, or eliminate them. Lower operating costs not only increase your net cash flows but also permit you to offer tenants more attractive rents. Here are some ideas to cut expenses.

Energy Audits

Utility companies will help you discover ways to reduce your gas and/or electric bills. Some will even audit and inspect your property. Others will provide booklets or brochures and, perhaps, a customer service department to answer specialized questions. You can also find dozens of articles and books at your local library that discuss energy conservation. Perform an energy audit on a building before you buy it. Then you can judge beforehand the extent to which you can feasibly reduce these costs.

Maintenance and Repair Costs

Savvy investors reduce or eliminate money-wasting property maintenance and repair expenses. Focus on the following:

1. *Low-Maintenance Houses and Apartment Buildings:* When shopping to buy, favor those properties that are constructed with materials and fixtures that require less maintenance: heating, ventilating, and air-conditioning. Nothing beats a property that's built to last with minimal care. Ditto for yards, shrubs, and landscaping.
2. *Tenant Selection:* Just as there are both low- and high-maintenance properties, so too are there low- and high-maintenance tenants. Avoid the latter and select the former. Watch out for chronic complainers and people who show no "house sense."

3. *Repair Clauses:* To promote tenant responsibility, a growing number of property owners shift the first $50 or $100 of every repair cost onto their tenants' shoulders. Also, I favor high security deposits.

4. *Handyman on Call:* Nothing eases the drain on your time and pocketbook as much as having a trustworthy and competent all-around handyman (or persons) to take care of your property maintenance and repairs.

5. *Preventive Maintenance:* You periodically inspect and maintain your car. Do likewise with your investment properties. Anticipate and alleviate when the cost is relatively small. Always ask your maintenance pros how to substitute high-maintenance items or materials with low-maintenance components.

Property Taxes

"If you think that your property taxes are too high," writes tax consultant Harry Koenig, "you're probably right! Research shows that nearly half of all properties may be assessed illegally or excessively." While Koenig probably overstates his point, millions of property owners do pay more in property taxes than they need to. With a little attention and planning, you can avoid this trap:

1. *Check the Accuracy of Your Assessed Valuation:* Usually, tax assessors base their tax calculations on a property's market value. Look closely at the assessor's value estimate on the tax bill. Can you find comparable sales of similar properties that would support a *lower* value for your property? If so, you have grounds to request a tax reduction. With prices now off their peaks in many cities, verify lower assessment when applicable.

2. *Compare Your Purchase Price to the Assessor's Estimate of Market Value:* Provide comp sales. Show the assessor that you

recently paid $390,000 for a property that he has appraised at $440,000. You've got a prima facie case for lower taxes. As property prices in some areas fall from their previous peaks, watch out for overassessments.

3. *Look for Unequal Treatment:* Under the law, assessors must tax properties in a neighborhood in an equal (fair) and uniform manner. Argue for lower taxes by showing that the assessor has assigned lower assessed values to similar nearby properties.

4. *Learn Tax Assessment Laws before You Improve or Rehabilitate a Property:* Property tax laws list the types of property improvements that are taxed and the applicable rates. After you discover the fine print of such laws, develop your property improvement strategy to add value without adding taxes.

GENTRIFICATION AND OTHER VALUE PLAYS

Gentrification refers to higher income (or higher earning professionals) moving into and revitalizing a moderate-priced neighborhood. In many cities throughout the world, gentrification has pushed property prices through the roof (e.g., Kerrisdale [Vancouver, Williamsburg [Brooklyn], South of Market [San Francisco], Chicago North Side, Chicago West Side, College Park [Orlando], "M Street" [Dallas], and Coconut Grove [Miami]). Most of these neighborhoods have become name brands.

In earlier years, though, most of these neighborhoods were modest, even low-priced neighborhoods. Several areas, such as Chicago Near North, San Francisco South of Market, and Manhattan's Soho districts, included industrial and commercial properties.

However, the close-in accessibility of these neighborhoods overwhelmed their negatives. Even prior to gaining cachet, these neighborhoods gave residents an easy walk, drive, or commute to major job districts. And their prices looked dirt cheap when compared with similarly accessible premier neighborhoods.

Many gentrified name-brand neighborhoods no longer represent good potential for investors. That's not to say that these areas won't appreciate. But, as a rule, their current rent levels probably won't cover mortgage payments and property operating expenses. While waiting for price increases, the negative cash flow alligator will chew through your bank account.

Play up your location. Point out every advantage. Turn every shortcoming into a positive.

The Good News

But here's the good news. In cities throughout the USA and the world, other emerging cities and neighborhoods are poised for turnaround, revitalization, and rapid appreciation of property values. By becoming a neighborhood entrepreneur, you can score the same large gains that those earlier investors earned in Brooklyn's Williamsburg, Chicago Near North, and others.

Revitalize the Neighborhood

You've probably heard this advice many times: "Buy in the best neighborhood you can afford. The best neighborhoods appreciate the most. You can change anything about a property except its location." At first glance, this advice sounds plausible. But think what the term *neighborhood* actually refers to:

- Convenience.
- Aesthetics.
- People: attitudes, lifestyles.
- Legal restrictions.
- Schools.
- Taxes/services.
- Microclimate (weather).

- Safety and security.
- Image/reputation.
- Affordability.

But, surprising, the neighborhoods where prices will rise fastest in the future may not be the name-brand or well-established neighborhoods. Often, the largest price increases occur in areas that are positioned and poised for turnaround or renewed popularity. The "best" neighborhoods don't always appreciate the fastest. (Remember, right place, right time, and right price.)

Entrepreneurs Improve Thornton Park (and Make a Killing)

"Florida's new urban entrepreneurs have the vision to see a bustling district of sushi bars, loft apartments and boutiques on a glass-strewn lot or rat-infested warehouse," writes Cynthia Barnett in an issue of *Florida Trend* magazine.

Phil Rampy is proud to have been one of those early entrepreneurs. Fifteen years ago, Rampy bought a property in the then-shunned Thornton Park neighborhood near trash-strewn Lake Eola (or, as they used to call is, Lake Erie-ola). Today, Thornton Park has climbed up the status ladder to rank among "the trendiest addresses" in Orlando. That $60,000 bungalow that Rampy renovated is now valued at more than $250,000. Although Thornton Park still sits on this Earth in the same place as it did 10 to 15 years ago, nearly everything else about this neighborhood has changed.

Many Neighborhoods Have Potential

When you compare neighborhoods, do not focus only on what you see, also envision the future of the neighborhood. Learn what people are saying. List all of a neighborhood's good points. How might you and other property owners join together to improve the area? List the neighborhood's weak points. How can you and others eliminate value-diminishing influences? Who can you enlist to promote your cause? Can you mobilize mortgage lenders, other investors, homeowners, real estate agents, not-for-profit housing groups, church leaders, builders, contractors, preservationists, police, local employers, retail businesses, schoolteachers, principals, community redevelopment agencies, elected officials, civic groups, and perhaps students, professors, and administrators of a nearby college or university? Involved people can and do spearhead neighborhood improvements and turnarounds.

Become a Neighborhood Entrepreneur

You need not live in an inner-city location to become an urban entrepreneur. You can do it anywhere. No neighborhood meets an ideal standard. I suspect that even Beverly Hills and London's Kensington could stand an improvement or two.

You can improve any location. Do something radical. Lead people to think about it in a new way.

Because neighborhood quality drives up property values and rent levels, generate ideas to initiate (or join in) to make the neighborhood a better place to live. When you simultaneously improve your property *and* its neighborhood, you more than double your profit potential. Follow these suggestions:

- *Add to Neighborhood Convenience:* Would a stoplight, wider road, or new highway interchange improve accessibility to the neighborhood? Where are the to-and-from traffic logjams? How can they be alleviated? Is the neighborhood served as well as it could be by buses and commuter trains? How about social service transportation? Could you get the vans that pick up seniors or the disabled to include this neighborhood on their route? What about the traveling bus for the library? Does it stop in the neighborhood? Try to attract new retailers, coffeehouses, and restaurants.

- *Improve Appearances and Esthetics:* Fix-up becomes contagious. Organize a civic pride group. Promote a cleanup and fix-up campaign. Plant trees, shrubs, and flowers in yards and in public areas. Lobby the city to tear down or eliminate eyesore buildings, graffiti, or trashy areas. Reduce on-street parking. Get junk vehicles towed. Enforce environmental regulations against property owners and businesses that pollute (noise, smoke, odors).

- *Zoning and Building Regulations:* Are property owners in the neighborhood splitting up single-family houses and converting them into apartments? Do residents run businesses out of their homes and garages? Are high- or mid-rise buildings planned that will diminish livability? Are commercial properties encroaching on the area? Then lobby for tighter zoning and building regulations. Or do areas within the neighborhood and those nearby make commercial and high-density uses desirable? Then lobby the city to rezone the area to apartments, office, or retail.

- *Eliminate Neighborhood Nuisances:* Do one or more households in the neighborhood make a nuisance of themselves? Junk cars in the driveway; barking dogs; loud music, motorcycles or cars; yelling and shouting; yards littered with trash—you and other property owners can force these annoying folks to conform to higher standards of behavior and property upkeep.

Pore over your local ordinances and any applicable homeowners' association rules and restrictions. Study regulations on zoning, aesthetics, noise, occupancy, use, parking, disturbing the peace, health, safety, loitering, drug dealing, and assault. You will find some regulatory code that you can cite to uphold a complaint. Rules seldom permit nuisances to continue if affected neighbors register complaints with the authorities.

If the troublesome folks continue to offend common decency, a judge can issue an order to stop or restrain their offensive actions. Further violations could then subject the riffraff to contempt of court penalties. They've now angered the judge. Each day their breach persists could rack up multiple fines and possibly jail time. In some cases, the government can directly remedy the problem—cut the weeds, haul off a junk car—and then bill the offenders.

- *Upgrade the Schools:* The *Wall Street Journal* reports that across the USA, "parents and property owners are aggressively pushing to improve their public schools." When you think that in many areas parents spend $5,000 to $25,000 a year to send their kids to private schools, it makes economic sense to reallocate those monies into the neighborhood schools. Improve school performance, and your property rents and values will set new highs.

- *Safety and Security:* Enhance safety within the neighborhood (especially for children and seniors) by slowing down or rerouting traffic. Get the city to lay down speed bumps, and you achieve both objectives at the same time. Speed bumps force motorists to let up on the gas pedal, and they direct drivers who want to speed to alternative streets.

- *Lobby the City Government:* You will pay property taxes. Insist that you get the city services that taxes support. The Berkeley experience shows that when neighborhood property owners and residents join together to form a force, they can push the city politicos to alleviate traffic problems, clean the streets, enforce ordinances, upgrade the schools, beef up police patrols, create parks, and provide other services that neighborhoods should expect.

  Also lobby for lower posted speed limits and intense enforcement. In Berkeley, California, neighborhoods persuaded the city to build concrete traffic blocks at select residential intersections. These road barriers transformed through streets into cul-de-sacs.

- *Add Luster to the Neighborhood's Image:* Friends of mine used to live in Miami, Florida, but now they live in the upscale Village of Pinecrest, Florida. Did they move? No. They and their neighbors persuaded the U.S. Postal Service to give them a new address that would distinguish them from that diverse agglomeration known as Miami. As part of their efforts to create an improved neighborhood, some residents of Sepulveda have formed a new community and renamed it North Hill. In Maryland, Gaithersburg changed its name to North Potomac, piggybacking on the prestige of its nearby, high-class neighbor, Potomac. Residents of North Hollywood got the official name for part of their community changed to Valley Village. "With the name change," says real estate agent Jerry Burns, "residents take more pride in their neighborhood." To improve perception, give your neighborhood (or micro area) or community a new name.

  Most properties have hidden potential. Find it and you earn nice profits.

- *Talk Up the Neighborhood:* Most people learn about various neighborhoods through word of mouth and articles they read in their local newspapers. As all good publicists know, you can positively influence these efforts to "get the word out." Talk up the neighborhood to opinion leaders. Comment to friends, coworkers, relatives, and acquaintances about the great improvements of the community. Convince a reporter to write about the neighborhood's potential for turnaround, quality of life, convenience, or affordability. Let everyone know that the area deserves a better image—that the old reputation no longer reflects reality. When you revitalize a neighborhood, your properties can double or triple in value within just 5 or 10 years. With (sensible) leverage, you can often earn a 10-fold or more increase in your equity.

11

MARKET YOUR PROPERTY FOR TOP DOLLAR

I create the best properties in the world. But I make sure my customers know it. Because my properties deserve promotion, the media regards me as a master of publicity and marketing.

Y OU'VE GIVEN your property curb appeal. You've renovated the interior to meet every want, need, and expectation of your potential tenants (buyers). You've revitalized the neighborhood. You know that your target market will reward you with their most valued property (MVP) award. So what's left to do?

Since you've built a better mousetrap, won't the world now beat a path to your door? Maybe, but don't count on it. To earn the highest profits, to reach and persuade your best prospects, plan your promotion and advertising (the *T*ransfer process) just as you have planned your property's set of benefits (*U*tility). (Transfer process falls under the *T* in DUST.)

WHOM DO YOU WANT TO REACH?

When you design your MVP strategy, think about how to appeal to select buyers or tenants. Learn all you can about these prospects. Who are they? Where do they work? Where do they shop? What publications do they read? What clubs, organizations, and trade or professional associations do they belong to? What faith-based institutions do they attend? In what colleges are they enrolled? Who are their friends, coworkers, or relatives who currently live in the area? What social service agencies cater to their needs? What do their demographics and psychographics look like?

Why So Many Questions?

Answer these and similar questions. Otherwise, you waste time, money, and effort with ill-worded, ill-designed, and misdirected promotions and sales messages. To rent or sell your property with the least amount of time, effort, and expense, work smarter. The more you know about your potential customers, the better you can figure out what to say and where to spread the word about your property.

Why spend big bucks for unproductive advertising in a major newspaper if a well-written notice on a bulletin board or web site will immediately make your telephone ring? Publicize, advertise, and promote your property in those places where you can reach your target market most cost effectively.

Sell Benefits, Not Just the Property

As you think about who you're trying to reach, remember the marketing maxim, "People don't buy features, they buy benefits." Yet, many property owners fail to craft a persuasive promotional message. They take five minutes to jot down the usual features of their property, then they phone in the ad to a newspaper—or maybe post it on a web site such as craigslist.org. What results is nothing more than a generic, unexciting property description such as the following:

> Park Terrace: Split plan, 3-br, 2-bth, den, 2-car garage, 1650 sq. ft., large lot, close to schools and shopping. For more information, call (555) 123-4567 after 5:00 PM.

Viewed by itself, this ad may seem okay. But listed with dozens—perhaps hundreds—of other ads (or property listings), it does little to grab the target prospect's attention and shout, "Here's the home you've been looking for. Here's why you will want to rush over to see this property right now."

Draw your market segment into the ad. Motivate them to act now. Emphasize benefits. Don't rely on their ability to easily see the great value you are offering. Don't believe that if prospects require more information, they will call or e-mail you. Your property competes with too many other properties for that approach to make your phone ring. Prospects rarely call or e-mail just to find out some basic facts about a property. They call only when—out of all the ads they look through—your ad wows them enough to make the final cut.

"Sell the sizzle, not just the steak." Describe a property's features in ways that push your prospect's hot buttons. Sergeant Friday of *Dragnet* may be pleased with a "Just the facts, Ma'am" approach. But to attract the most well-qualified prospects, sell the sizzle.

Sell the Sizzle

That advice to "sell the sizzle" returns us to these questions:

1. Who are your prospects?
2. What benefits do you offer that distinguish your property from competing properties?
3. Are your prospects looking for one or more of these benefits?
   - Bright with natural light.
   - Spacious open floor plan, wonderful for entertaining.
   - Quiet street, quiet building.
   - Home warranty, no repair costs for at least two years.
   - Top-rated school district.
   - Unlimited storage space.
   - Bargain price (rent).
   - Mortgage helper in-suite.
   - Warranted new roof.
   - Great appreciation potential.
   - Low cost of upkeep.
   - Choose your own cabinets, carpets, and colors.
   - Owner will carry financing.
   - Safe and secure neighborhood.
   - Prestigious address/community.
   - Energy-saving, low utility bills.

- Lowest price (rent) in neighborhood.
- Low down payment.
- Comfortable roommate living.
- Seller pays closing costs.
- Walk to shops, cafés, bookstores, and restaurants.
- Easy qualifying, assumable financing.
- Drop-dead-gorgeous kitchens and bathrooms.
- Private setting.
- Serene views.
- Immaculate condition, pride of place.
- Short-term lease/furnished.
- Internet with high-speed access.
- Utilities paid.
- Clean and fresh.
- Well-insulated, low utility bills.

Inspect your property and its competitors. Note every feature and matching benefit that will excite your tenants (buyers). Which of these features and benefits will best motivate your prospects to call? Which of these features and benefits do most of your competitors fail to provide? If you've strategically crafted your MVP, you can now strategically craft a promotional message that will get your property rented (or sold).

CRAFT YOUR AD OR PROMOTION

To cut costs, many owners write their ads or promotions too short. They list a few cold property facts and then expect prospects to call for more information. Don't waste your time and money with such meager efforts. Especially when selling (rather than letting) a property (if you choose to advertise), include the following:

- Sizzling hot buttons.
- Square footage.
- Room count.
- Street address.

- Rent (price).
- Terms, if any.
- Amenities.
- Open-house hours.
- Lot size/landscaping.
- Telephone number/e-mail/web site.

As a for rent by owner (FRBO) or for sale by owner (FSBO), avoid the tactics that property management and sales agencies follow. Contrary to what many people believe, real estate sales agents and property management firms do not typically run ads to rent or sell specific houses or apartments. They run ads to generate prospects for agents. Then, once the agent hooks the prospect, they set off to tour a number of properties. Eventually, the agent hopes to find some property the prospect wants, but agents don't particularly care which property (except they do prefer to push their own listings).

You can't play this numbers game. If you do not wow your targeted buyers with the information they're looking for, your ad won't get circled or bookmarked. Or your misdirected or sparsely worded ad may generate lots of calls from tire kickers, looky-loos, and people who want something other than what you're offering. Ill-written advertising (especially when linked with overpricing) goes a long way to explain why many owners fail to sell or rent their FSBO/FRBO properties and end up listing with a real estate firm (which costs them even more time and money). The more persuasive you tell, the better you sell.

Rather than merely ask people to call for more information, spark their enthusiasm to call with feature/benefit enticements. This ad suggests how to draft an effective sales message:

Affordable—Spacious—Stunning

Mint condition. 3/2, 1840 s. ft. $16,000 d.p., $1,830 per mo., romantic 400 sq. ft. Master BR suite with fplc., open living area, flower garden views, light and bright kitchen delight, unlimited storage. $360,000—compare at $395,000! 210 Pecan. Open Sat. & Sun. 12–5. Rare find, please call 555–1234.

Notice how this ad blends facts and benefits. It conveys a comparative advantage (a value proposition that beats competitors).

It emphasizes the need to "jump on this one before you lose it to someone else." This approach follows the well-known AIDA:

- *A*ttention (headlined benefits).
- *I*nterest (condition and affordability).
- *D*esire (prized features and benefits).
- *A*ction (open house, rare bargain, please call).

This ad will make the phone ring with motivated prospects. If you deliver as promised, you'll sell the first weekend. To lease rather than sell, incorporate the same AIDA principles. Only cite the rental amount instead of asking price, but still favorably compare your property to competing properties.

The Line Count Game

In most cities, newspaper classified ads don't come cheap (that's why more and more owners are relying on low-cost or free web sites). As you craft your ad for print or Web, look for ways to sell the sizzle—but do so with no more words than necessary. Write your ad, let it sit for a day or two, then revise for power and clarity. In the ad that is presented as an example, depending on line breaks, I may have dropped "rare find, please call."

By using "rare find," I wanted to emphasize scarcity—but most likely my prospects would know that without my telling them. With "please call," I wanted to convey "friendly, courteous" owner. Necessary? Worth another line charge? Maybe, maybe not.

To play the line count game, weigh the effectiveness of abbreviations. How many abbreviations are too many? Do your prospects easily understand your abbreviated words? To some degree, newspaper policy restricts the answer to these questions because many publications prohibit and limit some abbreviated terms. When using abbreviations, verify clear meaning. Realize that overuse of abbreviations cheapens your property. Draft cost-effective ads, not ads with the lowest cost. Because web sites tend to offer more space, avoid abbreviations in such ads.

Depend More on Flyers and Promotional Brochures

Advertising costs money—sometimes quite a lot. For less than the price of a three-day, four-line ad, you can print 500 (or more) promotional flyers. Plus, a flyer gives you much more space for your message and creativity. It also permits you to more closely target your market segment of prospects. As with advertising, make your flyer's message sizzle. Brochures and flyers provide an effective, low-cost way to inform, persuade, and motivate well-targeted prospects.

By-Owner Flyer

Avoid the bland, random lists of features that are shown in Figure 11.1, which illustrates how *not* to write a sales message. In addition:

1. *Never Let "For Sale by Owner" Dominate:* Use an attention-grabbing headline that conveys a strong benefit to the targeted prospects.
2. *Place One or More Photos of the Property on the Flyer:* Photos help jog the prospect's memory and, if done well, can accent the promotional message. Use a digital camera and print color flyers from your computer. Black-and-white photocopies cheapen you and the property.
3. *Organize Your Information in Related Sections:* Emphasize the strongest features and benefits.
4. *Explain Possibilities:* Notice that this property is zoned commercial. What does that mean for the value and uses of the property? Do not leave property potential to the buyer's

FOR SALE or RENT
BY OWNER

612 NW 3rd Street

4 Bedroom / 2 Bath

approx. **1550 sq. ft.**

Large corner lot with 6ft. wood privacy fence in backyard

Central Heat and A/C (one bedroom has separate wall mount A/C)

Appliances: Washer, Dryer, Refrigerator, Stove

Ceiling fans in each room

Zoned: Office/Residential (currently residential)

FOR SALE
$85,000

FOR RENT
$975 / month

Available 11-15
(First, Last, and $500 Security deposit required)

Call **(123)-456-7890** for more information or to schedule a visit.

Figure 11.1 By-Owner Flyer.

imagination. (Of course, as an entrepreneurial investor, you will actively search for properties that offer potential that sellers either do not recognize or undervalue.)

To communicate MVP, list and explain the advantages of your property. Otherwise, those prospects who would value your property most highly, might unknowingly zip right past your sales message. How many advertisements hit you and everyone else every day? Probably hundreds, maybe thousands. Persuasively motivate your prospects. Cut through the advertising clutter that dulls or blocks attention.

Rewrite of the By-Owner Flyer

Read through the rewrite in Figure 11.2 of the by-owner flyer. Notice that this rewrite raises the price. Why? Because the owner's ad promoted a run-down property. This revised message offers the benefit of making money. When the present lacks obvious appeal, sell the future. (As a buyer, pay for the present, get the future for free.)

Also notice that the rewritten flyer is loaded with facts and benefits. The more you tell (that relates to prospect wants and needs), the more you sell. Look at any successful immediate response sales message. Whether it's a television infomercial or a magazine ad, advertisers load their direct sales messages with features and benefits. They try to persuade prospects that their proposition offers customers the best value available (an MVP). Emphasize facts and benefits that strongly appeal to your market.

Distribute Flyers to Your Target Market

People drive through neighborhoods to look for "for sale" and "for rent" properties that interest them. Place the flyers in a waterproof tube or pouch and hang them on the large, easily read for-sale or for-rent sign that you place in the front yard of the property.

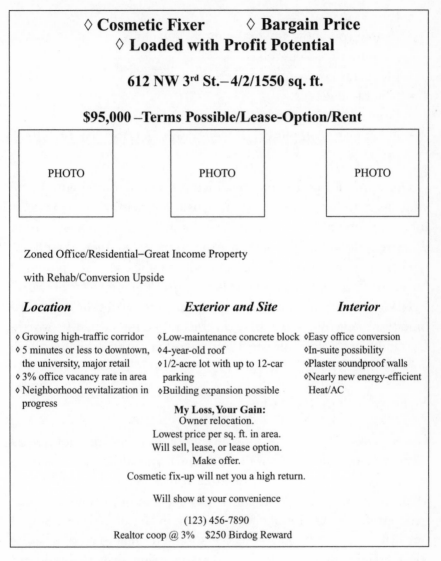

◊ Cosmetic Fixer   ◊ Bargain Price
◊ Loaded with Profit Potential

612 NW 3rd St.–4/2/1550 sq. ft.

$95,000 –Terms Possible/Lease-Option/Rent

| PHOTO | PHOTO | PHOTO |

Zoned Office/Residential–Great Income Property

with Rehab/Conversion Upside

| *Location* | *Exterior and Site* | *Interior* |

◊ Growing high-traffic corridor
◊ 5 minutes or less to downtown, the university, major retail
◊ 3% office vacancy rate in area
◊ Neighborhood revitalization in progress

◊ Low-maintenance concrete block
◊ 4-year-old roof
◊ 1/2-acre lot with up to 12-car parking
◊ Building expansion possible

◊ Easy office conversion
◊ In-suite possibility
◊ Plaster soundproof walls
◊ Nearly new energy-efficient Heat/AC

My Loss, Your Gain:
Owner relocation.
Lowest price per sq. ft. in area.
Will sell, lease, or lease option.
Make offer.

Cosmetic fix-up will net you a high return.

Will show at your convenience

(123) 456-7890
Realtor coop @ 3% $250 Birdog Reward

Figure 11.2   Rewrite of By-Owner Flyer.

In addition, distribute copies of the flyer anywhere your targeted prospects can see them:

- Neighborhood bulletin boards (such as those in grocery stores, libraries, and coffee shops).

195

- Employers.
- People you know at work, church, and clubs.
- Neighborhood churches.
- Mortgage companies and real estate firms.
- Schools, colleges.
- Home-buyer counseling agencies.
- Apartment complexes (if you don't get thrown off the property).

Don't wait for customers (qualified prospects) to find you. Bring your opportunity to them. At any given moment, many prospects for your property aren't actively searching. They're procrastinating. They're waiting for your sales message to motivate them. Hand out your flyers to anyone and everyone who might know of a potential buyer (or tenant). Unleash your bird dogs. Plug into your network.

I have bought, sold, and rented out many properties through word of mouth. Few by-owners play this technique for all that its worth. Certainly, in terms of prospecting, you often can find "diamonds in your own backyard."

Make Your Sign Stand Out

Use the largest for-rent or for-sale sign that the law (or your home-owners' association) allows. Place as much appealing sales information as possible on the sign. Just like your flyers, classified ad, and Web promotion, your sign must grab *A*ttention, create *I*nterest, generate *D*esire, and motivate passersby to *A*ction (AIDA). Someone driving by at 40 miles per hour should be able to recognize the MVP benefits that you offer. To read your sign, drivers should not have to stop and get out of their cars.

Sell with Honesty

Your sales message sells the sizzle, but you must deliver the steak. You're entitled to tout the advantages of your property. No one's entitled to fabricate features that don't exist or that mask serious shortcomings plaguing the property. If you misrepresent the property, you lose credibility, waste your own time, and waste the time and efforts of your prospects.

Don't con your customers. Bravado, hyperbole, that's the preview to the show. But when the curtain rises, deliver what the audience came to see.

Strive to give your tenants and buyers the best deal for their money. Do not dupe them into paying too much for too little. Establish a strong reputation, and prospects will come to you and inquire, "When do you think that you'll have something else coming for rent (sale)? Please give us a call." MVP not only stands for "most valued property" but also signals "most valuable player"—that's you.

DON'T MERELY SHOW THE PROPERTY, SELL IT

Your promotional efforts have worked their magic. Prospects are calling and e-mailing you. Are you now planning to *show* the property? Throw away that idea. Rewind your sales program. Erase the notion that you are going to *show* the property. You are going to *rent* or *sell* it, not merely show it. To *sell*, execute a proactive presentation.

When people *show* properties, they stand back in a passive role. They let the prospect wander around, and, if asked, they try to answer a question or two. When the person begins to leave, the *passive* "tour guide" says, "Thanks for coming by. Let me know if you have any questions or if you think you might be interested," or, "Here's a rental application. Would you like to take one with you?"

The persuasive showman knows that prospective tenants or buyers arrive full of hopes, fears, and uncertainties. The persuasive owner *prepares* to address these buyer (renter) concerns. "Let me know if you have any questions" does not make a sales presentation.

Sales Success: Your 12-Step Program

To progress beyond showing and on to selling, follow these 12 steps to a successful close (purchase or lease agreement). This 12-step program will convert prospects into renters or buyers.

Back Up Your Sizzle with Facts

Collect data on comparable for-rent or for-sale properties. Photocopy regulatory ordinances for your sales file. Provide a home warranty. Show school rankings. Map out the convenience of the location to important linkages (employers, shopping, culture, nightlife, parks, schools). Whatever persuasive points you want to make, present documentary proof or confirming evidence. Without facts, you're puffing.

Establish Rapport

Find common ground for chitchat. Before you talk kitchens and closets, inquire about their kids, cars, or hobbies. "You're wearing an American University of Sharjah sweatshirt. Is that where you went to college?" "Really? My son graduates from AUS this year. He's also signed up for Trump University courses. ..."

Segue into Likes and Dislikes

Never talk property features and benefits until after you learn the prospects' hot buttons and turnoffs. "What would you like to see first? What features prompted your call? Would you like ... ?" Too often, owners and real estate agents launch into a monologue about features that prospects care little about. Or, worse, they tout features that prospects find unappealing. This drives buyers into a socially distant position. Rapport vanishes.

Diplomatically Discover Their Feelings about Other Properties They've Shopped

You presume that you offer great property benefits that will win your prospect's MVP award. But what do your prospects think? Ask for feedback about the market from the only people who really count—your potential renters and buyers.

Really Listen to the Criticism That Prospects Give You

You've worked hard to renovate the property to outperform the competition. But, hey, none of us is perfect. Maybe you have overlooked something. Ask your prospects for objections and weak points. Until you obtain a signed contract, keep searching for profit-enhancing improvements.

Translate Features into Easily Understood Benefits

Your prospects won't necessarily see the meaning of R-38 insulation, thermo pane windows, a southern exposure, or R-1B zoning. Translate those features into benefits. "This heavy-duty insulation means that your heat and air conditioning costs will run less than $100 a month. Once this zoysia grass matures, your yard will look like a putting green, and you'll never have to pull crabgrass or weeds. Look at this photo. That's how the yard will look by the end of summer."

Inform the Prospective Buyers about Financing

First-time buyers, especially, may know little about down payments, monthly payments, and closing costs. They may not realize that they can buy your property with only a few thousand cash out of pocket (which they may be able to borrow from relatives). They may not realize that their after-tax monthly house payments might cost them less than rent (in lower-priced cities).

If you're selling to investors, work the numbers into your sales presentation. Investors want to learn about rents, cash flows, expenses, vacancy rates, and expected rates of return (see Chapter 15).

Monitor the Prospects' Dialogue, Emotional Responses, and Body Language

Are the prospects mentally and emotionally moving their furniture into the home and their kids into the local schools? Are they working through the financials in the context of their budget or investment goals? Do they object specifically to the rent, deposit, price, terms, property features, or neighborhood? Intensity of interest, either positive or negative, signals that they want to rent or buy—if you can relieve their concerns and strengthen the facts and evidence that support (what you believe to be) an MVP offer.

Make It Easy to Complete a Written Lease or Purchase Contract

Prepare your paperwork ahead of time. When you detect or elicit buy signals, move to the kitchen table (or sofa and coffee table) that you've brought into the unit (if it's unfurnished). When the prospects hesitate to commit, give assurances along with the reasons they need to act now and not let this great MVP go to someone else. If necessary, agree to include short-term contingencies. However, retain the right to accept backup offers. If such an offer does come in, agree to give the original buyers (tenants) 24 hours (maybe longer) to clear their contingency or else lose their chance to own (lease) the property.

Set Up an Earnest-Money Escrow for Buyers

To seal the deal, buyers will pledge an earnest-money deposit. If they're smart, they won't hand this check directly to you. So prearrange an escrow account with a title company (or other escrow agent). The buyers can then write the check directly to the trustee of the escrow account. This safeguard builds up the buyers' confidence that you're playing straight with them. (Tenants, of course, should write their deposit check directly to you. Although some landlord-tenant laws do require you to hold security deposits in an escrow account.)

Follow Up a Successful Signing

When you successfully sign your buyers or tenants, follow up to achieve two goals: (1) Make sure they proceed quickly to satisfy their contingencies (property inspection, mortgage approval, lawyer consultation) and (2) keep them motivated.

Some prospects suffer buyer's remorse. They begin to doubt their decision. You treat this disease with periodic positive updates: "A property down the street just sold for $10,000 more than you paid. The neighborhood elementary school has won an award for outstanding extracurricular programs. The city has just pledged $500,000 to upgrade neighborhood streets and parks."

After prospects sign an agreement, assure them that they've made the right decision. Do what you can to bolster their feelings of excitement. Alleviate their regret and uncertainty.

Follow Up a Failure to Close

When you set an appointment to rent or sell the property, get the full names of the prospects and their telephone numbers. If you meet prospects through an open house that you're holding, ask visitors to register (name, e-mail, and phone number) for a door-prize drawing. Or when convenient, directly ask for their names and numbers (or business cards).

Find out who your prospects are and how to keep in touch. Follow up a sales or rental presentation that failed to close with a thank-you note and more persuasive information about the property. Too many FRBOs and FSBOs let prospects walk out the door, never to be heard from again. Avoid that lapse. Act proactively. Reignite their interest, desire, and action with periodic updates about the property, the availability of lower-rate financing, or other potentially motivating enticements. Even prospects who are "just looking" today may become your tenants or buyers tomorrow.

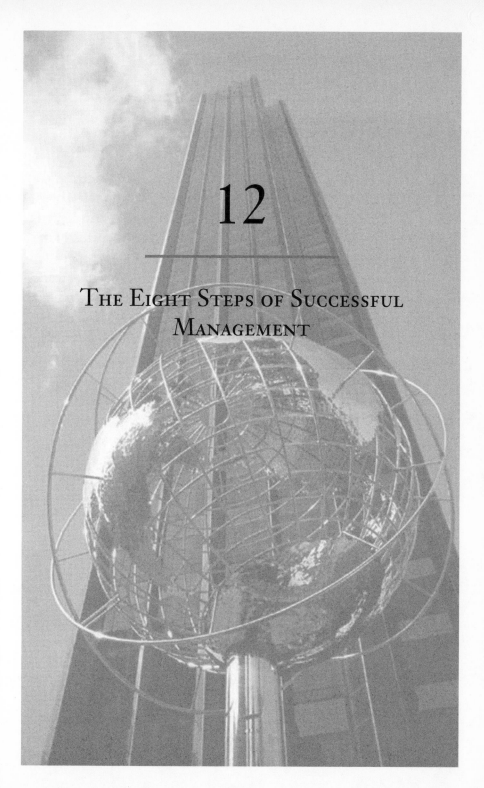

12

THE EIGHT STEPS OF SUCCESSFUL MANAGEMENT

> **You run your operation well, you make a good profit. Run it first class, you'll add 000s to your bank balances.**

Y OU'VE CREATED the most valued property (MVP) and attracted a quality prospect; you've verified credit, income, and references; and you are about to offer a lease. Your entrepreneurial strategy will soon begin to pay off. You are missing only one critical piece of the wealth-building puzzle. You need a management system.

In this chapter, you learn how to maximize your cash flows while minimizing your worry. A good management plan assures your customers that they will receive the benefits they expect. It assures you of wealth without worry. Your first managerial issue: Should you delegate property management or do it yourself?

> **Ferdinand Marcos (and other owners) mismanaged 40 Wall Street into steep disrepair. Their management destroyed value. My management system creates enormous value for the property because it blends together a great building, location, and exemplary tenant services.**

SELF-MANAGE OR EMPLOY A MANAGEMENT FIRM

I encourage beginning investors to self-manage their properties. Then, after you build a portfolio of rentals and experience, withdraw from the day-to-day activities if you choose to.

Why self-manage? You gain these advantages:

- Save money. You eliminate the costs that you would otherwise pay to a management company and, by self-contracting your own repair work (or by doing it yourself), you'll spend less.

- Your vacant units rent faster. Whenever I see a long-term vacancy, 90 percent of the time that property is being "professionally" managed. Management firms seldom work diligently to fill vacancies. They're content to put up a sign, *maybe* run an ad, and merely wait for a rental prospect to show up. You can do much better than that.
- Discover the ins and outs and the good and bad of property management. Although I do not now handle the day-to-day work of my property operations, the knowledge and experiences I gained from those early do-it-myself years still pay dividends. If you've never done it yourself, how will you be able to design (or critique) the management practices, policies, and procedures of your property manager?
- When you talk directly with prospective renters, look at competing properties, and monitor vacancies and rent levels, you build an invaluable firsthand base of market information. If you listen, that market knowledge will tell you how to choose the most profitable target market of tenants and how to adapt your property, lease terms, and rental rates to establish a competitive advantage (MVP).

For beginning investors, the benefits of self-management will beat hired guns who do it only for the money. Even Robert Griswald (author of *Property Management for Dummies* and owner of a large property management firm) agrees. Griswald advises:

> If you have the right temperament for maintaining a property and managing tenants, and if you have the time and live in the vicinity of your property(ies), definitely do it yourself.

The choice is yours. Even so, whether you or a firm provides management for your property, the following eight-step management system will help you achieve MVP status for yourself (most *valuable* property) and your tenants (most *valued* property).

The Eight Steps of Successful Property Management

1. Design a lease for your target market.
2. Create a flawless move-in.
3. Retain top-flight residents.
4. When the market supports it, raise rents.
5. Anticipate and prepare for special problems.
6. Maintain the property.
7. Process move-outs smoothly.
8. Continuously find ways to increase your cash flow.

Design a Lease for Your Target Market

Most new investors treat their lease strictly as a legal document that they can use to compel tenant performance. Although imperfect, written leases do give you better court-enforced protection than oral agreements. But leases also serve another important purpose: They help you achieve a competitive advantage over other property owners.

Your Lease Clauses

Before you decide on the specific clauses within your lease, review the leases of other property owners. Look for ways to differentiate your rental agreement that would encourage tenants (your target market) to choose your property over competing properties. For example, to gain a competitive advantage, you might lower your up-front cash requirements, offer a repair guarantee, shorten (or lengthen) your lease term, guarantee a lease renewal without an increase in rent, or place tenant security deposits and last month's rent in an investment of the tenant's choice to accrue interest or appreciation for the tenant's benefit.

Or, alternatively, perhaps you could develop "tight" or "restrictive" lease clauses and position your property as rentals that cater to more discriminating and responsible tenants. You could include severe restrictions on noise and other nuisances common to rentals.

In that way, you could promote your property as "the quiet place to live."

To create competitive advantage, adapt the features and benefits of your property to the wants of your tenant market, and custom tailor the clauses, language, and length of your lease to match target market needs.

Explain Your Advantages

Adapt your leases to fit the preferences of your target market and you increase your rental revenues, achieve a higher rate of occupancy, and/or lower your operating expenses. To realize these benefits, guide prospective tenants to the advantages you offer. Rather than casually hand the lease to prospects, explain (from the tenants' standpoint) the desirable features of your lease. Naturally, your lease will serve your interests, too. Explain the reasons and necessity for such clauses.

When you craft a lease to fit your market strategy, dozens of items, issues, and contingencies present themselves. Although "typical" lease clauses are featured in the discussions that follow, you should adapt (or omit) items to better appeal to your tenants. Properly drafted, your lease can boost your efforts to attract quality tenants. On the other hand, if you choose archaic legal jargon and an authoritarian demeanor, you can drive good tenants into the rentals offered by your more customer-friendly competitors.

Create a Flawless Move-In

Assure the cleanliness of the unit as well as the working condition of appliances, lights, electrical sockets, HVAC, water heater, and other components. Provide instructions for all appliances and keys for all locks. Point out light switches, circuit-breaker boxes, thermostats, and any operational advice. Anticipate everything. Make sure the tenants will enjoy their move-in week without complaint. As a special touch, give your tenants a welcome basket of flowers, fruits, beverages, and snacks. If the tenants are new to the neighborhood, provide a map and a list of nearby shops, stores, schools, services, and restaurants with addresses, web sites, and phone numbers.

Rules of Conduct

Do not arbitrarily post a list of rules for your tenants. Discuss the rules. Explain why each one adds to tenant welfare, property appearance, or upkeep. Ask the tenant to sign a copy of the rules and put it in your files with the lease, completed rental application, and credit reports. Remind the tenant in a friendly way that the rental agreement incorporates the rules. A breach of the rules means a breach of the lease and thus triggers whatever remedies your lease provides.

Verify Move-In Condition

When tenants move into your property, walk through the unit with them. If you have performed your make-ready, you should find no broken windows, soiled carpets, or dirty appliances. If you do find damage that remains unrepaired, note them on your move-in checklist. Once the tenants are satisfied that they have discovered (and you have listed) every flaw, ask the tenants to sign the list to certify the move-in condition of the property. Photograph or videotape the unit on move-in day. Should a damage dispute arise at move-out, your pictures can be worth a thousand dollars.

Retain Top-Flight Residents

You've moved your tenants into the property. Now retain them as long as possible. With tenants in the property, you become a customer service representative (not a mean ole landlord). To retain tenants, keep your customers happy—until those rare exceptions force you to become a taskmaster.

Keep Tenants Informed

Don't let tenants come home to find a backhoe noisily digging up the parking lot or a pest control man spraying in their apartment.

Notify and explain to tenants when anything out of the ordinary is about to happen on or within the property. Tenants don't like it when you thoughtlessly disrupt their lives or invade their privacy. Communication shows respect and concern for their welfare.

Plan Preventive Maintenance

Emergency repairs not only cost you big dollars but upset residents as well. No tenant likes a furnace that won't put out enough heat, a roof that leaks, or a sink that won't drain. To eliminate these problems, plan preventive maintenance. Don't wait for things to go wrong and then react. Anticipate what can go wrong and prevent it (or at least minimize the probabilities).

Control those seemingly minor expenses or you'll soon find they add up to major expenses. Even though I'm a billionaire, I still look for ways to save a thousand dollars.

Expect the Unexpected

Preventive maintenance programs won't prevent every appliance malfunction or HVAC breakdown. So, before they occur, set up a procedure for dealing with such problems when they do occur.

For routine repairs, provide tenants with a telephone number that's answered by a voice message machine. Ask your tenants to call and state their problem (you could also set up e-mail for this type of notice). Acknowledge their request within 24 hours. Repair within 72 hours (less is better). Nonresponsive landlords rank as one of the top three tenant complaints.[1] Make repairs courteously and quickly, and your tenants will sing your praises to their friends (and your future residents). For emergencies that threaten life, health, or

---

[1] Noise ranks number one. Other leading complaints include high utility bills, unkempt premises, too little parking, and thoughtless (troublesome) neighbors (other tenants).

property, provide tenants direct contact numbers (gas, roof, electrical, fire and police departments, and so on).

Enforce House Rules

Top-flight residents want you to enforce house rules consistently and without favor (or prejudice) among all tenants. Don't let those few bad apples spoil the barrel. Whether your rules regulate noise, parking, unauthorized residents (long-term "guests"), unruly pets, or mishandling of trash and garbage, you must not let violators go unnoticed (and uncorrected).

If you do, you soon will find that your good residents will move out and you will be able to replace them with only lower-quality residents. Draft rules for the benefit of all. Then enforce them against everyone equally.

When the Market Supports It, Raise Rents

When you raise rents, you risk losing a good tenant. Nevertheless, low rents depress your cash flows and diminish the value of your property. When your market study points toward higher rents (i.e., when you know top-flight tenants are willing to pay more than you're currently charging), raise the rents. MVP means that your target market gains a competitively superior value proposition. It does not require you to run a charitable operation.

You can alleviate tenant grumbling and nonrenewals when you offer something in return for that rent increase. How about covered parking, new carpets or appliances, installing ceiling fans, or a new security system? Don't wipe out the money you will gain from the rent increase. But if you enhance the desirability of the property, you can soothe tenant relations.

Anticipate and Prepare for Special Problems

On rare occasions, even the best selected residents may run into financial difficulty. Divorce, accident, ill health, unemployment, and bankruptcy represent several common problems that hit tenants. In my early years as a landlord, I was a soft touch for sob stories—real and fictional. Several times, with previously good-paying tenants, I offered forbearance. In every case, the tenants eventually moved and never paid the money they owed.

If your tenants need financial assistance, refer them to Master-Card or a social services agency. Forbearance seldom leads to a win-win outcome. If they can't borrow their rent money from a bank, pawn shop, relative, or friend, then it makes no sense for you to extend them credit.

If the tenants can't pay, encourage them to leave voluntarily. You may even forgive some of the monies they owe you. Sometimes, owners pay the tenants to move. In nearly all cases, it's better to get rid of a tenant and accept a minor loss than to drag out a bitterly fought eviction and possibly lose thousands in rent collections and attorney fees. When you must evict, however, follow lawful procedures. If you fail to dot your i's and cross your t's, the housing courts can pitch your case out and force you to refile.

Maintain the Property

In addition to preventive and corrective maintenance and repairs, schedule three other types of maintenance programs:

- *Custodial Maintenance:* Assign someone the tasks of yard care, picking up litter, and washing outside windows. Keep your property neat and clean.
- *Cosmetic Maintenance:* Periodically inspect the grounds, common areas, and rental units to freshen up their cosmetic appearance. Notice peeling paint, carpet stains, countertop burns, and other types of wear and tear. Consistent care for a property shows respect for its residents.
- *Safety and Security:* Keep your eyes open to spot problems of safety or security. Quickly repair stairs, lighting, locks,

window latches, or doors. Verify that all smoke alarms work. Require your tenants to call you immediately should they discover any potential threats to health, safety, or security.

Contain costs. I invest money to create the products and services my customers expect, but I don't waste money by paying more than I need to. People ask me, "Why are you quibbling over a few thousand?" Because anyone who doesn't watch their money will soon discover they have no money to watch.

Process Move-Outs Smoothly

At some point, your tenants will leave. When that time comes, process a trouble-free move-out.

Written Notice

Your lease should require your tenants to give you formal, written notice (typically 30 days, more or less) of their specific move-out date. This notice will give you time to get the word out to top-flight prospects that the area's best landlord (you!) will soon have a unit available for some lucky tenant. Early notice also gives you time to schedule work for make-ready cleaning, improvements, and repairs.

Final Walk-Through

Schedule a walk-through of the rental unit on the same day your tenants load their moving van. Compare the unit's condition to your move-in checklist, photos, or video.

With few exceptions, when I have treated my tenants with respect throughout their tenancy, when I document their damages, and when I don't try to overcharge, they honor their responsibility to pay reasonable costs of repair. Upon agreement, I immediately write a check for the balance remaining in their security deposit. In most cases, my tenants receive a 100 percent return of their deposit plus accrued interest.

Find Ways to Increase Your Cash Flow

Few of us perform at the top of our game. We get lazy. We fail to notice opportunities. We let negative self-talk and sloppy decision making rule our thought processes.

> **Enhance perceived value. Spend money where it creates the most lasting and emotional visual effect.**

Aggressively defend against such lapses. Persistently enhance your MVP and increase your cash flows. Set up systems to monitor competitors. Contemplate tenant complaints and suggestions. Solicit feedback from prospects. Talk regularly with your network. Read idea-generating books and articles. Attend investment seminars and workshops. Enroll in Trump University courses.

Then set a firm schedule. Every 90 days, review the knowledge you have gained. Apply your insights to revise, revitalize, or maybe revolutionize your entrepreneurial MVP benefits. Thousand-dollar bills lay waiting for those who will *stretch* to pick them up.

To Pyramid Wealth, Trade Up

Although Donald Trump was born into a relatively wealthy family, he still has followed the time-tested, wealth-builder plan. As his career progressed, he traded up to larger properties and larger deals. You can follow the same approach. Start with a small property, add value, trade up, and repeat the process. Over time, you, too, can build as much wealth as you choose.

Today's property prices greatly exceed those price levels that prevailed at the time Donald Trump and I began investing. But the technique of creating value through marketing and management, then trading up, still works. I've used it. Most professional investors use it. Likewise, you can use it. Manage your properties well. Like Donald Trump, you will plant acorns that will rapidly grow into oak trees.

13

PAY LESS THAN THE PROPERTY IS WORTH

Pay less than the property is worth, and you create immediate value for yourself. In addition, a "pay less than its worth" buying strategy sets up the potential most valued property (MVP) status for future customers. When you achieve a good buy at the time of purchase, you will find it much easier to provide tenants (or buyers) a superior value proposition.

How to Define Great Buy

How should you define "great buy"? When I say, "pay less than a property is worth," most people assume that advice means to "pay less than market value." That's one way. But I encourage you to look beyond that shortsighted view. "Pay less than a property is worth" actually includes multiple possibilities:

- Buy at a below-market-value price.
- Buy below use value.
- Buy below conversion value.
- Buy with below-market cost/terms of financing.
- Buy with below-average operating expenses.
- Buy with a short (discounted) payoff of liens.

Each of these approaches individually—or even better, in some combination, will place you on the fast track to wealth. In one way or another, each of these possibilities adds to your cash flow, builds your equity, or both.

Buy at a Below-Market-Value Price

Authors of "get rich in real estate" books often urge their readers to find motivated sellers who are so distressed financially that they will jump at the chance to get rid of their property to any buyer who agrees to give them a little walkaway money and perhaps pay for their moving van. In boom markets, you might find this "distressed-seller" approach tough to pull off. But in today's markets, such opportunities are yours for the asking. Banks, indebted homeowners, and overextended (and/or incapable) investors, present a bonanza of possibilities.

However, to buy at a price less than market value, you need not limit your search to people who are struggling through divorce, foreclosure, bankruptcy, or, perhaps, a neck-deep pile of credit card debt. In addition, you can negotiate attractive, below-market deals with other types of accommodating property owners.

To sell at market value, property owners need time, knowledge, and marketing expertise (or they need to employ someone who will provide the required knowledge and sales know-how). Also, market price sellers need to prepare their property for sale, show the property, negotiate the deal, and then worry about whether the supposed buyers who have signed the purchase offer will actually close the deal.

Turn these hassles and uncertainties to your advantage. Find owners who lack sufficient time, knowledge, or expertise—or those who want a quick, clean, no-ifs-ands-or-buts sale. Here are several types of owners (sellers) who lack the will or the ability to hold out for a market value price.

Opportunistic Sellers

These owners do not value their property nearly as much as they value some other perceived opportunity. They want to sell (the faster the better) so that they can move on with their lives. Maybe it's a retirement condo in Florida, a new job in San Diego, or a once-in-a-lifetime business venture. For these motivated owners, the grass is greener in other pastures. Agree to a quick and sure close and these sellers will discount their price, offer favorable terms, or maybe some combination of both.

Don't-Wanters

In contrast to those opportunistic owners who sell because they are motivated to chase other dreams, "don't-wanters" sell to get rid of a burden. Maybe the owner's a cranky landlord whose ill-designed or ill-executed management techniques have left him burnt out. Maybe a family moves into their new home before they sold their previous home. Now double mortgage payments, property taxes, and insurance premiums are eating up their take-home pay. Don't-wanters need relief more than they want to hold out for top dollar—or even a "fair" price. For any number of reasons, don't-wanters are eager to sell at any price that minimally meets their total needs.

Unknowledgeable Sellers

Some property owners lack knowledge about the current market price of their property. I favor for sale by owner (FSBOs) and out-of-town owners (recall my purchase at a below-market-value price example that you read about in Chapter 4). Such sellers often lack market knowledge.

On occasion, too, you'll find that real estate agents misprice properties. Fortunately for investors, some sellers choose to list their properties with real estate agents who are family, friends, or acquaintances—even though these favored agents may not know the property, the neighborhood, or the current market comparables.

Recently, a house went up for sale behind a property I own. A couple days later, I phoned the listing agent for details. "Oh, we went to contract on that house the first day," she said. "We had four full-price offers." The agent had sold the house at full listing price—but substantially below market value. In that neighborhood, the agent was out of touch (and the sellers lived out of town).

You can locate properties owned by out-of-towners by trolling through the owner addresses listed in the property tax assessor's records (now available online in many areas). To spot (potentially) mispriced, agent-listed properties, I keep an eye out for properties whose "for sale" signs name real estate firms that rarely appear in that neighborhood.

> **Originally, they wanted to sell Mar-a-Lago for $25 million. After several deals crashed, the caretaker foundation got frustrated. I offered $8 million—property and exquisite furnishings. With my assurances of a quick close, they took it.**

Windfall Gainers

Heirs inherit real estate. Do they want to go for the last buck, or the fast buck? The fast buck often seems more appealing. If the property were inherited from parents or other loved ones—for emotional reasons—the heirs may not feel like hassling with a drawn out listing and sales process. If the property is mortgaged, either the estate or the heirs will need to continue making payments for principal, interest, property taxes, and insurance. Under such circumstances, the fast sale looks even better. Assure these heirs a quick close, no-hassle, discount offer. Chances are, they will accept it.

> **Before they became hot commodities, property owners sold their air rights for peanuts—they considered any sum "found money."**

You Can Pay Less Than Market Value

Owners sell for less than market value every day. Some discount their price to end distress, delay, hassle, or expense. Others unknowingly give bargains. They lack firsthand knowledge and/or they rely on supposed experts who fail to offer competent, timely advice. Set up a property discovery system that will bring good deals to your attention.

But also, point your search in other profitable directions. Sometimes you pay *less than a property is worth—even if you pay market value* (or, when you must, even if you pay more than market value).

Buy Below Use Value

Market value—as a practical matter—typically refers to value according to current condition and use. However, when you inspect a property, you will find ways to enhance its value. Does the property include an extra large lot that permits an addition or separate housing unit? Does it include a garage, basement, or attic that could work as an efficiency apartment? Can you convert dead space to storage space or storage space to livable space? Can you rearrange the floor plan to improve privacy, traffic patterns, or create more desirable room sizes or room counts? Look for these and dozens of other value-creating ideas (see Chapter 10).

People pay for the benefits a property offers. Increase its usability, and you add an immediate gain in your equity. If you pay $250,000 for a property that has a market value of $300,000, you've made $50,000 (as long as you've studied the area enough to know that you're not stepping onto a down escalator). Likewise, if you pay market price of $300,000 for a property and immediately boost its use (rental) value by $50,000 (the present [discounted] value of the increased rent collections you will receive over time), you've made the same amount of gain as if you had bought at a price $50,000 below market. Either way, you have paid less than the property is worth. Pay market value or less when you can. But place other possibilities in view. Focus on the total value that you can realize from the deal. Maybe the seller's asking price still leaves a wide margin of profit potential. Maybe you just need to wipe clean the lens of your rose-colored glasses. (*Caution:* I am not saying you should pay any price—only that in many deals—you can pay market, or more, and still earn large gains.)

Buy Below Conversion Value

Neighborhoods change. Markets change. Relative prices and rent levels change: An apartment complex today, a condominium project tomorrow; a Victorian house today, an office building tomorrow; a warehouse today, artist lofts tomorrow; a church today, a discount outlet store tomorrow.

Always look for opportunities to convert properties from an older use that no longer yields maximum return to a use that better matches contemporary needs. Buy at the market price of the old; reap the gain from the new use and market strategy that you create.

Buy with Below-Market Costs/Terms of Financing

You pay for real estate in three ways: the cost of the property, the expenses necessary to operate it, and the cost of the financing. Say that you can buy a $300,000 property for below-market price of $275,000. You finance your purchase with a $250,000 loan at 7.5 percent (the going market rate) for 30 years. Alternatively, you find a seller who offers you a $300,000 property for $300,000. But you assume (take over) his current mortgage. That loan has an outstanding balance of $275,000, a fixed interest rate of 6.0 percent, and a remaining term of 27 years.

Other things equal, which deal would you choose? In this case, the mortgage assumption could give you the best gain. Many savvy investors look not only for below-market value purchases (and operating expenses), but also for below-market interest rates (or other favorable terms such as low down payment, a longer payback period, or any arrangement that will lead to increased cash flows).

Besides mortgage assumptions, you can sometimes arrange for lower interest through "subject to" purchases, seller carrybacks, and seller buy-downs. With a "subject to" purchase, you agree to make the payments on the seller's mortgage, but you do not process papers with his mortgage lender. With a seller carryback, the seller agrees to let you pay him on an installment plan. You negotiate terms and cost directly with the seller. (As noted, many of my purchase *and* sales agreements have included seller financing.)

A seller buy-down means that the seller pays a fee to a mortgage lender. In return, the lender gives you a below-market interest rate. Sellers sometimes use buy-downs in lieu of offering their property at a lower price. (For examples, see my book *The 106 Mortgage Secrets That All Borrowers Must Learn—but Lenders Don't Tell*, second edition, Wiley, 2008).

Buy with Below-Average Operating Expenses

Real estate agents and owners typically rely on the comparable sales method to price their houses, condos, and apartment buildings that they have listed for sale. The comparable sales method (as you will see in Chapter 15) usually compares and contrasts properties according to visible features such as square footage, floor plan, condition, and lot size. The comparable sales method figures that basically what you (or your inspector) see is what you get.

Low Expenses Boost Value

As a savvy investor, go beyond the obvious. When you inspect a property, consider whether that property offers low expenses (property taxes, utilities, insurance, maintenance, and so on) relative to the comparable properties. Most homebuyers and many investors more or less figure that operational expenses won't differ much among comparable properties. So estimates of market value tend to slight the actual amount of a property's operating expenses. As a result, when you find a low-expense property, you might buy it for less than it's really worth.

What's the Property Really Worth?

In addition to comp sales, investors use the capitalized income method to value a property:

$$V \text{ (Value)} = \frac{\text{NOI (Net operating income)}}{\text{R (Capitalization rate)}}$$

where NOI equals annual rent collections less annual operating expenses and R equals the market rate of return that typical real estate investors require. For example, assume that a property rents for $2,000 a month and property expenses total 40 percent of rents. For ease of calculation, assume the cap rate equals 10 percent:

$$V = \frac{\$24,000 \text{ (Rent)} \times (1 - 0.4) \text{ Expenses}}{0.10 \text{ Cap rate}}$$
$$= \frac{\$14,400 \text{ (NOI)}}{0.10 \text{ (R)}}$$
$$= \$144,000$$

The comparable sales approach also values this property within a range of $140,000 to $150,000.

Now say you find another similar property that's for sale. Comparable sales indicate a value of $140,000 to $150,000. This property could also rent for $2,000 a month ($24,000 for the year). However, unlike its comparables, this property's operating expenses total just 25 percent of rent collections versus 40 percent for the comps (more insulation; long-life roof; energy-efficient doors, windows, and heating, ventilating, and air-conditioning [HVAC]; low-maintenance exterior siding; and so on). When you apply the capitalized income method, you value the property at $180,000:

$$V = \frac{\$24,000 \times (1 - 0.25)}{0.10 \text{ (R)}}$$
$$= \frac{\$18,000 \text{ (NOI)}}{0.10 \text{ (R)}}$$
$$= \$180,000$$

Since you can buy this property at the "comp sale" market value of around $140,000 to $150,000, you've paid less than it is really worth when used as a rental (income-producing) property rather than as an owner-occupied residence.

To illustrate the point, I have simplified this example. (We explain further in Chapter 15.) But the principle holds. In the world of investment real estate (all other things equal), a low-expense property is worth more than its higher-expense comparables. Yet, on occasion, you will find low-expense properties priced at less than the real value the property will deliver.

Buy with a Discounted (Short) Payoff of Liens

You've now discovered multiple ways to buy properties for less than they are worth. You've learned about motivated sellers. Now you will see how to create a bargain price. Investors call this technique a short sale.

What Is a Discount (Short) Payoff?

The short-sale technique first gained popularity during the real estate recession that plagued California, Texas, and other parts of the country 15 to 20 years ago. Investors and lenders used the short sale to rescue *upside-down* property investors and homeowners who fell behind on their mortgage payments. Today, this technique has multiplied in importance. In some hard-hit areas of the United States, 20 percent of all sales involve a short payoff of one or more lien holders.

To illustrate a short payoff, say that during the recent speculative real estate boom you bought a home for $300,000. You put 5 percent down and borrowed $285,000 from a lender. Three years later, you were downsized. Even worse, the market value of your property falls to $265,000. You would like to sell the house, but now the property is worth less than you owe. You're upside down.

Even if a buyer gave you a full market-value offer, you wouldn't raise enough cash to pay your lender, closing expenses, a real estate commission, and any accumulated deferred maintenance (repair) costs. What can you do?

Without a job, you no longer can pay your mortgage payments. Nor is it likely that you can refinance. No job, inadequate collateral. Your lender threatens to foreclose. Your situation looks bleak.

Lenders, Too, Face Bleak (Money-Losing) Outcomes

The lender is threatening to foreclose, but it doesn't really want to. If the lender forecloses, it will want to collect its now outstanding balance of $280,000 plus other costs such as:

- Attorney fees.
- Court costs.
- Unpaid accrued mortgage interest.
- Property insurance premiums.
- Property tax payments.
- Miscellaneous costs (staff time, property upkeep, paperwork).

If these other costs total $20,000, the lender would have $300,000 sunk into this property.

How much would a speculator bid for the property at a foreclosure auction? Maybe $200,000. If the lender lets this speculator take the property, the lender loses around $100,000:

Total amount owed	$300,000
Speculator bid	200,000
Lender loss	100,000

Alternatively, the lender may not want to let the property go to a foreclosure speculator. The lender could place a bid of $300,001. If the lender wins its bid (which in reality only costs it $1—since it is owed $300,000), it then owns the property as an REO (which stands for real estate owned by the bank).

Does acquiring the foreclosed property solve the lender's problem? No. The lender continues to lose interest earnings on the money it has put out thus far on the property. It must still pay property taxes, premiums for property insurance, property upkeep, and repairs. To get the property sold, the lender will probably pay fix-up costs and a real estate commission.

Lenders lose with REOs. After these costs, will the lender eventually come out ahead with its REO? Still the answer is no. Remember, at most, the property will bring a market value price of $265,000. Here's how the numbers might look:

Balance owed at foreclosure	$300,000
REO repair costs	15,000
Sales commission/REO @ 6%	15,900 (on $265k)
Total	$330,900
REO sales price	265,000
Lender loss with REO	$(65,900)

Even with the REO alternative, the lender loses $65,900 (and that assumes an REO sale at full market value—which is not likely). So, ask yourself if, as an investor, you could work out a way for lenders with bad loans to lose less money. Would the lender accept your solution? Many times, the answer to that question is yes.

Solution: The Preforeclosure Workout
What if, before the lender filed foreclosure on a bad loan, you could get the lender to accept a short payoff—some amount less than the total balance the borrower owes? Quite likely you could save the lender from losing as much money as it otherwise would by going through with its foreclosure. You would help the borrowers salvage what's left of their credit record. (Late payments don't bring down a credit score nearly as much as would a foreclosure.)

What's in it for you? You acquire a property for less than its market value. Let's go back to the earlier example at the time when the borrowers owed $280,000—only now assume that you're the investor.

How the Numbers Look

You talk with the borrowers. You discuss their bleak upside-down situation. You offer them $1 for their property with the proviso that you can work out a short payoff on their loan with the lender. You succeed. The lender agrees to accept $230,000. In exchange, the lender grants a full release of the mortgage lien it holds against the property.

The sellers/borrowers begin a new financial life free of mortgage debt, free of mortgage payments they cannot make, and free of waking up in the middle of the night. The lender still loses—but not as much as it could have lost by foreclosing the borrowers and eventually adding to the growing pile of REOs that already plague its earnings and solvency.

As for you, the investor, you've just become the owner of a $265,000 property for an outlay of $230,001. You, the lender, and the prior homeowners all benefit.

How to Complete a Short Sale

To complete a short sale, negotiate tough but present your case factually. Then, diligently persevere. To earn your gain of $25,000 to $100,000 from the short-sale technique may require anywhere from several weeks to several months of back-and-forth talks and proposals. And even after this effort, you may still fail to put all of the pieces together.

But when you succeed, your efforts earn big rewards. Here are the steps you can take to beat the odds.

Find Sellers in Financial Distress (and Otherwise Motivated to Deal)

To complete a short sale, find sellers who are financially distressed and are otherwise eager to cut a deal that frees them from their property and mortgage obligations. How can you find these motivated sellers?

You've got dozens of possibilities. Remember, every day some people's lives change to make property ownership a burden. When you relieve that burden, you help the sellers and you help yourself.

Review the Sellers' Mortgage Payment Records

After you've established rapport with the sellers and set the tone for productive discussions, review their mortgage payment records and all collection letters thus far sent by their lender. Specifically, you want to learn:

- The current payoff amount on the loan including all back payments, late fees, and legal fees assessed by the lender (if any).
- How far along is the bank's collection/foreclosure process? In my experience, I've found lenders are more inclined to complete a short sale when the borrowers have missed multiple monthly payments. The borrowers are so seriously delinquent that the lender believes the property will almost certainly end up in foreclosure.
- How the full amount owed by the borrowers compares with the likely selling price of their mortgaged property.
- Whether it appears that a foreclosure will lose the lender a lot of money, after adding in continued lost interest and other expenses. If so, you've located a hot prospect for a short payoff.

Review the Sellers' Total Finances

Before a lender will accept a short payoff, the borrowers must prove destitution. By destitution, I do not necessarily mean that the borrowers will soon be sleeping in the back of their car and subsisting on food stamps. But the lender will probe to determine whether the borrowers own any valuable assets that they could sell to raise money.

The lender also will look at the borrowers' history of earnings and career prospects. If the borrowers merely want to shirk their mortgage obligations, the lender won't likely negotiate (unless you persuade the collections staff to rethink their position).

Place the Property Under Contract

When preliminary talks show that the borrowers can't pay and that the lender will lose money, place the property under a signed purchase contract with the sellers.

Offer the sellers some token amount ($1) in exchange for a deed to their property. In addition, you agree to permanently get the lender off their backs. You rescue the sellers' credit record and restore their peace of mind (at least as it relates to this imminent foreclosure).

Because you don't know whether the lender will accept a short payoff, include a contingency in your offer to the sellers that reads something like this:

> This agreement between ____[you] ____ and ____ [sellers] ____ is contingent upon ____ [you] ____ obtaining full satisfaction of all liens (mortgages, judgments, unpaid taxes, etc.) owed by the sellers.

Do not agree to pay the sellers any significant amount. The lender won't approve it. Only rarely will a lender permit borrowers to put cash in their own pocket from a short sale.

Obtain Permission to Negotiate with the Lender

At the time the sellers accept your offer, you also ask them to authorize the lender to release the sellers' loan information to you. This form allows you to verify mortgage loan data, and it gives the lender authority to negotiate a payoff with you.

Without this written release, the lender will not share confidential loan data about its borrowers with you. Make sure the sellers understand the need for this release.

Approach the Lender

When you first approach the lender, do not—I repeat, do not—even suggest the mortgage payoff price that you have in mind. During this preliminary meeting (most probably with a staff officer in the lender's loss mitigation department), learn the lender's views about short payoffs. Learn the criteria the lender applies. Learn the lender's operating procedures.

Lenders settle their bad loans in different ways. Some hardballers won't budge. Others are glad to see you. Some (perhaps the majority) will act standoffish but can be persuaded to negotiate when you show them why your solution will work to their advantage. (Never assume that the personnel who staff the bank's loss mitigation departments understand why short payoffs can benefit the lender—though during the past several years, their awareness has certainly grown.)

Prepare and Submit Your Offer

You've opened discussions with the lender and gathered information about its payoff policies. Ideally, during these talks, the lender will give you clues as to how much discount it's willing to accept. (Regardless, though, offer less than you're willing to pay.) You're now ready to prepare and submit an offer.

But wait. Don't just give the lender a number. First build your case. Submit a package of persuasive evidence. To enhance its effectiveness (and your chance for success), this package must include:

- *Cover Letter:* Here's where you describe the evidence that you've submitted to prove why a short payoff now will benefit the lender. Do not cite precise figures in this cover letter. Build up the merits of the idea before you start talking numbers. Talk benefits before price.

- *Condition of the Property:* Take *unflattering* photos of the property. Submit those that look the worst. Submit repair cost estimates (as high as you can reasonably justify).
- *Comparable Sales:* Choose the *lowest-priced,* best-looking comparable sale properties. Use comp sales to support your estimate of market value for the mortgaged property. The less the lender thinks the property will bring at foreclosure (or as an REO), the more likely that it will accept your short-sale offer.[1]
- *Owner Distress Pleas:* Include a hardship letter from the borrowers. This letter documents the tough times these folks are experiencing. For support, include threatening letters the borrowers have received from the IRS, those large unpaid medical bills, the electricity cutoff notice, and the newspaper article that explains why 800 laid-off workers at the local auto supplier plant (where both of the borrowers worked) will never be called back.
- *Credibility:* Provide evidence that you are ready, willing, and able to close. Prove to the lender that you will perform as promised.
- *Your Offer:* Calculate and show the amount of losses the lender will suffer if it continues the foreclosure process. Then, reveal your payoff. This figure should show that the lender will net more if it acts now to accept your offer.
- *Persistence Pays:* If the lender doesn't immediately respond to your offer, follow up, follow up, follow up. If the lender won't accept, then persuade the loss mitigation officer to suggest a number that might look good. Do whatever you can to keep the dialogue alive and productive.

---

[1] A lender will probably solicit one or more broker price opinions (BPOs). So, your figures should not wildly veer from reality. Support your offering price with reasons that will make sense to the lender. Lowball take-it-or-leave-it-offers rarely gain acceptance, and they can also damage your reputation and credibility.

Come Up with the Money

To maximize the attractiveness of your offer to the lender, talk cash. Lenders prefer to cash out their bad loans. It's usually tough to persuade a lender to accept a discounted payoff *and* carryback financing. (Yet, you can ask. With desperate lenders today, any reasonable proposition might win acceptance.) When I say "pay cash," though, I only mean cash to the foreclosing lender. I do not mean cash out of your own pocket. Most investors who deal in short sales arrange a line of credit or get preapproved for financing from their own bank or mortgage company. Then they close the transaction with these funds.

How to Find Good Deals

Where can you find good properties at a price less than they are worth? Anywhere and everywhere. Donald Trump succeeds as a deal maker because nearly everyone who's anyone knows that Donald Trump is open to investment proposals. From his early years, he mastered the art of self-promotion. He searches for opportunities *and* invites opportunities to come to him.

As I was heading in from the Palm Beach airport, a pair of newly built gleaming white towers caught my eye. I looked into who owned them and discovered that a bank had just foreclosed their mortgage. I soon bought the $120 million project for $40 million. You can find good deals everywhere if you just keep your eyes and your mind open to possibilities.

Likewise for you. Remain alert to discover or create deals. Get the word out. Just as important, encourage people to approach you with propositions before their deals get shopped all over town.

Competition for Properties

You can sometimes buy properties for less than their worth that have languished on the market for months—maybe even years. In today's depressed markets, those who want to sell greatly outnumber those who are seriously looking to buy. For many unsold properties, the "days on market" figures have passed 90, 150, even 180.

Search Opportunistically

To get your share of good deals, explore multiple avenues of search and discovery. Use any or all of these methods:

- *Word of Mouth:* Tell everyone you know. Ask if they're planning to sell or know somebody who might be thinking about it. Inquire about change-of-life possibilities (know anyone who's retiring, moving, getting divorced, in foreclosure, out of work, and so on?).
- *Bird Dogs:* In their business or occupation, some people (e.g., yard care, postal delivery, lawyers [divorce, foreclosures, probate, bankruptcy], barbers, hairstylists, condo association managers, locksmiths, handymen, painters, and so on) routinely learn of potential sellers before the news becomes more widely available. Agree to pay a standing bounty of $500 (more or less) for each lead your bird dogs point to that results in a closed deal.
- *Newspapers/Web Sites (For-Sale Ads):* Every morning, read through the ads of properties for sale. Especially focus on newly placed FSBO ads and agent ads that say "new listing." Look for those common deal signals such as "motivated seller," "foreclosure," "REO," "bank owned," "assumable financing," "seller will carry," "land contract," "lease option," "lease-purchase," "new listing," "won't last," "must sell," and other phrases that indicate a flexible or distressed seller.

Be wary, though. Sellers or agents may use such phrases to lure eager buyers into overpriced money traps. Nevertheless, give a call to learn whether they back their flash with substance.

Although "motivated" types of phrases signal possible good deals, unassuming ads also can offer promise. Look for plainly stated ads that state a low price (or some rare desirable feature) for that particular neighborhood. The ad might signal an unknowledgeable seller.

- *Newspaper/Web Sites (For-Rent/Lease Option):* Glance through the for-rent/lease option categories, too. You might spy some wording that signals a potential deal in the making. These "sleeping sellers" are generally more flexible as to terms since they do not necessarily need a firm sale or quick closing. Notice for-rent ads that have been running for more than two or three weeks. These ads may signal a "cranky" or otherwise disappointed landlord who is open to offer.

- *Newspaper Notices:* Newspapers include more leads than real estate ads. They list births, deaths, retirements, foreclosures, bankruptcies, and lawsuits. Any of these events might trigger the desire to sell a property. Many bargain hunters regularly pursue these types of leads with a letter or phone call.

- *Internet:* Thousands of real estate web sites list properties for sale—everything from eBay to foreclosures to FSBOs to real estate agents (multiple listing service [MLS] as well as specific firm/agent sites) to newspaper classifieds. Visit the sites that list properties in the areas that you believe promising. Keep track of the features, neighborhoods, and price ranges that appear to sell the fastest. (In addition to property searches, your local MLS site can help you stay abreast of market trends and conditions.)

- *Foreclosure Sales:* If a property owner who defaults on his mortgage(s) doesn't work out a remedy with his lender, the property goes to sale at a foreclosure auction. You can either bid at the auction or try to buy the foreclosed property from the winning bidder.

Generally, you can obtain a low price at the auction. But auctions present more risk. Bidders who win the auction may next need to resolve problems with title defects, holdover tenants or owners, and, perhaps, poor property condition with undisclosed problems.

Instead of bidding at the auction, you might buy from the winning bidder—most often the foreclosing lender or a property speculator. You'll usually pay a higher price (though not always), but the risk is less because you can inspect the property and require the new owner of the foreclosed property convey a deed that warrants title. (Foreclosure sales grant buyers a sheriff's deed or other type of title that may suffer clouds, encumbrances, and defects. You can listen to an extensive discussion of the pre- and postforeclosure buying opportunities in my Trump University audio CD, *The Real Estate Goldmine*).

- *Real Estate Agents:* Establish cordial relations with one or more real estate agents who will hustle on your behalf. Sharp agents cull new listings each morning to find properties that match the buying criteria of their favored clients. Agents, too, learn about properties that are not yet listed but are soon to come onto the market.

  Agents also harbor "pocket listings." A pocket listing refers to a juicy property that is held back from the MLS until after an agent notifies preferred clients that it has just come onto the market.

  Describe to a savvy agent the types of properties and deals you're looking for. As long as your criteria fit within the scope of reason, you will get some hits. A savvy agent not only saves you search time but can also bring you deals that you otherwise would never hear about.

- *Advertise and Promote:* Have you seen the "I buy ugly houses" billboards? They generate huge numbers of hot leads. Those billboards cost a small fortune, and they're up in cities all across the country. Although you may not want to spend that kind of money on promotion, follow the same principle.

Promote and advertise yourself as a property investor. Use mailers to selected neighborhoods. Hang flyers on door-knobs. Hand out your business card to every postman, taxi driver, and waitress you see. Tell them about your bird-dog bounty. Place a magnetic sign on your car. Paint your van with your logo and telephone number. Set up a web site. Place "wanted to buy" ads in newspapers, newsletters, and magazines. Post notices on college campus bulletin boards. If you want deals to come to you, take a tip from Donald Trump and the "I buy ugly houses" folks. Get the word out that you're ready to make offers.

- *Home Builders:* New single-family home (or condominium) builders sometimes offer good deals at two points in their sales campaign. At the beginning of a project, builders may price below market to generate buzz about their development and to sign enough preconstruction (off-plan) contracts to satisfy the requirements of their mortgage lenders.

   Near the end of a sales campaign, the builder wants to close its on-site sales office, cut expenses, and move on to the next project. At this stage, builders may slash prices to quickly sell their remaining 8 or 10 unsold units. Or they may provide incentives or concessions such as upgrades, HOA fees paid for the first two years, below-market interest rate, or a free parking space (that otherwise would sell for $25,000). Whatever method(s) the builder uses, you acquire a property at a price less than it's worth.

   In today's property markets that suffer overbuilding, you can really negotiate favorable deals on single-family houses and condominiums. In many instances, financially distressed builders will cut any type of deal that puts cash into their bank accounts and helps relieve them of their severe liquidity crises.

14

NEGOTIATE A GOOD DEAL

NEGOTIATING TIPS FROM DONALD TRUMP

Donald Trump titled his first book *The Art of the Deal* for good reason. Mr. Trump emphasizes that deal making requires "accommodation, adjustment, diplomacy, and not the least, finesse." Negotiation requires "persuasion more than power." A "razor-sharp mind, not a bulldozer."

To succeed, Mr. Trump advises, "Think just as hard about your negotiations strategy and tactics as you would think about the property itself." To profit from negotiation, follow these principles: (1) know yourself, (2) know the other party, and (3) prepare, prepare, prepare:

- *Know Yourself:* What do you want from the deal? You can't get what you want unless you know what you want and how to ask for it. Do not get hung up on price alone. Look for ways to structure financing, shift risks, and solve problems.

  Define your goals broadly so you can look for alternative ways to achieve them. "I always enter negotiations with Plan A, Plan B, and Plan C," says Mr. Trump. "The art of the deal is to figure out what you really want to accomplish and then persist in your creative efforts to achieve them."

- *Know the Other Party:* "If you're building a world-class skyscraper," says Mr. Trump, "you've got to know the materials you're working with—their strengths, their weaknesses, and how they will work together to create the effect you want. This same principle applies to building a deal—only instead of working with steal, glass, marble, and brass, your materials are people."

  "Don't even think about negotiating," advises Mr. Trump, "until you've learned everything about the hopes, dreams, personalities, and goals of the people you will be dealing with. If you're going to persuade people to accept your proposals, *you better first learn why they're even talking to you.*"

  "To a large extent, the art of the deal," Mr. Trump says, "is learning how to read other people. Top negotiators display a chameleon-like quality. They respond to the other party with their approach. They adapt their voice tone, body language, facts, and reasoning to the situation and the people involved." In Mr. Trump's view, only a rank amateur or egotistical smart guy rushes onto the negotiating field throwing hardballs. Savvy negotiators warm up and engage (not enrage) the other players.

- *Prepare, Prepare, Prepare:* Mr. Trump likes to talk about 40 Wall Street as one of his best deals—both for what he personally accomplished (restoring a tarnished gem to brilliance) and for the profits he has earned from it. To pull it off, he prepared meticulously.

  To learn more about the needs of the landowner, Mr. Trump flew to Germany to talk with him directly, thus bypassing the bevy of gatekeepers who were blocking the deal. But in addition to knowing the wants of the building owners and the land owners (yes, the building and the land were owned by different persons), Mr. Trump knew the building, the market, and the possibilities for the property better than anyone else.

  Did he gain this knowledge overnight? Hardly. He admits, "My personal and financial success from 40 Wall Street resulted all because I had my eye on that building for years. When the time came, I learned what the other parties needed, and I was prepared to act."

**We negotiated a great deal on Swifton Village
because we knew the FHA really wanted
a quick, sure sale.**

CREATE AND NEGOTIATE A GOOD DEAL

Sometimes good deals fall into your lap. The seller (for whatever reason) asks $375,000 for a property that's clearly worth at least $425,000. You offer $360,000. The seller counters at $370,000. You object and complain that the price is more than you can pay. You come to terms at $368,000. You're happy, the seller's happy.

That's the ideal. More often, to pay less than a property is worth, you will explore, propose, and negotiate.

Explore Possibilities

Before you negotiate price and terms, explore the possibilities for profit that the property offers. Remember, paying less than a property is worth refers to numerous possibilities for gain other than a below-market price. But even with a discount price, identify the potential offered by the property, the neighborhood, or even the owner.

Apply the benefit-creating ideas of Chapters 8, 9, and 10. Only when you've figured out what the property is worth to you can you outline the type of deal that will move you toward your $10 million (or greater) net worth.

Negotiate an Agreement

Some inexperienced negotiators mistakenly believe that a skilled negotiator dips into a bag of tricks and pulls out deceptive techniques such as lowballing, weasel clauses, shotgunning (multiple random offers), "dressing to impress" (pretending to be something you're not), bad-mouthing (deflating an owner's high opinion of his property), and eleventh-hour surprises (at the last minute before closing, insist on contract changes in your favor). One book on real estate negotiating advises, "Remember you are in a war and you must use every weapon available to win."

Unethical tricks and deceptions may temporarily pull chips into your pile. But more often than not, dishonesty backfires. Long-term successful investors negotiate to win an agreement that will actually close to the benefit of all parties. Working "with" creates more great deals than working "against." In other words, win-win does payoff for both parties.

In negotiations, look for leverage. What do you have that the other guy wants or, even better, can't do without. Don't go into a deal without first figuring out the power you possess to solve the other guy's problems.

As you negotiate win-win, you adopt a cooperative perspective. Win-win negotiators recognize that every negotiation brings forth multiple issues, priorities, and possibilities. They also recognize and respect the other party's (not opponent's) concerns, feelings, and needs. These negotiators do not push and pull along a single line of contention (e.g., price). Win-win negotiators work to create a strong, mutually beneficial agreement that all parties want to see completed. It serves little purpose to negotiate a tough deal over a period of weeks or months only to see the other party walk away and refuse to close because they have changed their mind or found a better deal.

Should you sue for specific performance or damages? Possibly, but that route seldom proves practical or profitable. Moreover, the other party will not obstinately refuse to close, but instead will invent some plausible or defensible reason.

In your efforts to keep a deal on track, never stoop to an accommodating position while the other party hurls hardballs at you. When push comes to shove, win-win negotiators either shove back to restore a cooperative endeavor or they walk away with their dignity and finances intact.

Develop a Cooperative Attitude

Most important, win-win demands willing cooperation. Bob Woolf, agent, attorney, and past negotiator for many well-known sports figures and entertainers, has said, "When I enter a negotiation, my attitude is, 'I'm going to make a deal.' I don't start with a negative thought or word. I try to foster a spirit of cooperation. I want the other party to feel that I'm forthright, cheerful, confident, and determined to reach their goals. If I'm sufficiently sensitive to the other party, I firmly believe they will be inclined to make an agreement with me. To a degree, your attitude will become a self-fulfilling prophecy."

Bob Woolf's advice applies whether you are negotiating a big-time sports contract or a purchase agreement for an investment property. Act in good faith. Play by the rules of courtesy. You want to buy a property. The sellers want to sell a property. Your best chance for success comes when all parties cooperate to help each other.

Every time you communicate with a buyer, seller, or tenant, you're negotiating or setting the stage for negotiations. Plan and prepare for what result you want.

Learn as Much as You Can about the Sellers

Some lawyers and sales agents do everything they can to keep buyers and sellers away from each other. They fear that the deal might fall through because you and the seller personally clash with each other. Or you might inadvertently give away a choice bit of information that will help the other side.

Although the keep-the-buyers-and-sellers-apart sales strategy sometimes is best, as a principle, reject it. Before you think offer, learn about the sellers. What kind of people are they? Do they seem generous and open? Are they rigid and argumentative? Do they show pride in their property? Are they reluctantly moving? Are they eager to sell? Why are they selling? Have they bought another property? What are their important needs: emotional, personal, and financial? What are their worries and concerns? What deal points can you highlight that will captivate their attention, set aflame their desire, and motivate action?

What Do the Sellers (Really) Want?

The sellers aren't merely trying to sell a property. A sale represents a means to some other goal. The sellers will judge your offer by how well it helps them move toward what they want to achieve. That's why you must get to know the sellers. Without understanding their needs, you miss the opportunity to find issues of a high-value/low-value win-win trade-off that benefit both of you.

**Rely on negotiations to explore and discover . . .
"I was just thinking about something you said. How would you feel if we could . . ."**

Say the sellers previously accepted two offers that fell through because the buyers couldn't arrange financing. With these experiences lurking in the background, the sellers don't want to be strung out again. If you can assure them that you have the resources to buy (bank statements, credit report, preapproval letter, job security), they likely will give you a lower price or other concessions.

Establish Rapport and Emotional Connection

Frequently, investors aim their 16″ guns toward price. The sellers want to fly high. Investors want to shoot them down. Antagonism and stalemate result. Steer around this trap. Meet the sellers, talk with them, and learn all you can about their perceptions, their past property experiences, their feelings, and their needs. Except for show, play it cool; avoid clashes with the sellers.

- *Get to Know the Sellers:* The sooner you get a fix on who the sellers are and what they're like, the better you can begin to map your negotiation strategy. Sellers respond more openly with information when you first look at their property. At that point, they're eager to please. They want to excite your interest. If you wait to meet them until after you've made an offer, they'll guard their admissions and concessions more tightly.

243

- *Before You (Explicitly) Begin to Negotiate, Innocently Suggest Concessions:* "You're asking $825,000, is that right? Just so I can fairly compare your property to others I'm looking at, have you thought about how much you would really be willing to accept?" Or, "You're asking $825,000, right? What personal property—appliances, drapes, rugs, patio furniture does that price include?" Or maybe, "Have you considered the type and terms of the financing you're willing to carry back?" By suggesting concessions in this way, you do not appear to be negotiating with the sellers. You're not even directly asking for concessions. You're merely gathering information to rank the sellers' property against other properties that are up for sale. Sensing that you are exploring other options, many sellers will sweeten the deal before you even write your offer.

- *Inquire, Don't Interrogate:* The way you ask your questions is far more important than the information you request. Phrase inquiries as innocuously as you can. Don't intimidate, accuse, threaten, or debate. You might recall Peter Falk as Columbo, the perpetually "disoriented" detective. Columbo didn't interrogate suspects. He gently probed. Use similar tactics. Encourage the easy flow of information. Don't extract it like an impacted wisdom tooth.

- *Establish Rapport:* Find common ground. Talk about the last Cubs game, the weather, or perhaps a shared hobby. Negotiations are about people, just not money. Treat the sellers as people, not as impersonal owners of a property that you might want to buy.

Artful negotiators persuade with style rather than flatten with power.

- *Compliment, Don't Criticize:* As you inspect the property (especially when talking with homeowners), compliment; do not immediately try to pull the property down to justify a lower price. Sincerely note the beautiful grandfather clock, "Does it have an interesting history? How long have you owned it?" Comment on other belongings the owners seem to take pride in. What about the yard? Do the sellers have a green thumb? Can you genuinely admire their tomatoes or roses?

At this *first* meeting, put forth a cordial attitude. Establish a *relationship* bank account to draw on later when you will need it. To sharply criticize the sellers' property at this time won't loosen them up to accept a lower price. But it may turn them against you. Even though the property will need work and improvement, wait until later in the negotiations to mention the repairs and fix-up the property will need. During your first visit with the sellers, discovery pays off better than critique.

Conciliate, Avoid Compromise

A mother tires of hearing her two children bicker at the dinner table. Each child wants the only remaining slice of pie. Upset over this debate, the mother grabs the remaining piece, slices it in two, and gives half to Craig and half to Chris. "There," she says, "you've got to realize that you can't have everything you want. You must learn to compromise. Remember this as an important lesson."

This mother thought she was teaching her kids exemplary behavior. In fact, she imprinted an obstacle to win-win negotiating. Why? Because practically speaking, she "split the difference" before she discovered her children's real wants and a range of options. This mother mistakenly framed her kids' debate along a single continuum. Compromise simply mandated a presumably fair way to split the piece of pie.

Look for Ways to Enhance Potential Outcomes

Had the mother framed the problem multidimensionally, more than likely she could have figured out a better solution. What if

Chris preferred the crust and Craig preferred the filling? What if the children shared a television set and each preferred different programs? What if the children shared after-dinner cleanup responsibilities? What if the children had money from an allowance? What if Chris didn't want the pie but simply liked to torment Craig?

Had the mother recognized a range of wants, trade-offs, and outcomes, she may have achieved results that satisfied better and at the same time yielded a more valuable lesson about life as a negotiator (i.e., win-win tradeoffs) for both children. The true art of the deal does not refer to how quickly you strike a compromise. It depends on how well you see beyond a single either/or issue. Thoughtful and exploratory conciliation beats an everyone-loses (or someone-loses) compromise.

Compromise Provokes Extremes

People who negotiate to compromise typically open with offers at the extreme. If you believe the sellers will split the difference, it's to your advantage to offer $550,000 for a property that's worth $650,000. Should the sellers agree to meet you halfway, they will sell you the property for $600,000.

Few sellers are that obliging. The tactic of bid low and compromise is too familiar to work effectively. As negotiating expert Herb Cohen emphasizes, "A tactic perceived is no tactic at all." You will close more good deals when you broaden your knowledge of wants, needs, trade-offs, and possibilities. To paraphrase Emerson, "Foolish compromises are the hobgoblins of little minds."

Learn the Sellers' Reasons and Reference Points (Valuation Metrics)

When the sellers say, "This property is worth at least $425,000," learn their reference points. Why do they think $425,000 represents a low price? When the sellers say, "We need at least $425,000," find out why. When the sellers say, "We couldn't afford to carry back financing, we need every net dollar in cash," gently inquire why. No matter what objections sellers raise to your offer, never accept "no" as the final word. Find the underlying reasons and the supposed factual foundation that the sellers are building on to support their decision (or their counteroffer).

Pushy sales agents deal with objections like a steamroller. They push forward and flatten the buyer's concerns. Do not *overcome* (or overpower) objections with the methods taught in those high-pressure sales training classes. Correct, alleviate, or eliminate the sellers' misperceptions through better understanding and explanation.

When the sellers' facts or perceptions make sense, work toward resolve. A confused mind always says no. To progress toward a yes, assuage the concerns of the sellers that provoke doubt or delay.

Use an Agent as an Intermediary, but Negotiate for Yourself

Property sales agent Gus Brown tells of an offer he received on one of his listings. Gus says that after receiving the purchase offer from a *buyer's agent* (an agent who presumably owes a fiduciary duty to his clients), this agent told Gus, "This $290,000 is my clients' [first] offer, but I know they will go up to $350,000."

"Of course," Gus adds, "I passed along that information and countered with several offers—eventually settling on $345,000. My clients were pleased."

Never let your real estate agent or lawyer control your negotiations. Provide your agent only the information you want the other side to learn. Do not tell your agent that you are willing to pay a price higher than your first offer. Use your agent as a fact finder and intermediary, but guard your emotions, intentions, and especially your confidences.

Some investors mistakenly rely on their agents or lawyers to actually come up with the terms of an offer and then carry out their negotiations. These naive investors will ask their agents, "What price do you think I should offer? What's the most you think I should pay? Will the sellers concede points or agree to carryback financing?" The buyers then follow whatever the agent recommends.

Control the lawyers. Left unleashed, their attacks can kill good deals (and drain your bank account).

Abdicate your negotiating responsibilities and you set yourself up for the "relying on experts" mistakes discussed in Chapter 4 ("Make Great Decisions").

Leave Something on the Table

Negotiator Bob Woolf says, "There isn't any contract I have negotiated where I didn't feel I could have gone for more money or an additional benefit."

Why does Woolf "leave money on the table?" Because skilled negotiators know that "the deal's not over until it's over." Push too hard, and you draw resentment and even hostility from the other party. If they have signed a contract, they'll start thinking of all the ways they can get out of it. Worse, if you stumble on the way to closing, they won't help you up. Resentful sellers (buyers) will just kick dirt in your face.

Especially in the purchase of real estate—where emotions run strong—leave something on the table. The purchase agreement only ends the *first stage* of your negotiations. It does not end the negotiations, per se. Before you close a deal, problems might arise with property inspections, appraisal, financing, possession date, closing date, surveys, zoning, building permits, or any number of other issues. Without goodwill, trust, and cooperation, unpleasant setbacks on the way to closing can throw your signed agreement into a deal-killing dispute.

Deal Points

Naturally, negotiate price. But price represents just one chip, not your entire pile. Even simple purchase agreements include at least 8 or 10 other critical deal points. As you negotiate, look for high-value/low-value tradeoffs—tradeoffs benefit you and the seller. What can you offer in trade for a lower price? What can the seller offer that tempts you to concede a higher price than you otherwise would agree to pay?

1. *Terms:* Will the seller offer owner-assisted financing? If so, how much up-front cash? What interest rate? What amount of monthly payments? Exactly what type of financing assistance (lease option, lease purchase, land contract, first mortgage, second mortgage, and so on)?

2. *Closing Costs:* In most areas, custom dictates who pays what settlement expenses. But negotiation can override custom. With settlement costs ranging upwards of 2 to 5 percent of the purchase price, smart investors place these sums on the table for discussion.

3. *Earnest-Money Deposit:* To show your commitment to a deal, you will support your offer with an earnest-money deposit. How much? That's subject to negotiation.

4. *Repair Allowance:* In lieu of (or along with) a price reduction, you can negotiate a repair allowance for some of the fix-up work you plan for the property.

5. *Personal Property:* Would you like the seller to include window air conditioners, appliances, or other personal property in the sale? Write them into your offer.

6. *Financing Contingencies:* If the seller does not provide all your financing, you will probably include a financing contingency in your offer. This clause will give you a specified amount of time to raise the money you will need to close the deal. It will also set the terms, such as interest rate, loan-to-value (LTV) ratio, down payment amount, and so on, that a lender must offer you. Otherwise, you're released

from the agreement and entitled to a return of your earnest money.

7. *Inspection Contingencies:* Get the property professionally inspected for physical condition, termites, and environmental hazards. How long do you have to complete these inspections? Who pays how much for any unanticipated or previously unknown problems? In what situations can you withdraw from the agreement without sacrificing your earnest money deposit—or subjecting yourself to a potential lawsuit for damages or specific performance? Negotiation touches on all these issues.

8. *Closing Date:* To gain a bargain price, many investors offer a fast (or delayed) closing as dictated by seller preferences.

9. *Possession Date:* Generally, sellers relinquish possession on or around the date of closing. Sometimes, though, you may want a delayed closing with early possession (such as with a lease purchase or lease option). Or, alternatively, the sellers may want to seal the deal but hold on to the property until, say, the school year ends, their new home is ready for them to move into, or if the property is already a rental, the sellers may want time to locate a replacement property for a Section 1031 tax-deferred exchange.

10. *Warranties:* Is the seller providing you a warranty for building components such as the roof, HVAC, or appliances? What *exactly* do any warranties cover? For what amounts? For what period of time?

Every purchase-sale agreement addresses many significant deal points. To negotiate entrepreneurially, view these issues as connected to each other. Combine terms and deal points to work for you and the other party.

Reduce Seller Anxiety

Sellers may agree to accept your offer if you prove that you are a solid buyer and that your contract offer will actually close. Serious buyers can win more concessions that the "shotgunners" who throw out offers like buckshot:

1. Increase the amount of your earnest-money deposit.
2. Produce a tentative commitment letter from a mortgage lender. Perhaps, reveal your bank balances and credit score to assure sellers that you possess the money and credit to close the purchase.
3. If you're paying cash or making a large down payment, emphasize that strength. Cash counts. If you've got it, use it to boost the credibility of your position.
4. Emphasize the strength of your character, stability in your job and community, investment experience, and other factors that prove you're able and willing to quickly close the deal.
5. Eliminate weasel clauses. A weasel clause is any contract clause that lets you escape easily from a contract without obligation. One of the easiest and most obvious weasel clauses states, "This offer is subject to the approval of my attorney." If you need to consult an attorney, do it before you begin negotiations. (In some states, by custom, attorneys routinely get involved in negotiating property purchase agreements. Nevertheless, the same advice holds. The firmer your offer, the more likely the sellers will treat you as a serious buyer and make concessions toward an agreement.)
6. Avoid indefinite contingency clauses such as "Offer subject to raising $10,000 from my business partners" or "Subject to locating a 1031 replacement property." Sometimes homeowners write into their purchase offer, "Subject to the sale of our current home." Clauses like these raise doubts and increase anxiety. If you load your offer with "ifs, ands, or buts," sellers will hesitate to accept it.
7. When you write contingency clauses into your offer, make them definite and short term: "Buyer will secure a property inspection report within five days," "Buyer agrees to submit

mortgage loan application within 48 hours," or "Sellers are released from obligation if buyers do not produce a letter of mortgage credit approval within three days." These clauses show that you're not going to drag your feet through the transaction.

8. Make your contingency clauses realistic. Don't condition your purchase on finding mortgage money at 6.0 percent if market rates are at 7.5 percent. Don't expect a 27-year-old property to be free of defects.

Plan your offer with no more escape hatches than you need (but no fewer either). Sellers will agree to a better price and terms in exchange for the peace of mind of a near-certain sale. Buyers who pay cash, for example, nearly always gain more seller concessions than those investors who load their contracts with weasel clauses.

You will compete for the best deals with other sharp, entrepreneurial investors. While you're fiddling with contingencies and thinking things over, someone else will grab the prize.

When you find a property that you think you can buy for less than it's worth, put it under contract immediately. Use short-fuse contingencies when prudence dictates. But otherwise, come to the negotiating table prepared to deal.

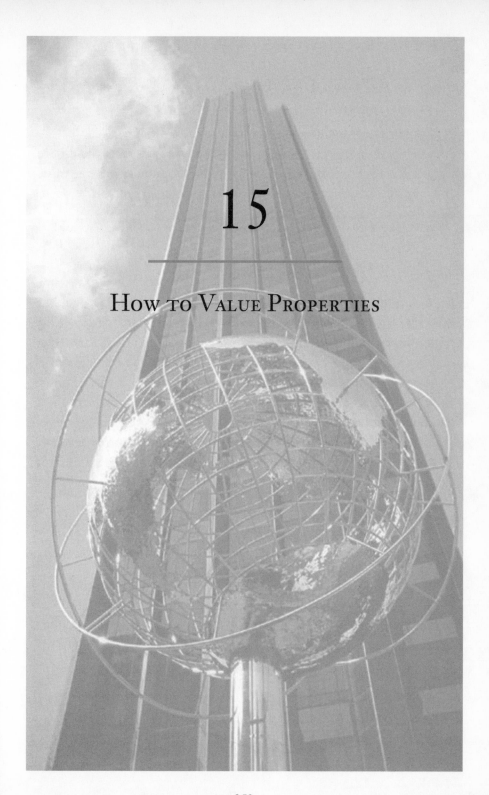

15

How to Value Properties

At the right price, I'd buy it.

Y OU NOW KNOW how to identify and negotiate great deals—
except for one remaining issue: How do you actually figure
value? So, we begin this chapter with a discussion of market value
and then illustrate other techniques that investors also rely on to
benchmark their offering price and terms.

THE UNIFORM RESIDENTIAL APPRAISAL REPORT

Market value should never serve as your sole measure of value, but
do refer to it as one useful data point. To estimate the market value
of houses, townhouses, and condominiums, most lenders, investors,
and appraisers follow a form similar to that shown in Figure 15.1.

The two leading sources of mortgage money in the United States,
Freddie Mac and Fannie Mae, have both approved this form and
promulgate its widespread use. Lenders and investors in countries
other than the United States also follow a similar appraisal process.
No matter where a property is located, the principles of market
value remain the same.

A Word of Warning

Beware: Too many lenders, homebuyers, and investors merely look
at an appraisal's conclusion of market value. But market value conclusions are worth no more than the accuracy of the data and the
quality of the reasoning that support them. Regrettably, experience
proves that appraisals often err in facts, reasoning, and judgment.

Regardless of whether you perform your own appraisal or review the work of an appraiser, verify all input data and question all
inferences and conclusions.

In the following pages, we discuss each section of an appraisal
(Figure 15.1) and highlight some frequent sources of mistakes and
questionable judgments.

Uniform Residential Appraisal Report   File

The purpose of this summary appraisal report is to provide the lender/client with an accurate, and adequately supported, opinion of the market value of the subject property.

<table>
<tr><td>Property Address</td><td>City</td><td>State</td><td>Zip Code</td></tr>
<tr><td>Borrower</td><td>Owner of Public Record</td><td colspan="2">County</td></tr>
<tr><td colspan="4">Legal Description</td></tr>
<tr><td>Assessor's Parcel #</td><td>Tax Year</td><td colspan="2">R.E. Taxes $</td></tr>
<tr><td>Neighborhood Name</td><td>Map Reference</td><td colspan="2">Census Tract</td></tr>
<tr><td colspan="4">Occupant ☐ Owner ☐ Tenant ☐ Vacant   Special Assessments $ ☐ PUD   HOA $ ☐ per year ☐ per month</td></tr>
<tr><td colspan="4">Property Rights Appraised ☐ Fee Simple ☐ Leasehold ☐ Other (describe)</td></tr>
<tr><td colspan="4">Assignment Type ☐ Purchase Transaction ☐ Refinance Transaction ☐ Other (describe)</td></tr>
<tr><td colspan="4">Lender/Client   Address</td></tr>
<tr><td colspan="4">Is the subject property currently offered for sale or has it been offered for sale in the twelve months prior to the effective date of this appraisal? ☐ Yes ☐ No</td></tr>
<tr><td colspan="4">Report data source(s) used, offering price(s), and date(s).</td></tr>
</table>

I ☐ did ☐ did not analyze the contract for sale for the subject purchase transaction. Explain the results of the analysis of the contract for sale or why the analysis was not performed.

Contract Price $ Date of Contract   Is the property seller the owner of public record? ☐ Yes ☐ No   Data Source(s)

Is there any financial assistance (loan charges, sale concessions, gift or downpayment assistance, etc.) to be paid by any party on behalf of the borrower? ☐ Yes ☐ No
If Yes, report the total dollar amount and describe the items to be paid.

Note: Race and the racial composition of the neighborhood are not appraisal factors.

Neighborhood Characteristics		One-Unit Housing Trends			One-Unit Housing		Present Land Use %	
Location ☐ Urban ☐ Suburban ☐ Rural		Property Values ☐ Increasing ☐ Stable ☐ Declining			PRICE	AGE	One-Unit	%
Built-Up ☐ Over 75% ☐ 25-75% ☐ Under 25%		Demand/Supply ☐ Shortage ☐ In Balance ☐ Over Supply			$ (000)	(yrs)	2-4 Unit	%
Growth ☐ Rapid ☐ Stable ☐ Slow		Marketing Time ☐ Under 3 mths ☐ 3-6 mths ☐ Over 6 mths			Low		Multi-Family	%
Neighborhood Boundaries					High		Commercial	%
					Pred.		Other	%

Neighborhood Description

Market Conditions (including support for the above conclusions)

Dimensions	Area	Shape	View
Specific Zoning Classification	Zoning Description		

Zoning Compliance ☐ Legal ☐ Legal Nonconforming (Grandfathered Use) ☐ No Zoning ☐ Illegal (describe)
Is the highest and best use of the subject property as improved (or as proposed per plans and specifications) the present use? ☐ Yes ☐ No If No, describe

Utilities	Public	Other (describe)		Public	Other (describe)	Off-site Improvements–Type	Public	Private
Electricity	☐	☐	Water	☐	☐	Street	☐	☐
Gas	☐	☐	Sanitary Sewer	☐	☐	Alley	☐	☐

FEMA Special Flood Hazard Area ☐ Yes ☐ No FEMA Flood Zone   FEMA Map #   FEMA Map Date
Are the Utilities and off-site improvements typical for the market area? ☐ Yes ☐ No If No, describe
Are there any adverse site conditions or external factors (easements, encroachments, environmental conditions, land uses, etc.)? ☐ Yes ☐ No If Yes, describe

General Description	Foundation	Exterior Description materials/condition	Interior materials/condition
Units ☐ One ☐ One with Accessory Unit	☐ Concrete Slab ☐ Crawl Space	Foundation Walls	Floors
# of Stories	☐ Full Basement ☐ Partial Basement	Exterior Walls	Walls
Type ☐ Det. ☐ Att. ☐ S-Det./End Unit	Basement Area sq. ft.	Roof Surface	Trim/Finish
☐ Existing ☐ Proposed ☐ Under Const.	Basement Finish %	Gutters & Downspouts	Bath Floor
Design (Style)	☐ Outside Entry/Exit ☐ Sump Pump	Window Type	Bath Wainscot
Year Built	Evidence of ☐ Infestation	Storm Sash/Insulated	Car Storage ☐ None
Effective Age (Yrs)	☐ Dampness ☐ Settlement	Screens	☐ Driveway # of Cars
Attic ☐ None	Heating ☐ FWA ☐ HWBB ☐ Radiant	Amenities ☐ Woodstove(s) #	Driveway Surface
☐ Drop Stair ☐ Stairs	☐ Other Fuel	☐ Fireplace(s) # ☐ Fence	☐ Garage # of Cars
☐ Floor ☐ Scuttle	Cooling ☐ Central Air Conditioning	☐ Patio/Deck ☐ Porch	☐ Carport # of Cars
☐ Finished ☐ Heated	☐ Individual ☐ Other	☐ Pool ☐ Other	☐ Att. ☐ Det. ☐ Built-in

Appliances ☐ Refrigerator ☐ Range/Oven ☐ Dishwasher ☐ Disposal ☐ Microwave ☐ Washer/Dryer ☐ Other (describe)
Finished area above grade contains: Rooms   Bedrooms   Bath(s)   Square Feet of Gross Living Area Above Grade
Additional features (special energy efficient items, etc.).

Describe the condition of the property (including needed repairs, deterioration, renovations, remodeling, etc.).

Are there any physical deficiencies or adverse conditions that affect the livability, soundness, or structural integrity of the property? ☐ Yes ☐ No If Yes, describe

Does the property generally conform to the neighborhood (functional utility, style, condition, use, construction, etc.)? ☐ Yes ☐ No If No, describe

Figure 15.1 Uniform Residential Appraisal Report.   *(continued)*

255

Uniform Residential Appraisal Report

File #

| There are | comparable properties currently offered for sale in the subject neighborhood ranging in price from $ | | to $ |
| There are | comparable sales in the subject neighborhood within the past twelve months ranging in sale price from $ | | to $ |

FEATURE	SUBJECT	COMPARABLE SALE # 1	COMPARABLE SALE # 2	COMPARABLE SALE # 3
Address				
Proximity to Subject				
Sale Price	$	$	$	$
Sale Price/Gross Liv.Area	$ sq. ft.	$ sq. ft.	$ sq. ft.	$ sq. ft.
Data Source(s)				
Verification Source(s)				

VALUE ADJUSTMENTS	DESCRIPTION	DESCRIPTION	+(-) $ Adjustment	DESCRIPTION	+(-) $ Adjustment	DESCRIPTION	+(-) $ Adjustment
Sale or Financing							
Concessions							
Date of Sale/Time							
Location							
Leasehold/Fee Simple							
Site							
View							
Design (Style)							
Quality of Construction							
Actual Age							
Condition							
Above Grade	Total Bdrms. Baths	Total Bdrms. Baths		Total Bdrms. Baths		Total Bdrms. Baths	
Room Count							
Gross Living Area	sq. ft.	sq. ft.		sq. ft.		sq. ft.	
Basement & Finished Rooms Below Grade							
Functional Utility							
Heating/Cooling							
Energy Efficient Items							
Garage/Carport							
Porch/Patio/Deck							
Net Adjustment (Total)		☐ + ☐ -	$	☐ + ☐ -	$	☐ + ☐ -	$
Adjusted Sale Price of Comparables		Net Adj. % Gross Adj. %	$	Net Adj. % Gross Adj. %	$	Net Adj. % Gross Adj. %	$

I ☐ did ☐ did not research the sale or transfer history of the subject property and comparable sales. If not, explain

My research ☐ did ☐ did not reveal any prior sales or transfers of the subject property for the three years prior to the effective date of this appraisal.

Data source(s)

My research ☐ did ☐ did not reveal any prior sales or transfers of the comparable sales for the year prior to the date of sale of the comparable sale.

Data source(s)

Report the results of the research and analysis of the prior sale or transfer history of the subject property and comparable sales (report additional prior sales on page 3).

ITEM	SUBJECT	COMPARABLE SALE # 1	COMPARABLE SALE # 2	COMPARABLE SALE # 3
Date of Prior Sale/Transfer				
Price of Prior Sale/Transfer				
Data source(s)				
Effective Date of Data source(s)				

Analysis of prior sale or transfer history of the subject property and comparable sales

Summary of Sales Comparison Approach

Indicated value by Sales Comparision Approach $

Indicated value by: Sales Comparison Approach $ Cost Approach (if developed) $ Income Approach (if developed) $

This appraisal is made ☐ "as is", ☐ subject to completion per plans and specifications on the basis of a hypothetical condition that the improvements have been completed, ☐ subject to the following repairs or alterations on the basis of a hypothetical condition that the repairs or alterations have been completed, or ☐ subject to the following required inspection based on the extraordinary assumption that the condition or deficiency does not require alteration or repair:

Based on a complete visual inspection of the interior and exterior areas of the subject property, defined scope of work, statement of assumptions and limiting conditions, and appraiser's certification, my (our) opinion of the market value, as defined, of the real property that is the subject of this report is
$, as of   , which is the date of inspection and the effective date of this appraisal.

Figure 15.1 *(Continued)*

Uniform Residential Appraisal Report

File #

ADDITIONAL COMMENTS

COST APPROACH TO VALUE (not required by Fannie Mae)

Provide adequate information for the lender/client to replicate the below cost figures and calculations.

Support for the opinion of site value (summary of comparable land sales or other methods for estimating site value)

COST APPROACH

ESTIMATED ☐ REPRODUCTION OR ☐ REPLACEMENT COST NEW	OPINION OF SITE VALUE .... =$
Source of cost data	Dwelling Sq. Ft. @ $ =$
Quality rating from cost service Effective date of cost data	Sq. Ft. @ $ =$
Comments on Cost Approach (gross living area calculations, depreciation, etc.)	
	Garage/Carport Sq. Ft. @ $ =$
	Total Estimate of Cost-New =$
	Less Physical Functional External
	Depreciation =$ ( )
	Depreciated Cost of Improvements.. =$
	"As-is" Value of Site Improvements.................................... =$
Estimated Remaining Economic Life (HUD and VA only) Years	Indicated Value By Cost Approach .... =$

INCOME APPROACH TO VALUE (not required by Fannie Mae)

INCOME

Estimated Monthly Market Rent $ X Gross Rent Multiplier   = $ Indicated Value by Income Approach

Summary of Income Approach (including support for market rent and GRM)

PROJECT INFORMATION FOR PUDs (if applicable)

PUD INFORMATION

Is the developer/builder in control of the Homeowners' Association (HOA)? ☐ Yes ☐ No Unit type(s) ☐ Detached ☐ Attached

Provide the following information for PUDs ONLY if the developer/builder is in control of the HOA and the subject property is an attached dwelling unit.

Legal name of project

| Total number of phases   Total number of units   Total number of units sold |
| Total number of units rented   Total number of units for sale   Data source(s) |

Was the project created by the conversion of an existing building(s) into a PUD? ☐ Yes ☐ No If Yes, data of conversion

Does the project contain any multi-dwelling units? ☐ Yes ☐ No Data source(s)

Are the units, common elements, and recreation facilities complete? ☐ Yes ☐ No If No, describe the status of completion.

Are the common elements leased to or by the Homeowners' Association? ☐ Yes ☐ No If Yes, describe the rental terms and options.

Describe common elements and recreational facilities

Figure 15.1 *(Continued)*

257

Uniform Residential Appraisal Report

This report form is designed to report an appraisal of a one-unit property or a one-unit property with an accessory unit; including a unit in a planned unit development (PUD). This report form is not designed to report an appraisal of a manufactured home or a unit in a condominium or cooperative project.

This appraisal report is subject to the following scope of work intended use, intended user, definition of market value, statement of assumptions and limiting conditions, and certifications. Modifications, additions, or deletions to the intended use, intended user, definition of market value, or assumptions and limiting conditions are not permitted. The appraiser may expand the scope of work to include any additional research or analysis necessary based on the complexity of this appraisal assignment. Modifications or deletions to the certifications are also not permitted. However, additional certifications that do not constitute material alterations to this appraisal report, such as those required by low or those related to the appraiser's continuing education or membership in an appraisal organization, are permitted.

SCOPE OF WORK: The scope of work for this appraisal is defined by the complexity of this appraisal assignement and the reporting requirements of this appraisal report form, including the following definition of market value, statement of assumptions and limiting conditions, and certifications. The appraiser must, at a minimum: (1) perform a complete visual inspection of the interior and exterior areas of the subject property, (2) inspect the neighborhood, (3) inspect each of the comparable sales from at least the street, (4) research, verify, and analyze data from reliable public and/or private sources, and (5) report his or her analysis, opinions, and conclusions in this appraisal report.

INTENDED USE: The intended use of this appraisal report is for the lender/client to evaluate the property that is the subject of this appraisal for a mortgage finance transaction.

INTENDED USER: The intended user of this appraisal report is the lender/client.

DEFINITION OF MARKET VALUE: The most probable price which a property should bring in a competitive and open market under all conditions requisite to a fair sale, the buyer and seller, each acting prudently, knowledgeably and assuming the price is not affected by undue stimulus. Implicit in this definition is the consummation of a sale as of a specified date and the passing of title from seller to buyer under conditions whereby; (1) buyer and seller are typically motivated; (2) both parties are well informed or well advised, and each acting in what he or she considers his or her own best interest; (3) a reasonable time is allowed for exposure in the open market; (4) payment is made in terms of cash in U. S. dollars or in terms of financial arrangements comparable thereto; and (5) the price represents the normal consideration for the property sold unaffected by special or creative financing or sales concessions* granted by anyone associated with the sale.

*Adjustments to the comparables must be made for special or creative financing or sales concessions. No adjustments are necessary for those costs which are normally paid by sellers as a result of tradition or law in a market area; these costs are readily identifiable since the seller pays these costs in virtually all sales transactions. Special or creative financing adjustments can be made to the comparable property by comparisons to financing terms offered by a third party institutional lender that is not already involved in the property or transaction. Any adjustment should not be calculated on a mechanical dollar for dollar cost of the financing or concession but the dolar amount of any adjustment should approximate the market's reaction to the financing or concessions based on the appraiser's judgment.

STATEMENT OF ASSUMPTIONS AND LIMITING CONDITIONS: The appraiser's certification in this report is subject to the following assumptions and limiting conditions:

1. The appraiser will not be responsible for matters of a legal nature that affect either the property being appraised or the title to it, except for information that he or she became aware of during the research involved in performing this appraisal. The appraiser assumes that the title is good and marketable and will not render any opinions about the title.

2. The appraiser has provided a sketch in this appraisal report to show the approximate dimensions of the improvements. The sketch is included only to assist the reader in visualizing the property and understanding the appraiser's determination of its size.

3. The appraiser has examined the available flood maps that are provided by the Federal Emergency Management Agency (or other data sources) and has noted in this appraisal report whether any portion of the subject site is located in an identified Special Flood Hazard Area. Because the appraiser is not a surveyor, he or she makes no guarantees, express or implied, regarding this determination.

4. The appraiser will not give testimony or appear in court because he or she made an appraisal of the property in question, unless specific arrangements to do so have been mede beforehand, or as otherwise required by law.

5. The appraiser has noted in this appraisal report any adverse conditions (such as needed repairs, deterioration, the presence of hazardous wastes, toxic substances, etc.) observed during the inspection of the subject property or that he or she became aware of during the research involved in performing this appraisal. Unless otherwise stated in this appraisal report, the appraiser has no knowledge of any hidden or unapparent physical deficiencies or adverse conditions of the property (such as, but not limited to, needed repairs, deterioration, the presence of hazardous wastes, toxic substances, adverse environmental conditions, etc.) that would make the property less valuable, and has assumed that there are no such conditions and makes no guarantees or warranties, express or implied. The appraiser will not be responsible for any such conditions that do exist or for any engineering or testing that might be required to discover whether such conditions exist. Because the appraiser is not an expert in the field of environmental hazards, this appraisal report must not be considered as an environmental assessment of the property.

6. The appraiser has based his or her appraisal report and valuation conclusion for an appraisal that is subject to satisfactory completion, repairs, or alterations on the assumption that the completion, repairs, or alterations of the subject property will be performed in a professional manner.

Figure 15.1 *(Continued)*

Subject Property

This first section of the standard form appraisal report sets up the appraisal problem. Most of this information is relatively straight-forward. Yet, it still pays to verify accuracy. Besides inspecting the physical property (site, buildings, improvements, onsite amenities), be sure you also examine the relevant property rights.

To value real estate, confirm that the title to the appraised property can be conveyed free of judgment liens, tax liens, clouds, or encumbrances (such as mortgages or adverse easements). If not "free and clear," you will need to adjust your offering price accordingly. You do not just buy land and buildings. You buy the legal rights that govern use, occupancy, transfer, redevelopment, and so on. Most professionally prepared appraisals *assume* that property rights present no significant issues. Do not rely on such assumptions. Consult a title company or an attorney who specializes in property law.

When you buy a rental property with existing tenants, examine the leases. Until those leases expire, you must operate your property under the terms and rent levels of those previously signed leases. Watch out for options—especially in commercial leases. Often a commercial tenant might sign a five-year lease, for example, but also obtain an option to renew for as many as four new five-year periods.

Remember, too, the divisible bundle of freehold property rights may include (or exclude) air rights, oil and gas, coal, minerals, timber, water, grazing, development, various subsidiary estates, and many other technical rights issues. Some of these may diminish the value of the property—if already conveyed to someone else. Or in some instances, divisible rights can present an entrepreneurial opportunity through your sale or purchase of such rights—as Donald Trump proved when he bought air rights from nearby property owners to increase the legally permitted height of Trump World Tower from 40 to 80 stories.

If you buy internationally, consult local, competent, and experienced legal counsel. Often countries set up different types of rights for nationals, expat residents, retirees, nonresident owners, and other potential buyer categories. In addition, some countries permit only that country's nationals to own land. Other buyers obtain ownership of their buildings subject to a leasehold on the site itself. Likewise, you may face much more uncertain title and usage claims than you would in the U.S., U.K., and other more mature property rights countries. (Of course, title and usage issues can arise in all countries. But in some countries, your rights may not gain the security of 200-plus years of court enforcement. Factor this risk into your decision to buy and the price you offer.)

Many U.K. buyers who had purchased second homes in Spain have recently learned that their properties will be taken from them by the government without compensation. Many foreign homebuyers in the popular vacation island of Northern Cypress run the risk that a Greece-Turkey settlement of decades old grievances could jeopardize the land titles of thousands of recent buyers. Many foreign property buyers in Dubai were promised three-year residency visas. Then the government revoked that buyer incentive retroactively. (A new shorter six-month UAE residence visa has now been proposed.) For years, Thailand winked at straw man purchases of Thai properties on behalf of foreigners. Then the Thai government announced such practices were illegal and rights claims may not be honored. (I will not even go into the property rights issues now arising in Zimbabwe or Venezuela. Suffice it to say, many foreign owners have not fared well.)

When you contract to buy real estate, you are really contracting for both the physical property as well as the bundle of rights that will permit you to enjoy and use the property as you intend. Whether buying in your home country or internationally, never assume that those rights attach to the property automatically or securely. Know and adhere to local law—and understand the risk that the law could change to your detriment.

Contract of Sale

Most lenders lend against the contract price *or* the market value of a property—whichever is *less*. Say you negotiate a price of $160,000 for a property that's valued at $200,000. You figure that with an 80 percent loan-to-value (LTV) ratio (80% × $200,000), the bank will loan the full purchase price of $160,000. Nice idea, but unfortunately most banks would loan you only $128,000 (80% × $160,000).

Never Lie to a Lender (False Contracts, Liars' Loans)

To gain a larger loan, some dishonest buyers would scheme to write a side deal with the sellers and draft a second contract that lists a $200,000 purchase price. Then they show that false contract to the bank. Such a deception exposes you to a charge of bank fraud. *Do not do it.*

Never lie to a lender about your true contract price or any other fact material to a loan application or loan agreement. As current criminal investigations move forward, many property appraisers, loan reps, and borrowers who falsely filled out mortgage paperwork will find themselves in jail. Those once-popular "liars' loans" have contributed greatly to recent loan losses and bank failures.

Seller Concessions

Say you agree to pay sellers an above-market price. In exchange, sellers offer to pay your down payment, mortgage fees, or closing costs. Or maybe the sellers include an unusually large amount of furniture, household furnishings, and appliances with the sale. In such instances where sellers provide valuable concessions to their buyers, the bank wants to know the property's market value, not merely the contract price. To calculate the maximum amount of loan, the bank applies its loan-to-value (LTV) ratio to the appraised value of the property—not the higher purchase price.

Neighborhood

In the USA, federal law does not permit appraisers to discuss the existing or evolving racial composition of a neighborhood. No professionally prepared appraisal report will mention racial neighborhood demographics. In other nations without such restrictions, appraisers may choose to include data on population ethnicity, religion, or nationality—if they believe such demographics influence the property values within a neighborhood—as they most certainly do in some countries. Through my international travels, I have witnessed such demographic value discrepancies firsthand.

Neighborhood Supply, Demand, and Price Ranges

Appraisal reports do briefly refer to the types and uses of properties in a subject neighborhood, the prevailing price ranges, and whether the number of "for sale" and "for rent" properties are stable, increasing, or decreasing.

As an investor, pay attention to these trends. Whereas market value appraisals focus on the present (or actually, the recent past), you must envision the future.

Economic Base and Neighborhood Effects

Because market value appraisals emphasize the present, they slight neighborhood trends and omit a thorough review of an area's economic base, employment, and future growth or decline. As a smart investor, research these topics more diligently. (See Chapter 6.)

Just as important, watch how changes in jobs, roads, rail lines, and growth patterns within a metro area affect specific neighborhoods. Even within larger declining areas, some neighborhoods might prosper. And even in high-growth cities and regions, some neighborhoods might deteriorate. Market value appraisals rarely

262

point to future changes that entrepreneurs recognize as signals of loss or gain.

SITE

In some cities, lot value can total 30 to 60 percent (sometimes more) of a property's market value. Weigh carefully this part of an appraisal. First, walk the site boundaries as shown on a credible survey. Measure the site dimensions. Learn the site dimensions both visually and by size.

Zoning and Land-Use Laws

As Chapter 8 discusses, zoning, building codes, local ordinances, and land-use laws regulate properties in dozens of ways. Knowing the ins and outs of these rules opens the door to creative opportunities. Or they may shut out your otherwise brilliantly conceived entrepreneurial plans. Learn these laws in detail, not just by broad classification (e.g., residential, commercial, industrial, agricultural). Each zoning district includes multiple sub-districts within the broad classification scheme. And some districts permit mixed uses such as retail, residential, and office all within the same building—as is the case with Trump Tower.

A market value appraisal may or may not accurately note whether a property adequately conforms to applicable zoning and building regulations. But few appraisals would spell out how you could take advantage of such laws (including the possibility of rezoning) to add value to the property.

Utilities

Contrary to what city slickers might believe, not all sites are serviced by all utilities. I know an experienced investor who bought a house without realizing that it lacked a sewer connection and thus used a septic tank for waste disposal. Other things equal, no sewer connection reduces a property's value.

Verify the gas, water, sewer, cable, security (e.g., alarm services), and Internet connections to the property. Although appraisals seldom mention utility costs per se, these expenses can add or subtract from a property's value. Anticipate how much these costs will run. Consult the relevant service providers for past usage rates and billing amounts.

IMPROVEMENTS

In real estate lingo, improvements include not only building(s) but also sidewalks, landscaping, pools, tennis courts, fencing, basements, storage sheds, fireplaces, appliances, decks, patios, porches, driveways, garages, and so on. To value a property, itemize and assess the quality of all site and building improvements.

Inspect square footage, room counts, closets, floor plan, energy efficiency, insulation, windows (energy, design, safety, and usability), architectural design, livability, age, and condition. Each of these details can prove important to a property's value and your efforts to create MVP for your tenants or buyers. These features and details provide input data for three valuation techniques.

RESIDENTIAL VALUATION TECHNIQUES

To estimate market value, appraise the property from three perspectives:

1. *The Comparables Sales Approach* compares the features and recent selling prices of similar properties to the subject property (see Figure 15.2).

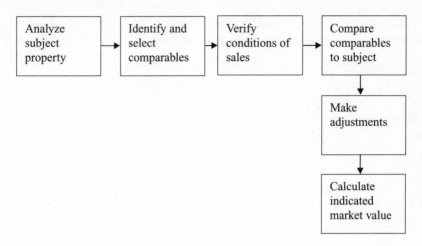

Figure 15.2 Comparable Sales Approach.

2. *The Cost Approach* calculates the cost you would have to pay to reconstruct the property (plus land value) today and then subtracts an amount for depreciation (see Figure 15.3).
3. *The Capitalized Income Approach* capitalizes the net rental income of a property and converts that income into a market value estimate (see Figure 15.4).

In addition, another income approach called the gross rent multiplier calculates value as a multiple of potential rent collections.

After you figure the indicated market values with each of these three approaches, you next set a market value range for the property and decide your best estimate of market value (see Figure 15.5). Generally, you emphasize the comp sales approach for houses, townhouses, co-ops, and condominiums, and the income approach for multiunit residential properties as well as office buildings and

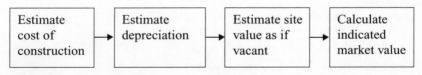

Figure 15.3 Cost Approach.

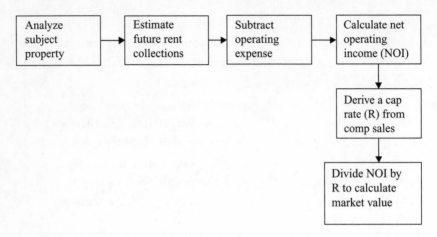

Figure 15.4 Capitalized Income Approach.

shopping centers. In practice, appraisers rely on the cost approach primarily to cross-check the comp sales and income approaches.

Special Note: As mentioned in an earlier chapter, the cost approach also helps you determine future price increases or decreases.

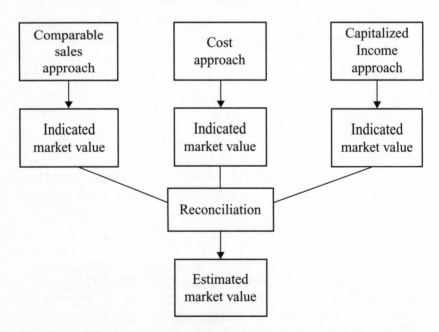

Figure 15.5 Three Approaches to Market Value.

When properties sell for prices that substantially exceed their replacement costs, builders rush to construct new properties. This stampede to earn huge profit margins soon brings forth losses as newly built *Supply* temporarily outpaces *Demand*. To work off excess inventories of unsold (or unrented) properties, builders slash prices and rents and offer generous buyer (renter) incentives and concessions (e.g., upgrades, below-market financing, two months of free rent, $99 move-in specials). Too many houses and condos for sale (from overbuilding and the resulting increase in foreclosures) have pushed down property prices in cities such as Miami, Las Vegas, and Phoenix.

When properties sell for substantially less than their cost of construction (as occurs during recession or the latter stages of oversupply when builders slash prices to liquidate their inventories), builders pull back from the market. Eventually, growth areas generate a larger population, more jobs, and higher incomes. Excess "for sale" and "for rent" properties are absorbed. New buyers and renters compete for a diminishing number of unsold or vacant units. They bid rents and property prices up. Entrepreneurial investors monitor replacement costs, builder profits, builder inventories of unsold (unrented) properties, and other trends in property pricing and supply.

The Comparable Sales Approach

Refer now to page 2 of Figure 15.1, where you can see the specific information that appraisers incorporate into their comparable sale value estimates.

The comp sales method works best when you closely inspect and itemize the features of the subject property and the comparable properties. That's why I encourage you to look at every property that comes up for sale in the area where you would like to buy. Record their features in detail. Take photographs. Write out comments and notes. Over time, as these properties sell, you develop a thorough knowledge of property prices and features.

When you monitor property sales, you discover what features create market appeal, quick sales, and price premiums. With such market savvy, you can recognize when properties that hit the market are priced less than they are worth. If you lack ready knowledge, bargain-priced properties will sell to someone who is better prepared to act now—while you are still trying to figure things out.

Factual market knowledge also supports your offers and purchase (or sales) negotiations (selected and interpreted in your favor, of course). When you persuade with facts, you win more negotiations. "That's my offer. Take it or leave it," rarely gains a positive response from sellers.

The blanks provided in the comp sale section of the appraisal form (Figure 15.1) do not provide much room for explanation or differentiation. That's why professional appraisers often err in judgment. They paint their pictures of value with a broad brush. They slop over details that can provide benefits (or perhaps present problems).

Even more troubling, appraisers often fail to inspect the interiors of the comp properties they select. An appraiser typically obtains this information secondhand from the sales agents who were involved in the previous sales transactions. Or (and I have seen these shortcomings in many appraisal reports), appraisers make stuff up or ignore differences between a subject property and its comp because the appraisers do not recognize that such differences exist.

For these and other reasons, I assure you that neither I nor Donald Trump rely on appraisers or real estate agents to tell us what a property is worth. We listen, we review, we critique, and then we decide for ourselves. You should too.

Address of Comps and Proximity to Subject

Other things equal, the closer your comp properties sit to your subject property, the better. (In fact, comp properties should match a subject property in every way possible.) In contrast to this ideal, appraisers often choose comps that are located outside the neighborhood of the subject property.

Check to see whether a comp property is located in a different zone of desirability—such as on the wrong side of a border street; in a different school district; or farther from the bus line, subway, MTR, or freeway interchange. Verify accuracy. Drive by the comps that an appraiser includes within an appraisal report. Are the neighborhoods and locations truly comparable? What differences that make a difference can you identify?

Sales Price and Price per Square Foot

Investors and mortgage lenders prefer to see the value of a subject property come in at least 10 to 20 percent below the top end of the neighborhood price range. Properties priced at or below the prevailing price range of a neighborhood tend to show better marketability.

If you can't find comps that suitably match the subject property, select several comps that stand either superior or inferior to the subject. Bracket the value of the subject between the inferior and superior. When all comps run superior (or inferior) to the subject, it is more difficult to answer "how much less" or "how much more" the subject property is worth.

For example, say, superior properties have recently sold at around $450,000 to $500,000 and inferior properties have sold for $400,000 to $420,000. By bracketing the subject property, you know that its market value probably lies between $425,000 and $440,000. You've narrowed your range of value.

Price per square foot (psf) provides another useful indicator of market value. To calculate psf, divide sales price (less concessions, if any; see the following equation) of a property by the square footage of its gross living area. (Do not count garages, basements, attics, storage sheds, and so on.) Assume that a property sold at a price of $380,000 and includes 1,843 square feet of living space:

$$\text{psf} = \frac{\$380,000}{1,843} = \$206$$

Price per square foot gives you a starting figure, but never give that value much weight until you compare features among comparable properties.

Data Sources and Verification

On occasion, appraisers cite "personal inspection" as a data source for comps. More often, appraisers cite public records, multiple listing service, and real estate agents. Although no appraiser (or inspector) could work without relying on secondhand data, verify sources. Secondhand data multiply possibilities of error.

Value Adjustments

Following through Figure 15.1, you see a list of property features. No subject property can precisely match the comp properties on every feature. So, market value estimates require you to "adjust" the price of the comps according to whether their features (*U*tility) differ favorably or unfavorably from the subject property.

The adjustment process answers this question: At what price *would the comp property have sold* if its features had matched exactly the subject property's features? To figure the answer to this question, compare the subject property—feature by feature—to each comp. If the feature matches, you need not adjust the price of the comp.

If the comp feature proves superior to the subject, then to make it equivalent, the estimated value of its favorable feature is *subtracted* from the comp's selling price. If the comp proves inferior to a subject on a specific feature, the estimated value of that disadvantage is *added* to its sales price. In this way, the adjusted sales price for each comparable fairly indicates the market value of the subject property.

Table 15.1 illustrates this adjustment process through a simple example.

In the Comp 1 sale, the sellers carried back a 90 percent loan-to-value ratio (LTV) mortgage (10 percent down) on the property at an interest rate of 6.5 percent. At the time, investor financing usually required a 75 percent LTV (25 percent down) and a 7.5 percent interest rate on this type of property. Without this favorable owner financing, Comp 1 would probably have sold for $11,250 less than its actual sales price of $225,120. Because the definition of market value requires financing on terms typically available in the market, you

Table 15.1   Adjustment Process (Selected Features)

	Comp 1	Comp 2	Comp 3
Sales price	$225,120	$213,440	$211,060
Features			
Sales concessions	Similar	−7,500	Similar
Financing concessions	−11,250	Similar	Similar
Date of sale	Similar	+7,500	Similar
Location	Similar	Similar	−15,000
Floor plan (design)	Similar	+3,750	Similar
Garage	+8,250	Similar	+12,750
Pool, patio, deck	−6,750	−9,750	Similar
Adjusted sales price of comparables	$215,370	$207,440	$208,810

Property	Sales Price	Monthly Rent	GRM
214 Jackson	$220,000	÷ $1,250	= 176
312 Lincoln	247,000	÷ 1,350	= 183
107 Adams	210,000	÷ 1,175	= 179

Subject House (Estimated Value Range)

GRM		Monthly Rent	Value
176		× $1,225	= $215,600
183		× 1,225	= 224,175
179		× 1,225	= 219,275

must subtract the premium created by this owner will carry (OWC) financing from Comp 1's sales price. Here are the explanations for several other adjustments:

Comp 1 Garage at (+) $8,250: The subject property includes an oversized double-car garage, but Comp 1 only has a single-car garage. With a garage like the subject's, Comp 1 would have brought an $8,250 higher sales price.

Comp 1 Pool, Patio, and Deck at (−) $6,750: Comp 1 is superior to the subject property on this feature because the subject lacks a deck and tile patio. Without this benefit, Comp 1 would have sold for $6,750 less.

Comp 2 Date of Sale: Market value presumes current sales comparison data. Because Comp 2 sold six months earlier in a rising market, it would likely sell at a price $7,500 higher today.

Comp 2 Sales Concession at (−) $7,500: The $213,440 sales price in this transaction included the seller's custom-made drapes, a washer and dryer, and a storage shed. Because these items aren't customary in this market, you must adjust the sales price downward to equalize this feature with the subject property, the sale of which will not include these items.

Comp 2 Floor Plan (Design) at (+) $3,750: Unlike the subject property, this house lacked convenient access from the garage to the kitchen. The garage was built under the house, and residents had to carry groceries up an outside stairway to enter the kitchen. With more conventional access, the selling price of Comp 2 would probably have increased by $3,750.

Comp 3 Location at (−) $15,000: This house was located on a cul-de-sac and its backyard bordered an environmentally protected wooded area. The subject property sits on a typical subdivision street, and its rear yard looks toward a neighboring house. Because of its relatively inferior backyard view, the subject property is expected to sell for $15,000 less than Comp 3.

After adjusting for inferior and superior features (or concessions), add up each column of numbers. The resulting figure tells you the sales price each comp would have commanded if it simply cloned the subject property. I now hear you ask, "How do I come up with the specific dollar amounts for each of the adjustments?" To that question, there's no easy answer. It comes from the knowledge you will gain by monitoring many sales transactions over months or even years. You also draw on the knowledge of professionally competent real estate agents and appraisers.

Still, test the opinions of the pros against your own judgments. Ask questions. Explore their reasoning. Verify their facts. Identify features and benefits (**Utility**) that could make a difference. Remember, you inspect and evaluate not just to estimate market value. Envision how you can add value to the property.

Transfer (Sales) History

Regulators of financial institutions now require appraisers to investigate the frequency of past sales transactions for both the subject property and its comps. Properties that get flipped at higher and higher prices with a short number of years (or months) often signal a property market that's heading for a fall. When regulators see such signals, they are supposed to urge mortgage lenders to tighten their credit standards and appraise properties and LTV ratios more cautiously. In the speculative markets of the early- to mid-2000s, regulators failed to perform their jobs.

You also should show restraint. Or, if you wish to play the flipping game, sharpen your skills of market timing. During booms, such skills become ever more critical to your solvency and success. (In this sense, I refer primarily to speculative flippers, not investors who buy properties for renovation and resale—though even here, timing can matter greatly, especially for renovators who become overextended financially. If flipping attracts you, maintain strong cash reserves as well as Plans B, C, and D. In fact, that advice applies to all investors who want to reduce their risks and enlarge their opportunities.)

Indicated Value by Sales Comparison Approach

After you compare sales concessions, dates of sale, features, benefits, and transfer history, make an *informed judgment* about the market value of the subject property. Although many people claim to know property values, only a thorough methodology with accurate data can give you the confidence to quickly make offers (when you need to).

The Cost Approach

Although many residential market value appraisals do not require the cost (or income) approaches, as an investor, stay informed about a property's cost of reconstruction.

Calculate the Cost to Build New

To see the methodology of the cost approach, refer to the lower half of page 257, Figure 15.1. First, calculate how much it would cost to construct the subject property using the dollars-per-square-foot construction costs that would apply for the type of property you're valuing.

Replacement cost considers both the size and quality of the building. Account for the cost of upgrades and extras (e.g., crystal chandelier, high-grade wall-to-wall carpeting, Subzero appliances or Kohler plumbing fixtures, sauna, or hot tub as well as a swimming pool, garage, carport, patios, porches). Then add these extras to the basic psf construction costs.

Subtract Depreciation

After you calculate the cost to reconstruct a property, you estimate three types of depreciation: (1) physical, (2) functional, and (3) economic (external). An older building is generally worth less than a similarly built new building because of physical depreciation (wear and tear). Properties deteriorate from age, weather, use, and abuse. Frayed carpets, faded paint, cracked plaster, rusty plumbing, and leaky roofs bring down a building's value. How much? Estimate a percentage for wear and tear relative to new. Usually, "well maintained" might warrant a 10 to 20 percent figure. For really "run down," depreciation could total 50 to 70 percent of new construction costs. Instead of applying a percentage depreciation figure, you could also itemize the costs of the repairs and renovations that would put the property in top condition.

Next, estimate *functional* depreciation. Unlike wear and tear that naturally occurs through use and abuse, functional depreciation refers to a loss of value because of out-of-favor dark-wood paneling, an ill-designed floor plan, unpopular room count or room sizes, low-amperage electrical system, unpopular color schemes, or unappealing architectural design. A property might suffer little wear and tear (physical depreciation), yet still fall victim to functional depreciation because the features of the property no longer please potential buyers (or renters).

> **The Bonwit Teller building—a faux Art Deco box—had outlasted its usefulness. It was functionally obsolete. The site was ready for a higher and more profitable use.**

External (locational) depreciation occurs when a property no longer reflects the highest and best use for a site. Say you find a well-kept house located in an area that's now predominantly stores and offices. Zoning of the site has changed from residential to commercial. More than likely, the house would add little or nothing to the site's value. When someone buys the property, they will tear down the house (or possibly convert) to create a retail store or office building. This same principle applies when neighborhoods move upscale and well-kept, three-bedroom, two-bath houses of 1,600 square feet are torn down and replaced with 4,000-square-foot $1.5 million houses.

Economically obsolete properties are called "teardowns." Teardowns can include buildings that boast excellent repair as well as those junkers that could collapse at any time. If you buy a teardown, pay only for the lot value less the cost of demolition and removal of the building.

Site Value

To estimate lot value, find similar (vacant) lots that have recently sold or lots that have sold with teardowns on them. To value similar sites, compare features such as size, frontage, views, topography, zoning and building regulations, subdivision rules, and other characteristics that buyers seek.

Estimate Market Value (Cost Approach)

As you can see on the appraisal form (Figure 15.1), after completing these three steps—(1) calculate a property's replacement construction cost as if newly built, (2) subtract each type of depreciation, and

(3) add in site value—you have estimated market value. Because no one can precisely measure construction costs, accrued depreciation, and site value, the cost approach rarely stands alone. It mainly cross-checks the comparable sales approach and the income approach.

The Income Approach

Just below the section "Cost Approach to Value" (Figure 15.1), notice an entry labeled "Income Approach to Value." That income approach refers to an appraisal technique called the *gross rent multiplier* (GRM).

To use GRM to calculate market value, research the monthly rents and sales prices of similar houses or apartment buildings. Assume these sales of rental houses: (1) 214 Jackson was rented at $1,250 a month and sold for $220,000, (2) 312 Lincoln was rented at $1,350 a month and sold for $247,000, and (3) 107 Adams was rented at $1,175 a month and sold for $210,000. With this information, you can calculate a range of GRMs for this neighborhood:

$$\text{GRM} = \frac{\text{Sales price}}{\text{Monthly rent}}$$

If a house (or condonminium) could rent for $1,225 a month, figure the market GRM from your comps as follows:

Subject House (Estimated Value Range)

GRM	Monthly Rent	Value
176	× $1,225	= $215,600
183	× 1,225	= 224,175
179	× 1,225	= 219,275

The market value would range from $215,600 to $224,175.

Because the GRM method does not directly adjust for sales or financing concessions, features, location, condition, or operating expenses, this technique "roughly" estimates market value. Nevertheless, many investors use it as a quick indicator. As with price-per-square-foot, GRM works best when you find nearly identical rental properties in the same neighborhood.

The GRMs shown in these examples *do not necessarily* correspond to the GRMs in your city. *Even within the same city*, different neighborhoods show differences in their GRMs. In the San Diego area, GRMs for single-family homes in La Jolla could range upward of 400; in nearby Clairemont, you may find GRMs in the 250 to 300 range; and in National City, GRMs may drop below 200. Within the same neighborhood, GRMs for single-family houses often run higher than those of condominiums.

During the early- to mid-2000s boom, GRMs climbed upward. During down cycles, GRMs typically fall as property prices return to levels more closely aligned with the rental amounts that you can collect. As with all appraisal methods, use timely, locally relevant data before you apply GRMs.

> **You can get killed paying top dollar for a superb location. Or by buying a poor location, even at a low price. You've got to know the value of the deal. Never pay more than the deal is worth.**

Reconciliation of Value Estimates

Once you complete the three approaches to estimating market value, interpret the results. For single-family houses, the comp sales approach provides the best guide to market value. The cost method and GRM provide crosschecks. For apartment buildings, the appraisal principles remain steadfast but the techniques used for the comparable sales and income approaches differ somewhat from houses and condominiums.

VALUING INCOME PROPERTIES

To illustrate how to value an income property, I will use a simple example: the 20-year-old, Royal Terrace apartment building. Royal

Terrace consists of 38 efficiency apartments that each measures 550 square feet in size. This property is located in Middleton, Iowa, a low-cost midwestern American city that offers economic stability and a typical small-town quality of life, but little growth in jobs, incomes, or population.

After inspecting the physical features, location, and services of Royal Terrace, we found (quite fortunately) two similar properties in the same neighborhood that had sold within the past six months. Data on these comparables are as follows.

2735 Maple (Comparable No. 1)

This building is 25 years old and contains 33 efficiency apartments. It shows more wear and tear than the subject, but otherwise it's similar in construction, quality, style, and condition. One major unfavorable feature (because of noise from band practice and traffic): Comp 1 is located directly across from a new high school. Its units are presently rented at $285 per month, and each unit contains 525 square feet. Information obtained from the property manager shows that vacancy in the building has been stable at about 4 percent and that operating expenses are 52 percent of gross potential income. (Of course, the smart investor never trusts just one source of information and will verify and crosscheck multiple data points while also exercising keen powers of observation.) Public records and talks with real estate agents reveal that this Comp 1 property sold with a 20 percent down payment and a 25-year, fixed-rate mortgage at 7.0 percent interest. The price was $506,700.

1460 Elm (Comparable No. 2)

Comp 2 is 16 years old and houses 40 efficiency apartments. As positives, Comp 2 shows better construction than the subject property, and it is located two blocks from a neighborhood park with tennis courts, pool, and a nine-hole golf course. The units are presently

Table 15.2   Royal Terrace Owner-Prepared Income Statement

Actual rents collected		$123,120
Expenses		
Property insurance (three-year policy)	$19,200	
Property taxes (pd. 2/8/86 for year 1985)	3,682	
Caretaker salary	12,000	
Gas and electric	16,590	
Water and sewage	3,200	
Trash collection	1,847	
Repairs and maintenance	4,383	
Mortgage interest	18,390	
Depreciation	15,444	94,736
Net income		$28,384

rented at $315 per month, and like the subject, each contains 550 square feet. Vacancies average 4 percent, and operating expenses total 49 percent of grow potential income. Public records show that the property was financed with an 80 percent LTV ratio for 30 years at 6.75 percent interest. The selling price was $772,400.

To estimate replacement cost for the subject property, we spoke with several building contractors and consulted the *Marshall and Swift Valuation Service*. From this research, we figure that to construct a building like the subject would cost about $72 per square foot.

From the Royal Terrace owner's bookkeeper, you obtained income and expense data (see Table 15.2) for the calendar year ended this past December 31.

GRM

The GRM technique is used for income properties in much the same way as it is for rental houses and condominium units. From market comparables, you calculate a gross income multiplier. Then you multiply that figure by the subject property's gross potential income. However, for rental houses and condominiums, it's customary to calculate the multiplier on the basis of gross monthly rentals. For apartment buildings, investors calculate the GRM on an annual basis. Consider that the GRMs for our two comparables are 4.49 (506,700/112,860) and 5.10 (772.400/151,200). If, say, we decide on a 4.75 multiplier for the subject property, Royal Terrace, its indicated market value using the GRM technique would equal $638,970:

$$4.75 \times \$134,520 = \$638,970$$

The GRM is used extensively in some areas and for certain types of apartment buildings. But investors do not give it as much importance as capitalized net operating income (NOI). Only when the selected comparables are very much alike does the GRM provide a somewhat useful estimate of market value. Investors seldom value office buildings or shopping centers via the GRM because such properties differ widely in lease terms as well as property features. The GRM ignores too many important details. Still, the GRM adds another benchmark of value that increases your level of confidence through use of multiple valuation metrics.

Income Capitalization

To estimate market value with the income capitalization method, use the following formula:

$$V = \frac{NOI}{R}$$

Where V represents market value, NOI represents the net operating income of the property, and R represents the overall rate of return on capital (i.e., the capitalization rate, or, for short, the cap rate) that buyers of similar income properties typically require. (Remember, here we are estimating *market value*, not what the property may be worth when you execute your entrepreneurial strategy.)

If Royal Terrace is expected to earn an NOI of $63,174 per year and the market cap rate is 0.096, you calculate its market value as follows:

$$V = \frac{63,174}{0.096}$$
$$= \$658,062$$

This simple division doesn't yet tell us how to calculate the inputs of NOI and R.

Net Operating Income

To calculate NOI, total up the annual gross potential rental income expected from a property and subtract from that amount vacancy and collection losses, operating expenses, replacement reserves, property taxes, and property and liability insurance.

Many small investors do not know how to construct an NOI statement for purposes of income capitalization.

Moreover, some sellers purposely overstate rental income and understate vacancies and operating expenses. By overreporting income and underreporting expenses, such sellers represent that their properties yield more NOI—and thus are worth more—than is really justified by the *facts*.

So, whether you buy from amateurs or pros, caveat emptor applies. Never accept the numbers sellers (or their agents) give you. Instead, reconstruct the NOI figures from your own research and market knowledge.

Contrast the owner's income statement and the reconstructed version for Royal Terrace (Tables 15.2 and 15.3). The reconstructed version more accurately reflect the amount of NOI that the property can be expected to earn under generically competent, management during the coming year:

- *Reconstruct Income:* To reconstruct effective gross income, use market rental and vacancy rates—not those actually experienced by the subject property. What rent and vacancy levels are reasonable? Research the rent levels of the

Table 15.3   Your Reconstructed Royal Terrace Income Statement

Gross potential income (38× 12× $295)	$134,520
Vacancy and collection @ 4%	5,381
Effective gross income (123,120)	$129,139
Expenses*	
Property management (0)	5,165
Promotion and advertising (0)	600
Property insurance (19,200)	6,400
Property taxes (3,682)	6,500
Caretaker salary (12,000)	9,000
Gas and electric (16,590)	18,900
Water and sewage (3,200)	3,800
Trash collection (1,847)	2,100
Repairs, maintenance, and reserves (4,383)	11,500
Miscellaneous	2,000
Total expenses	$65,965
Net operating income	$63,174

*Owner's reported income and expense amounts are shown in parenthesis. For purposes of market value appraisals, depreciation and mortgage interest are not included in calculating net operating income.

selected comparable properties as well as the rents achieved by other apartment buildings in that neighborhood (or like neighborhoods). Rely on a current market investigation. With income recalculated, next enter reasonable amounts for the operating expenses.

- *Management and Promotion:* The owner's statement omits management and promotion expenses. The owner had self-managed the building, and because of his below-market rental rates, he compiled a waiting list of potential tenants just through word of mouth. A new owner, though, would expect to incur both management and promotional expenses.

- *Insurance and Property Taxes:* The property insurance amount in the owner's statement errs because it wasn't prorated over the full three years of coverage. The annual amount should have been one-third of $19,200, or $6,400. Also adjust the expense amounts reported by the owner's accountant for property taxes because the increase in property taxes was figured to reflect the reassessed value that the tax appraiser will use after sale. The tax assessor's office gets behind in its appraisal of properties. Therefore, many properties remain undervalued on the tax rolls. But when a sale is recorded, the tax assessor revises the property's value per current market prices. Plus, because (in this example) property tax rates have been increased by the county council. Next year's taxes will go up even without an updated tax appraisal of the property. (In down cycles, you may be able to persuade the tax appraiser to lower the assessed value of a property.)

- *Utilities, Caretakers, and Others:* Check the utility companies for property usage rates. On the basis of these reported rates, you can figure the likely utility costs for the coming year. The caretaker's salary was reduced in the reconstructed statement because some of these duties will be performed by the new property management firm. Through your due diligence, you found that the current owner performed some repair and maintenance chores. Because you plan to purchase Royal Terrace as an investment—and not as a source of self-employment—you should increase this expense amount accordingly.

- *Repairs, Maintenance, and Reserves for Replacement:* Property sellers routinely understate the costs necessary to maintain their properties and replace components (carpets, roof, appliances, and so on) as they wear out. So, increase that amount to represent a more realistic expense figure.

- *Miscellaneous Items:* As a final item, notice that $2,000 was added for miscellaneous expenses. Such items include costs such as legal and accounting fees, cleaning supplies, and re-decorating materials (paint, wallpaper), but you should exclude mortgage interest and depreciation expenses that are reported on the owner's income statement. Although interest and depreciation will certainly cost you, they are not counted as *operating* expenses for purposes of calculating NOI.

- *NOI:* After you reconstruct all income and expense items, the coming year's NOI for Royal Terrace equals $63,174.

Table 15.4   Deriving a Market-Based Cap Rate

Comparables	NOI ($)	Sales Price ($)	Rate ($)
2735 Maple	49,658	506,700	0.098
1460 Elm	71,064	772,400	0.092
Subject	63,174	?	?

Deriving Capitalization Rates

To come up with a reasonable market capitalization rate for Royal Terrace, look at the cap rates applied by the investors who bought 2735 Maple and 1460 Elm (Table 15.4). For 2735 Maple, a property somewhat inferior to the subject (it's five years older, shows more wear, and is located across from Hot Rod High), we can see that the buyer applied a capitalization rate of 9.80 percent. For the superior 1460 Elm (it's located in a quieter, beautifully treed area; brick construction; and was financed at a below-market rate of 6.75 percent); its buyer applied a capitalization rate of 9.20 percent.

In reasoning out the cap rate for the subject property, you figure that it will fall between 0.092 and 0.098. All other things equal, investors typically prefer brick properties to frame. Brick buildings require less maintenance. The income streams of such properties will probably last longer. Based on these criteria, we place the Royal Terrace between the two comparables, so will its capitalization rate.

Next judge whether the subject property lies closest in character to 2735 Maple or 1460 Elm. After you weigh similarities and differences, you estimate a number: How about 0.096?

Like other decisions in appraisal and investing, a cap rate calculation requires facts *and* judgment. No two properties are identical; no two buyers are exactly alike; no one has full market or property information. Here you reasoned that Royal Terrace was most similar to 2735 Maple. Plus, the subject apartments probably would be financed at 7.0 percent, rather than at the 6.75 percent rate that applied to 1460 Elm. So, you chose a market-based capitalization rate of 0.096.

Direct Capitalization Approach

To calculate market value, divide $63,174 (NOI) by 0.096, which equals $658,062:

$$V = \frac{63,174}{0.096}$$
$$= \$658,062$$

Comparable Sales Approach

In addition to the capitalized income method, you will use comp sale figures to verify the reasonableness of your income valuation. Typically, you set up price-per-unit and price-per-square-foot figures as shown in Table 15.5.

From the market data in Table 15.5, you estimate the market value of Royal Terrace via comp sales as follows:

$$38 \text{ units} \times \$16,800 \text{ ppu} = \$638,400$$
$$20,900 \text{ sq.ft.} \times \$31.50 \text{ price psf} = \$658,350$$

These comp sale value estimates support the cap rate conclusion. As with all appraisals, you never obtain a precise answer. Facts,

Table 15.5   Per Unit Comparisons

Features	2735 Maple	1460 Elm	Royal Terrace
Physical conditions	Slightly inferior	Somewhat better	Average
Age	25 years	16 years	20 years
Location	More traffic noise Inferior	Park nearby Superior	Average
Financing	80% LTV 7.0% 25 years	80% LTV 6.75% 30 years	
Sales price	$506,700	$772,400	?
No. of suites	33 efficiencies	40 efficiencies	38 efficiencies
No. of rooms	33	40	38
No. of sq. ft.	17,325 sq. ft.	22,000 sq. ft.	20,900 sq. ft.
Price per unit	$15,354	$19,310	$16,800*
Price per sq. ft.	$29.25	$35.10	$31.50*

*We estimated these per unit amounts after comparing the subject property comparables.

interpretations, judgments, and reasoning differ among investors. So, you always work within a range of values that you judge reasonable.

The Cost Approach

In Table 15.6, the cost approach shows that the property's market value equals $822,525.

The cost approach indicates a market that exceeds those estimates using the comp sale and income approaches. Why? Because Middleton, Iowa, lacks a dynamic local economy. Building construction costs (which to a large degree are set by the national and international prices of materials) have increased faster than properties in Middleton have appreciated.

As a result, the investor who buys Royal Terrace will not likely face much competition from newly constructed apartments or houses. To earn a profit, newly built properties must charge much higher rents (or sales prices). Otherwise, the builder's revenues won't cover the costs he pays to construct the units.

Consequently, you face less risk from new competitors. You might also enjoy good opportunities to upgrade and create value for the property. Since investors do not expect properties in Middleton to appreciate much, they emphasize cash flows more than price gains. Cash flows—with a stable economic base—yield a more dependable, less risky source of return.

Table 15.6   The Cost Approach: Royal Terrace

Estimated reproduction costs	$1,504,800
(20,900 sq. ft. × $72)	
Depreciation	
Physical	$610,275
Functional	$172,000
Locational	$0
Depreciated value of improvements	$722,525
Land value	$100,000
Indicated market value	$822,525

All in all, at a price of $650,000 or less, Royal Terrace seems like an excellent investment. But before deciding whether to place an offer, you want to run the numbers to calculate cash on cash return on investment (ROI) and total return over time—which will include equity buildup through amortization (paying off the mortgage financing) and any capital gains. But first let's look at some tips on how to obtain the financing you might need.

How to Obtain Financing

Because the power of (sensible) leverage multiplies your returns, you will typically borrow anywhere from 75 percent to 90 percent (sometimes even more) of the purchase price of the property you are buying. The exact LTV, terms, conditions, costs, and underwriting standards that lenders will apply to you will depend on where you are in the credit cycle (easy money, normal times, tight money), the property, and your financial profile. Overall, you should persuade the lender that you and your property present little or no risk of default. You want to build up the lender's confidence that you will repay the loan on time, every time.

How do you accomplish this? Focus on these five criteria:

1. *Credit Record and Credit Score:* The famous banker, J.P. Morgan once told Congress that he did not consider collateral as the most important part of the lending decision. "I would not lend money to a man I did not trust—no matter how much collateral he provided...." Throughout the early to mid-2000s (when liar's loans became the loan of choice), many bankers and loan companies seem to have forgotten J.P.'s stricture—much to their later regret. Your credit record and credit score provide the most important evidence of trust—that you honor your obligations. So, not only guard your business reputation, but also go to myfico.com and follow the advice on how to arrange your finances and borrowing to score as high as possible.

2. *Down Payment:* Equity speaks loudly. Lenders want to believe that you will pay off your loan according to schedule (or before). The larger your down payment, the more confidence the lender has that you will not walk away from the mortgaged property if times get tough for you. Contrary to what many people believe, although a larger down payment increases the collateral value available to the lender, that's not its major role. Rather, it shows that you are committed to the property—you have skin in the game.

3. *Business Plan:* Throughout this book, we have emphasized the importance of entrepreneurial management and marketing. The DUST framework provides you with the system of thought and action that can guide you to positive cash flows and increased equity. Although a market value appraisal informs the lender that the property seems to be worth the amount you are paying, your business plan (much more importantly) shows the lender that you will operate the property profitably.

4. *Debt Coverage Ratio:* When you buy a home, the lender will qualify you according to the amount of your personal income. With investment property, your personal income plays a smaller role. Instead, the lender primarily emphasizes the debt coverage ratio (DCR). To calculate DCR, the lender will divide the expected NOI of the property by the annual amount of payments required by the mortgage loan on the property. For example, if NOI equals $25,000 and your loan will require annual payments (called debt service) of $20,000, the DCR equals 1.25. In general, lenders like to see a DCR of at least 1.15. But for riskier properties or borrowers the required DCR might increase to 1.4 (or higher). A well thought out business plan will help you persuade the lender that your property can meet the lender's specified DCR.

5. *Cash Reserves:* During the easy money period of mortgage lending, lenders relaxed or eliminated their requirements

for cash reserves, which was a bad idea for both lenders and borrowers. Too many borrowers overextended themselves and when unexpected vacancies or repairs hit them, they could not make their mortgage payments. Today (though perhaps not tomorrow) lenders want to see investors maintain a cash cushion—the more the better.

Now the question becomes, what if you are weak on one or more of these criteria? Does that mean that real estate investing is off the table for you? Not at all. You still might use seller financing, a master lease, a lease option, an option to purchase, assignments, or other techniques of creative financing (for more on this topic, see my book, *The 106 Mortgage Secrets that All Borrowers Must Know—But Lenders Don't Tell*, second edition, 2008). Nevertheless, no matter what technique you use to raise the money you need, you still should work as hard as you can to match your financial profile to the five criteria listed.

No right-minded person wants to do business with someone whom they cannot trust to carry out their obligations. The better you develop your financial fitness and entrepreneurial know-how, the faster you will build wealth with less risk.

Cash on Cash Return on Investment

Let's now return to Royal Terrace. You decide to pay $650,000. To complete your purchase, you invest $130,000 cash out-of-pocket (20 percent down payment) and you borrow $520,000 (80 percent LTV) at 7 percent for 30 years. To calculate your first year, before tax cash flow (BTCF) subtract your annual mortgage payments from your first year expected NOI.

$$NOI = \$63,174$$
Annual mortgage payment = $41,905
($520,000 @ 7%, 30 years)
_____

$$BTCF = \$21,269$$

289

Next, divide your out-of-pocket cash investment (down payment) of $130,000 into your BTCF.

$$\text{ROI} = \frac{\text{BTCF}}{\text{Cash investment}}$$
$$= \frac{\$21,269}{\$130,000}$$
$$= 16.3\%$$

Based on these figures (and providing your economic base, market, and property studies support such numbers), your cash on cash ROI looks quite good. Through leverage, you have increased the property's return from 9.6 percent (the cap rate equals the pretax, unleveraged ROI) to 16.3 percent. Today, most income property investors would find a 16.3 percent cash on cash ROI quite attractive.

Total Return on Investment

The above cash on cash return, though, does not include the additional benefits that you will achieve from amortization (paying off loan principal) and property price gains. To calculate your total return on investment (TROI), forecast annual BTCF over an expected period of ownership (say five years) and the cash proceeds that you will gain when you sell the property.

To illustrate, assume that because Middleton lacks dynamic economic growth, Royal Terrace BTCFs increase just 2 percent per year, and similarly, the property's market value goes up just 2 percent a year. After five years, your mortgage balance will have fallen from $530,000 to $488,343.

Refer to Tables 15.7 and 15.8. You can see that a 2 percent rate of price gain leaves a net proceeds of sale (after deducting 5 percent of

Table 15.7   Net Proceeds of Sale of Property at Different Appreciation Rates

Property Appreciation	0%	2%	5%
Sales price	$650,000	$717,653	$829,583
Less 5% sales expense	$32,500	$35,883	$41,479
Less mtg. balance	$488,343	$488,343	$488,343
Net proceeds of sale (pretax)	$129,157	$193,427	$299,761

Table 15.8 TROI Calculation Using BTCF Increases of 2 Percent per Year with Differing Rates of Property Appreciation

Appreciation	Year 0	Year 1	Year 2	Year 3	Year 4	Year 5	TROI
Before tax cash flow (BTCF)		$21,269	$22,425	$23,600	$24,793	$26,006	
No appreciation	($130,000)	$21,269	$22,425	$23,600	$24,793	$129,157	
						$155,163	17.78%
Before tax cash flow (BTCF)		$21,269	$22,425	$23,600	$24,793	$26,006	
2% appreciation	($130,000)	$21,269	$22,425	$23,600	$24,793	$193,427	
						$219,433	23.86%
Before tax cash flow (BTCF)		$21,269	$22,425	$23,600	$24,793	$26,006	
5% appreciation	($130,000)	$21,269	$22,425	$23,600	$24,793	$299,761	
						$325,767	31.67%

the selling price to cover the sales expense) of $193,427. Table 15.7 also shows the net sales proceeds that would result if the property incurred no price gains (pessimistic view) or 5 percent price gains (optimistic view).

Using an Excel spreadsheet (or similar software), you can next generate your total return on investment figures, such as those shown in Table 15.8.

Under different rates of price gain, your expected total rate of return—not including any gains you plan to generate from your entrepreneurial efforts to create value—for Royal Terrace ranges from a low of 17.78 percent to a high of 31.67 percent.

The figures in Table 15.8 show just a few of the results that spreadsheet software enables you to calculate. You could also vary rates of growth for rents and operating expenses, changes in mortgage interest rates, mortgage term, amount of down payment, and any other variables. You also use spreadsheets to forecast and compare the profits that your improvements generate. As Donald Trump and I emphasize throughout this book, you will earn your most attractive gains by using your entrepreneurial talents to create value.

When you explore multiple potential outcomes, you review a series of possible results that range from pessimistic to optimistic. Because no one can perfectly forecast the future, a range of possibilities not only helps you make better decisions, it helps you anticipate and manage those periods when your market heads into a down cycle.

Conclusion

Thanks for sticking with us. You now know more about how to profit through real estate investing and entrepreneurship than the majority of "landlords" who have owned and managed rental properties for years. You now realize that real estate always offers superior opportunities for those individuals who read, listen, and seek out new places and new ideas. Even better, the current down cycle presents an incredible starting point for your wealth building.

Donald Trump says, "Sometimes I'm hard on people because I know they can do more, and I know they are not living up to their potential. I do not want to fire them, I want to fire them up to achieve in ways that I know they can. When you persist with a solid plan, you succeed. Respect yourself! Take advantage of the possibilities and promises that await you. I expect you to succeed, and accept no excuses."

You have gained the know-how. You have gained the entrepreneurial mindset. Now, act. Think 5, 10, 20 years into the future. Let me repeat that. Think 5, 10, 15, 20 years into the future. What level of financial and personal freedom would you like to live? Make it happen.

Mr. Trump and I want you to prosper: for yourself, for your family, and for those you serve. We wish you good fortune. Please let us know how you're doing. You can contact me directly at b-prof@hotmail.com.

INDEX

INDEX

INDEX

SPECIAL BONUS #2

FREE Advanced Training

If you're serious about investing in real estate, you need to know everything you can about what you're doing. **Trump University** offers its members free continuing education events around the country so that they can stay current on the latest investing trends and strategies. These invitation-only events feature three-days of intensive training where you will learn how to:

- Develop a winning investment strategy
- Build a long-term portfolio
- Finance your deals with minimal capital
- Invest in projects out of state
- Use the internet to source profitable deals

To receive an invitation to the next training event in your area simply register by logging onto:

TrumpUniversity.com/Bonus2

SPECIAL BONUS #3

Wealth Builders Network 14 Day FREE Membership

Now that you're a part of the **Trump University** community we would like to offer you a free trial in the Wealth Builders Network, our premium membership community. As a member you will be able to:

- Participate in live training webinars every week

- Access a forms library for invaluable contracts, etc.

- Network with other success-oriented entrepreneurs

- View archived webinars

- Download audio classes to your iPod

To accept this free trial invitation please log onto:
TrumpUniversity.com/Bonus3